Entrepreneurship

Entrepreneurship

Nitin Johri

RANDOM

RANDOM PUBLICATIONS

NEW DELHI (INDIA)

Entrepreneurship

ISBN 978-93-5111-346-1

Published in 2014 in India by

RANDOM PUBLICATIONS

4376-A/4B, Gali Murari Lal, Ansari Road
New Delhi-110 002
Phone : +91-11-43580356, +91-11-23289044
e-mail: randomexports@gmail.com, sales@randompublications.com,
info@randompublications.com

Reprinted 2026

Type Setting by : Keystoneprintads, Delhi-110051

Preface

"Entrepreneurship" may result in new organizations or revitalize mature organizations in response to a perceived business opportunity. A new business started by an entrepreneur is referred to as a startup company. In recent years, the term has been extended to include social and political forms of entrepreneurial activity. Entrepreneurship within a firm or large organization has been referred to as intra-preneurship and may include corporate ventures where large entities spin off subsidiary organizations.

Entrepreneurial activities differ substantially depending on the type of organization and creativity involved. Entrepreneurship ranges in scale from solo projects, and even just part-time projects, to major undertakings that create many job opportunities. Many "high value" entrepreneurial ventures seek venture capital or angel funding in order to raise capital for building the business. Angel investors generally seek annualized returns of 20-30% and more, as well as extensive involvement in the business. Many organizations exist to support would-be entrepreneurs including specialized government agencies, business incubators, science parks, and some NGOs. More recently, the term entrepreneurship has been extended to include conceptualizations of entrepreneurship as a specific mindset resulting in entrepreneurial initiatives e.g. in the form of social entrepreneurship, political entrepreneurship, or knowledge entrepreneurship.

I thank all associates of my group who have helped in the preparation of the book. My individual thanks go to "Random Publications" who have in print the book.

— Nitin Johri

Contents

1

Introduction

CONCEPTS OF ENTREPRENEURSHIP

The workshop participants were introduced to various aspects of entrepreneurship, namely the importance of getting ideas for an enterprise, how to get ideas, identifying the appropriate trade, factors to consider in selecting a business, factors to consider in deciding to initiate an enterprise, and the functions of an enterprise.

The topics discussed during the session are as follows:

- *Importance of Getting Ideas for an Enterprise*:
  - Basic ideas are required in all cases to perform any work successfully
  - One should acquire the basic concepts of entrepreneurship before getting involved in running an enterprise
  - This knowledge helps an entrepreneur to run the enterprise smoothly and also to explore the possibility of taking new initiatives
  - It also helps in correct decision making
- *How to Get Ideas*:
  - Consult with those who are currently in the business
  - Observe other enterprises to identify problems and think about possible solutions
  - Discuss with friends and neighbours
  - Get ideas from the existing available merchandise in the market
- *Identifying the Appropriate Trade*:
  - Be selective in identifying one's trade.
  - Select just as to the ability and interest of the entrepreneur.
  - Decide only after getting enough relevant information about a particular trade or business. It will help to:

a. Run the business smoothly

b. Avoid loss from major mistakes

- Factors to Consider in Selecting a Business
  - Possibilities of success
  - What risks are involved
  - Profitability
  - Attractiveness
- Factors to Consider when Deciding about Initiating an Enterprise
  - Availability of experienced and knowledgeable persons to consult with
  - Mobilization of sufficient capital
  - Adequate demand for the products/goods in the market
  - Facility for marketing
  - Facility for storage of goods
  - Availability of raw materials
  - Ability to get support from Government
- Functions of an Enterprise
  - Preparing business plan
  - Surveying the market
  - Mobilizing capital
  - Analysing costs
  - Pricing goods
  - Marketing products
  - Keeping accounts
  - Identifying risk factors
  - Looking for ways to become self-reliant

MEANING

Entrepreneurship is the act of being an entrepreneur, which can be defined as "one who undertakes innovations, finance and business acumen in an effort to transform innovations into economic goods".

This may result in new organizations or may be part of revitalizing mature organizations in response to a perceived opportunity. The most obvious form of entrepreneurship is that of starting new businesses; however, in recent years, the term has been extended to include social and political forms of entrepreneurial activity.

When entrepreneurship is describing activities within a firm or large organization it is referred to as intra-preneurship and may include corporate venturing, when large entities spin-off organizations. Paul Reynolds, entrepreneurship scholar and creator of the Global Entrepreneurship Monitor, "by the time they reach their retirement years, half of all working men in the United States probably have a period of self-employment of one or more years; one in four may have engaged in self-employment for six or more years. Participating in a new business creation is a common activity among U.S.

workers over the course of their careers." And in recent years has been documented by scholars such as David Audretsch to be a major driver of economic growth in both the United States and Western Europe. Entrepreneurial activities are substantially different depending on the type of organization that is being started.

Entrepreneurship ranges in scale from solo projects to major undertakings creating many job opportunities. Many "high value" entrepreneurial ventures seek venture capital or angel funding in order to raise capital to build the business.

Angel investors generally seek annualized returns of 20-30% and more, as well as extensive involvement in the business. Many kinds of organizations now exist to support would-be entrepreneurs, including specialized government agencies, business incubators, science parks, and some NGOs.

In more recent times, the term entrepreneurship has been extended to include elements not related necessarily to business formation activity such as conceptualizations of entrepreneurship as a specific mindset resulting in entrepreneurial initiatives *e.g.* in the form of social entrepreneurship, political entrepreneurship, or knowledge entrepreneurship have emerged.

DEFINITION OF ENTREPRENEURSHIP

Entrepreneurship is more than simply "starting a business." The definition of entrepreneurship is a process through which individuals identify opportunities, allocate resources, and create value. This creation of value is often through the identification of unmet needs or through the identification of opportunities for change.

Entrepreneurs see "problems" as "opportunities," then take action to identify the solutions to those problems and the customers who will pay to have those problems solved. Entrepreneurial success is simply a function of the ability of an entrepreneur to see these opportunities in the marketplace, initiate change and create value through solutions.

CHARACTERISTICS OF ENTREPRENEUR

The Department of Labour predicts that the #1 employer in 2010 will be"self." An Internet poll of 25-44 year olds revealed that 90% of them hoped to own their own businesses. A survey conducted by Ernst and Young found that 75% of influential Americans believe that entrepreneurship will be the defining trend of the 21st century. Some of the factors that have attributed to the rise of the modern day entrepreneurial spirit are access to technology, a global economy and corporate stagnation. Many workers have experienced feelings of discontent - likely due to the upsizing, downsizing, and right-sizing of corporations.

But whatever the reason, modern workers want to have more control over the work they do. And they want work that is meaningful and important to them. Now is a great time to become your own boss. In fact, the number of Americans who are running their own businesses will continue to grow as we move further into the millennium..

As workers' values are changing and people want more time to do the things they love with those they love, having employment that allows for a greater balance in their lives is critical to today's worker. In fact, it is downright un-American not to believe in the principles of entrepreneurship. We started out working on the family farm or in the family-owned grocery store but as our country became more industrialized, families were pulled apart. We had to go where the work was.

We left our homes and hometowns and ventured into the big cities. Big companies, industries and corporations popped up all over the country, and we became reliant on them to take care of us. Today, with the advent of the computer, we don't even have to leave home to conduct business. It frees us up to concentrate on the"business of life" again. The new world of work encourages the entrepreneurial mindset, in that we need to learn to use our imagination to dream up new ideas, challenge assumptions and belief systems to find a better way, and break through worn-out thinking to create new and innovative products and services.

This way of thinking is helpful whether you are working for yourself or someone else. The characteristics of entrepreneur can be defined as'anyone who undertakes a commercial risk for profit and/or tackles new challenges'. They are the change agents of society because they see a problem and want to find a way to solve it. They believe in being self-reliant and taking action to better their communities. Robert Schwartz's definition:"An entrepreneur is essentially a visualizer and actualizer. He can visualize something and when he visualizes it, he sees exactly how to make it happen." Successful entrepreneurs realise that if it is to become a reality, they are the ones to make it happen.

An entrepreneur is someone who is able to continually reinvent himself, and to rethink an entire project if he finds that something is not right. Thus, someone who has vision, flexibility, and a risk-taking nature fares very well in self-employment ventures. Of course, like anything else, there are pros and cons to becoming an entrepreneur. One pro is that you are the boss. The con is that you still have other co-workers, customers, and vendors to rely on to get the job done. People who are self-employed often only have illusions of control. For instance, you may think you have everything under control and then something happens that puts everything out of your control.

The difference is that being the boss means that it all comes down to you. You are fully responsible for your success. For many people this level of personal responsibility is part of the challenge and enjoyment. The truth is that any successful entrepreneur rolls with the punches and moves with the winds of change. Take this test to find out if you have what it takes to be an entrepreneur.

Characteristics of Entrepreneur:

- *Check if these entrepreneurs characteristics are applicable to you*:
  - Responsible
  - Hard Worker
  - Risk Taker
  - Creative
  - Flexible
  - Follows through with ideas
  - Personable
  - Optimistic
  - Perceptive
  - Self-confident
  - Determined
  - High degree of energy
  - Innovative
  - Independent
  - Ability to anticipate needs
  - Effective communicator
  - Responsive to criticism
  - Able to take the lead
  - Learn from mistakes
  - Self-directed
- *Would you say that you are always, sometimes, or never like these statements*:
  - I am goal and action-oriented.
  - I am a self-starter.
  - I am self-confident.

- I am a persistent person.
- I like taking risks.
- I am flexible and adaptable when necessary.
- I am a problem-solver.
- I am an innovative thinker.
- I can sell myself and/or my product to others.
- I accept responsibility for my actions.
- I enjoy networking.
- I can function in an environment of uncertainty.
- I like being in charge.
- I am willing to devote whatever time and energy it takes to be successful.
- I am able to see what needs to be done and then do it

THE GROWTH OF ENTREPRENEURSHIP IN INDIA

Through unrecognized by policy statements, entrepreneurial initiative was breaking new grounds in the small industry scene over the past four decades banking mainly upon the ingenuity and determination of individuals. The late sixties and early seventies also witnessed a few sporadic attempts to create entrepreneurs from non traditional communities with a view to breaking the monopoly of the dominant groups and diversifying the entrepreneurial base in the country.

The state of Gujarat was the forefront of this movement. By the late sixties it became quite evident that two resources are the most critical for development of entrepreneurship, finance and managerial capabilities. The industrial policy exercises were woefully oblivion of these two basic factors though there were incentives and special institutions.

When industrial development picked up in the sixties the bankers limited credit mainly to established industrialists and merchants for existing projects with assured success and sufficient collaterals. A study of 53 projects financed by banks and the Gujarat State Financial Corporation during the period 1965-68 revealed many interesting things. More than two thirds of institutionals loans were for diversifications and expansion of existing enterprises. Of the new new loans, 30% were given to merchants and traders with adequate financial resources and hence the required collateral.

The entrepreneur's financial stake stood very high in the transactions tat a debt equity ratio 1:1. Such policies evidently were holistic to an aspiring and an otherwise competent young entrepreneurs but without enough financial resources and tangible assets. As an innovative alternative to the conventional banking system an Industrial Investment Corporation was set up as a State company in Gujarat in 1968 with attractive and unconventional credit schemes. The task next was to identify and groom potential new entrepreneurs from a variety of socioeconomic backgrounds.

The entrepreneurship development programme with well ell designed inputs for motivating, informing and skilling entrepreneurial individuals was pioneered in 1970. Something started as an experiment soon spread to other parts of the country and became a deeply entrenched strategy for new enterprise creation over the years. Difficult models and methodologies have been evolved and tasted by different organizations.

Several modifications have been carried out to suit the profile and needs of various groups of trainees. For example, potential micro enterprises in the rural sectors by the poor, whose ventures have only limited investment and low levels of technology must be addressed differently from those of enterprising women whose talents and creativity have been suppressed by age-old socio-cultural norms and practices.

Both need appropriate approaches so that they become capable of manifesting their entrepreneurial competence. Despite efforts made made by a host of institutions, only less than 20% of the new entrepreneurs have access to training every year. This means that a large mass of potential entrepreneurs are still outside the reach of training interventions.

ROLE OF ENTREPRENEURSHIP IN ECONOMIC DEVELOPMENT

ENTREPRENEUR

An entrepreneur can be regarded as a person who has the initiative skill and motivation to set up a business or enterprise of his own and who always look for high achievements. He is the catalyst for social change and works for the common good. They looks for opportunities, identifies them and seizes them mainly for economic gains. An action oriented entrepreneur is a highly calculative individual who is always willing to undertake risks in order to achieve their goals.

NEED FOR ENTREPRENEURSHIP DEVELOPMENT

Economic development essentially means a process of upward change whereby the real pr capita income of a country increases over a period of time.Entrepreneurship has an important role to play in the development of a country. It is one of the most important inputs in economic development. The number and competence of entrepreneurs affect the economic growth of the country.

The economic history of the presently advanced countries like USA, Russia and Japan supports the fact that economic development is the outcome for which entrepreneurship is an inevitable cause. The crucial and significant role played by the entrepreneurs in the economic development of advanced countries has made the people of developing and under developed countries conscious of the importance of entrepreneurship for economic development.

It is now a widely accepted fact that active and enthusiastic entrepreneurs can only explore the potentials of the countries availability of recourses such as labour, capital and technology. The role of entrepreneurs is not identical in the various economies. Depending on the material resources, industry climate and responsiveness of the political system, it varies from economy to economy.

The contribution of entrepreneurs may be more in favourable opportunity conditions than in economies with relatively less favourable opportunity conditions.

ENTREPRENEURSHIP AND ECONOMIC DEVELOPMENT

Entrepreneurship helps in the process of economic development in the following ways:

- *Employment Generation*: Growing unemployment particularly educated unemployment is the problem of the nation. The available employment opportunities can cater only 5 to 10% of the unemployed. Entrepreneurs generate employment both directly and indirectly. Directly, self employment as an entrepreneur and indirectly by starting many industrial units they offer jobs to millions. Thus entrepreneurship is the best way to fight the evil of unemployment.
- *National Income*: National Income consists of the goods and services produced in the country and imported. The goods and services produced are for consumption within the country as well as to meet the demand of exports. The domestic demand increases with increase in population and increase in standard of living. The export demand also increases to meet the needs of growing imports due to various reasons. An increasing number of entrepreneurs are required to meet this increasing demand for goods and services. Thus entrepreneurship increases the national income.
- *Balanced Regional Development*: The growth of Industry and business leads to a lot of Public benefits like transport facilities, health, education, entertainment etc. When the industries are concentrated in selected cities, development gets limited to these cities. A rapid development. When the new entrepreneur grow at a faster rate, in view of increasing competition in and around cities, they are forced to set up their enterprises in the smaller towns away from big cities. This helps in the development of backward regions.
- *Dispersal of economic power*: Industrial development normally may

lead to concentration of economic powers in a few hands. This concentration of power in a few hands has its own evils in the form of monopolies. Developing a large number of entrepreneur helps in dispersing the economic power amongst the population. Thus it helps in weakening the harmful effects of monopoly.

- *Better standards of living*: Entrepreneur plays a vital role in achieving a higher rate of economic growth. Entrepreneurs are able to produce goods at lower cost and supply quality goods at lower price to the community just as to their requirements. When the price of the comedies decreases the consumers get the power to buy more goods for their satisfaction. In this way they can increase the standard of living of the people.
- *Creating innovation*: An entrepreneur is a person who always looks for changes. Apart from combining the factors of production, he also introduces new ideas and new combination of factors. He always try to introduce newer and newer technique of production of goods and services. An entrepreneur brings economic development through innovation.

Entrepreneurship also helps in increasing productivity and capital formation of a nation. In short, the development of the entrepreneurship is inevitable in the economic development of the country.

The Role played by the entrepreneurship development can be expressed in the following words:

" *Economic development is the effect for which entrepreneurship is a cause*"

WOMEN ENTREPRENEURSHIP: GROWTH AND DEVELOPMENT

WOMEN ENTREPRENEURSHIP

Description

Historically, women have experienced special problems as entrepreneurs or aspiring entrepreneurs. It probable is still true in some locales that women cannot get business loans without a husband's or father's co-signature. For this sort of reason, specially focused programmes for women can be important for a community to obtain the full benefit of this important sector for business development, quite apart from questions of equity.

Programmes in women entrepreneurship may, but ordinarily do not also serve men, although much of the content of such programmes would be no different if they happened to be organized for a group of men. For example, there are, of course, no gender differences in the processes of feasibility studies or market analyses. However, an emphasis, for example, on networking among solely women entrepreneurs provides a significant support for sharing experiences with gender-related obstacles and techniques or dealing with them. Moreover, seminars and other training sessions restricted to women probable offer a greater opportunity for the participants to gain from them than if the usual pattern of male-dominated interactions in the school and other training settings must otherwise be countered.

In rural communities, families on farms must seek supplementary income, and the woman who considers a side-business is particularly a potential client for an entrepreneurship programme. Similarly, women dependent upon welfare supplements are another client base when these seek some means of self-employment in a very restricted labour market. A women entrepreneurship programme should not be limited to working with individuals or groups of entrepreneurs.

An important function for such a programme is to act as a collective advocate for women in business in the local community or in wider venues, including the province and the nation. For example, WRED (Women and Rural Economic Development) has been especially active in advocacy at the provincial and national level.

It as also addressed the problem of credit for women business by getting a credit union to establish a loan programme. It this instance, WRED offered to guarantee loans so as to encourage the credit union's participation. Through WRED's advocacy efforts the lenders are also making some financial contribution by offering the loans at minimal rates.

Benefits

All too often the ideas, energy, and effort of women have been denied by and to a community's business development activities. This onerous handicap can be overcome by the techniques considered here. Thus today's national trend in which most new businesses are being started by women can be capitalized on in a CED strategy that promotes women entrepreneurship.

Major Challenges

The biggest problem to address is the need for comprehensiveness in programming, especially in rural areas. It is not enough to simply encourage women to start their businesses; they will need a variety of supportive services to sustain the businesses, including access to capital. And probable most important is access to continuing consultation as they try to grow their businesses. These, of course, are the needs of all new businesses, but in rural areas, the infrastructure of support is so sparse.

Thus a women entrepreneurship programme, to be most effective, has to step in to do a variety of tasks that in urban settings are being addressed by other agencies or groups – *e.g.*, basic numeracy and literacy training. Or failing that, the programme would have to restrict its clients to those who do not need the full range of supportive services and preparatory training. In that case, the programme neglects those who most need aid in moving into self-employment, particularly considering that they are least able to access any government programmes.

WOMEN AS ENTREPRENEURS IN INDIA

Women owned businesses are highly increasing in the economies of almost all countries. The hidden entrepreneurial potentials of women have gradually been changing with the growing sensitivity to the role and economic status in the society. Skill, knowledge and adaptability in business are the main reasons for women to emerge into business ventures.

'Women Entrepreneur' is a person who accepts challenging role to meet her personal needs and become economically independent. A strong desire to do something positive is an inbuilt quality of entrepreneurial women, who is capable of contributing values in both family and social life. With the advent of media, women are aware of their own traits, rights and also the work situations.

The glass ceilings are shattered and women are found indulged in every line of business from pappad to power cables.

The challenges and opportunities provided to the women of digital era are growing rapidly that the job seekers are turning into job creators. They are flourishing as designers, interior decorators, exporters, publishers, garment manufacturers and still exploring new avenues of economic participation.In India, although women constitute the majority of the total population, the entrepreneurial world is still a male dominated one.

Women in advanced nations are recognized and are more prominent in the business world.

But the Indian women entrepreneurs are facing some major constraints like:

- *Lack of confidence*: In general, women lack confidence in their strength and competence. The family members and the society are reluctant to stand beside their entrepreneurial growth. To a certain extent, this situation is changing among Indian women and yet to face a tremendous change to increase the rate of growth in entrepreneurship.
- *Socio-cultural barriers*: Women's family and personal obligations are sometimes a great barrier for succeeding in business career. Only few women are able to manage both home and business efficiently, devoting enough time to perform all their responsibilities in priority.
- *Market-oriented risks*: Stiff competition in the market and lack of mobility of women make the dependence of women entrepreneurs on middleman indispensable. Many business women find it difficult to capture the market and make their products popular. They are not fully aware of the changing market conditions and hence can effectively utilize the services of media and internet.

- *Motivational factors*: Self motivation can be realised through a mind set for a successful business, attitude to take up risk and behaviour towards the business society by shouldering the social responsibilities. Other factors are family support, Government policies, financial assistance from public and private institutions and also the environment suitable for women to establish business units.
- *Knowledge in Business Administration*: Women must be educated and trained constantly to acquire the skills and knowledge in all the functional areas of business management. This can facilitate women to excel in decision making process and develop a good business network.
- *Awareness about the financial assistance*: Various institutions in the financial sector extend their maximum support in the form of incentives, loans, schemes etc. Even then every woman entrepreneur may not be aware of all the assistance provided by the institutions. So the sincere efforts taken towards women entrepreneurs may not reach the entrepreneurs in rural and backward areas.
- *Exposed to the training programmes*: Training programmes and workshops for every type of entrepreneur is available through the social and welfare associations, based on duration, skill and the purpose of the training programme. Such programmes are really useful to new, rural and young entrepreneurs who want to set up a small and medium scale unit on their own.
- *Identifying the available resources*: Women are hesitant to find out the access to cater their needs in the financial and marketing areas. In spite of the mushrooming growth of associations, institutions, and the schemes from the government side, women are not enterprising and dynamic to optimize the resources in the form of reserves, assets mankind or business volunteers.

Highly educated, technically sound and professionally qualified women should be encouraged for managing their own business, rather than dependent on wage employment outlets. The unexplored talents of young women can be identified, trained and used for various types of industries to increase the productivity in the industrial sector. A desirable environment is necessary for every woman to inculcate entre-preneurial values and involve greatly in business dealings.

The additional business opportunities that are recently approaching for women entrepreneurs are:

- Eco-friendly technology
- Bio-technology
- IT enabled enterprises

- Event Management
- Tourism industry
- Telecommunication
- Plastic materials
- Vermiculture
- Mineral water
- Sericulture
- Floriculture
- Herbal and health care
- Food, fruits and vegetable processing

Empowering women entrepreneurs is essential for achieving the goals of sustainable development and the bottlenecks hindering their growth must be eradicated to entitle full participation in the business. Apart from training programmes, Newsletters, mentoring, trade fairs and exhibitions also can be a source for entrepreneurial development. As a result, the desired outcomes of the business are quickly achieved and more of remunerative business opportunities are found. Henceforth, promoting entrepreneurship among women is certainly a short-cut to rapid economic growth and development. Let us try to eliminate all forms of gender discrimination and thus allow 'women' to be an entrepreneur at par with men.

RURAL ENTREPRENEURSHIP: MEANING, NEED/OBJECTIVE

ENTREPRENEURSHIP AS AN ECONOMIC FORCE IN RURAL DEVELOPMENT

Rural development is more than ever before linked to entrepreneurship. Institutions and individuals promoting rural development now see entrepreneurship as a strategic development intervention that could accelerate the rural development process. Furthermore, institutions and individuals seem to agree on the urgent need to promote rural enterprises: development agencies see rural entrepreneurship as an enormous employment potential; politicians see it as the key strategy to prevent rural unrest; farmers see it as an instrument for improving farm earnings; and women see it as an employment possibility near their homes which provides autonomy, independence and a reduced need for social support.

To all these groups, however, entrepreneurship stands as a vehicle to improve the quality of life for individuals, families and communities and to sustain a healthy economy and environment. The entrepreneurial orientation to rural development accepts entrepreneurship as the central force of economic growth and development, without it other factors of development will be wasted or frittered away. However, the acceptance of entrepreneurship as a central development force by itself will not lead to rural development and the advancement of rural enterprises.

What is needed in addition is an environment enabling entrepreneurship in rural areas. The existence of such an environment largely depends on policies promoting rural entrepreneurship. The effectiveness of such policies in turn depends on a conceptual framework about entrepreneurship, *i.e.*, what it is and where it comes from.

This deals with the following three issues: firstly, it sets out the reasons why promoting entrepreneurship is a force of economic change that must take place if many rural communities are to survive; secondly, it deals with what policies are necessary in order to create an environment in rural areas conducive to entrepreneurship; and thirdly, it considers women and entrepreneurship.

Entrepreneurship Concept

The entrepreneurship concept, what it means and where it comes from, is the foundation for policies promoting entrepreneurship and the key to understanding the role of entrepreneurship in development.

What, Who and Why?

Defining entrepreneurship is not an easy task. There are almost as many definitions of entrepreneurship as there are scholar books on the subjects. To some, entrepreneurship means primarily innovation, to others it means risk-taking? to others a market stabilising force and to others still it means starting, owning and managing a small business.

The entrepreneur is then viewed as a person who either creates new combinations of production factors such as new methods of production, new products, new markets, finds new sources of supply and new organizational forms; or as a person who is willing to take risks; or a person who, by exploiting market opportunities, eliminates disequilibrium between aggregate supply and aggregate demand, or as one who owns and operates a business.

To choose the definition of entrepreneurship most appropriate for the rural area context, it is important to bear in mind the entrepreneurial skills that will be needed to improve the quality of life for individuals, families and communities and to sustain a healthy economy and environment.

Taking this into consideration, as suggested, find that each of the traditional definitions has its own weakness. The first definition leaves little room for innovations that are not on the technological or organizational cutting edge, such as, adaptation of older technologies to a developing-country context, or entering into export markets already tapped by other firms. Defining entrepreneurship as risk-taking neglects other major elements of what we usually think of as entrepreneurship, such as a well-developed ability to recognise unexploited market opportunities. Entrepreneurship as a stabilising force limits entrepreneurship to reading markets disequilibria, while entrepreneurship defined as owning and operating a business, denies the possibility of entrepreneurial behaviour by non-owners, employees and managers who have no equity stake in the business.

Therefore, the most appropriate definition of entrepreneurship that would fit into the rural development context, argued here, is the broader one, the one which defines entrepreneurship as: "a force that mobilises other resources to meet unmet market demand", "the ability to create and build something from practically nothing", "the process of creating value by pulling together a unique package of resources to exploit an opportunity" It combines definitions of entrepreneurship by Jones and Sakong, 1980; Timmons, 1989; Stevenson, *et al.*, 1985.

Entrepreneurship so defined, pertains to any new organization of productive factors and not exclusively to innovations that are on the technological or organizational cutting edge, it pertains to entrepreneurial activities both within and outside the organization. Entrepreneurship need not involve anything new from a global or even national perspective, but rather the adoption of new forms of business organizations, new technologies and new enterprises producing goods not previously available at a location. This is why entrepreneurship is considered to be a prime mover in development and why nations, regions and communities that actively promote entrepreneurship development, demonstrate much higher growth rates and consequently higher levels of development than nations, regions and communities whose institutions, politics and culture hinder entrepreneurship.

An entrepreneurial economy, whether on the national, regional or community level, differs significantly from a non-entrepreneurial economy in many respects, not only by its economic structure and its economic vigourousness, but also by the social vitality and quality of life which it offers with a consequent attractiveness to people.

Economic structure is very dynamic and extremely competitive due to the rapid creation of new firms and the exit of 'old' stagnant and declining firms. It is populated with rapidly growing firms, gazelles as they are called in the literature of entrepreneurship. Gazelles are the key to economic development. As described by Twaalfhoven and Indivers, they are run by dynamic entrepreneurs, who manage and lead their companies not only to remain in the business but to expand it. Dynamic entrepreneurs look for growth, they do not have only a vision but are also capable of making it happen.

They think and act globally, look for expansion, rely on external resources, seek professional advice or they work with professional teams. They challenge competitors instead of avoiding them and take and share risks in a way that leads to success. In this way economic vitality of a country largely depends on the overall level of entrepreneurial capacity, *i.e.*, on its ability to create rapidly growing companies, gazelles.

Equally important is the speed by which new small companies are created. These phenomena explain why countries, regions and communities with a similar number of large and small firms show a completely different economic vitality. Economic vitality of a country is no doubt a necessary condition for social vitality. Without it other important factors that make living attractive in certain areas, such as education, health, social services, housing, transport facilities, flow of information and so on, cannot be developed and sustained in the area in the long run.

As evidence suggests, it is false to assume that socially and economically depressed areas will transform into fast growing areas by injection of external investment funds and external expertise. Without entrepreneurial capabilities which are well developed or potentially available, external funds will be wasted on projects that will not provide long term economic growth. Consequently instead of becoming more and more integrated into other economically and socially rich areas, such areas will become increasingly isolated, depopulated, poorer and therefore less and less capable of attracting people who, given other available resources, would make an impact from a development standpoint.

Entrepreneurial, orientation to rural development, contrary to development based on bringing in human capital and investment from outside, is based on stimulating local entrepreneurial talent and subsequent growth of indigenous companies. This in turn would create jobs and add economic value to a region and community and at the same time keep scarce resources within the community.

To accelerate economic development in rural areas, it is necessary to increase the supply of entrepreneurs, thus building up the critical mass of first generation entrepreneurs, who will take risks and engage in the uncertainties of a new venture creation, create something from practically nothing and create values by pulling together a unique package of resources to exploit an opportunity. By their example they will stimulate an autonomous entrepreneurial process, as well as a dynamic entrepreneurship, thereby ensuring continuous rural development.

It is important to stress that rural entrepreneurship in its substance does not differ from entrepreneurship in urban areas. Entrepreneurship in rural areas is finding a unique blend of resources, either inside or outside of agriculture.

This can be achieved by widening the base of a farm business to include all the non-agricultural uses that available resources can be put to or through any major changes in land use or level of production other than those related solely to agriculture. Thus, a rural entrepreneur is someone who is prepared to stay in the rural area and contribute to the creation of local wealth. To some degree, however, the economic goals of an entrepreneur and the social goals of rural development are more strongly interlinked than in urban areas. For this reason entrepreneurship in rural areas is usually community based, has strong extended family linkages and a relatively large impact on a rural community.

Sources of Entrepreneurship

From the policy viewpoint? the promotion of entrepreneurship, the understanding where entrepreneurship comes from is as equally important as understanding the concept of entrepreneurship. It indicates where the governments, national, regional or local, should target their promotional efforts.

If entrepreneurial skills, for example, are innate, active promotion policies have a small role to play. If instead, only certain entrepreneurial characteristics are innate, then active promotion policies can contribute to entrepreneurship development in the community in the region and in the nation, since entrepreneurial skills can be acquired through training. Empirical research on the sources of entrepreneurship is extensive, particularly within the discipline of psychology and sociology.

The standard perception is that entrepreneurship is a special personal feature, either a person is, or is not an entrepreneur. This perception entrepreneurial traits, such as the need to achieve, risk taking propensity, self-esteem and internal locus of control, creativity and innovative behaviour, the need for independence, occupational primacy, fixation upon goals and dominance, are all inborn.

Therefore, policies directed specifically towards promoting the development of entrepreneurship would not help much since chose characteristics cannot be acquired by training. Risk talking propensity here is understood as the perceived probability of receiving rewards as opposed to the perceived probability of incurring a failure. Another perception is that some cultures or some social groups are more conducive to entrepreneurial behaviour than others.

The factors that contribute to the supply of entrepreneurs are an inheritance of entrepreneurial tradition, family position, social status, educational background and the level of education.

Based on research into the origins of business owners, it is believed that persons who come from small business owner families, are more likely to become entrepreneurs than others. Studies of family position of existing entrepreneurs demonstrate that entrepreneurs are often found among elder children, since just as to the explanation, they are pressed to take more authority and responsibility at earlier stages than younger members of the family. The outsider group, ethnic minority, or the outsider individual, the marginal person, who are by a combination of different factors rendered outsiders in relation to the social groups with whom they normally interact, are both viewed as a significant source of entrepreneurship.

It is claimed that to minorities small business ownership means escape form marginality. Whether educational background influences potential entrepreneurs or not is a matter of debate. The popular idea of an entrepreneur is that of a totally self-made man, lacking in formal qualifications. This of course is not in conflict with findings that entrepreneurs who are better educated are more successful than the less educated ones.

Apparently two things are involved simultaneously: propensity to start an entrepreneurial venture and skills to run the venture successfully. The research which tries to explain, by personal traits and/or other social aspects, why certain individuals become entrepreneurs, has not yet produced convincing results. Consequently, a widely accepted view is the following: while personal characteristics as well as social aspects clearly play some role, entrepreneurship and entrepreneurs can also be developed through conscious action.

Development of entrepreneurs and of entrepreneurship can be stimulated through a set of supporting institutions and through deliberate innovative action which stimulates changes and fully supports capable individuals or groups.

It is argued, that controllable variables such as a stable system of property rights and freedom of action in the economic sphere, availability of other inputs in the economy as well as education and training, contribute significantly to the development of entrepreneurship.

Therefore, policies and programmes designed specifically for entrepreneurship promotion, can greatly affect the supply of entrepreneurs and thus indirectly represent an important source of entrepreneurship. This view has important implications for entrepreneurship development in rural areas. If currently entrepreneurial activities in a given rural area are not thriving? one should not jump to the entrepreneurship is something inherently alien to rural areas.

While this feeling could have some legacy due to the slower pace of changes occurring in rural areas compared to urban ones, proper action can make a lot of difference with respect to entrepreneurial behaviour of people living in rural areas.

Many examples of successful entrepreneurship confirm this statement and there is no reason why there should not be plenty of them. By bringing together different capabilities and different experiences in entrepreneurship development, everyone could enhance his/her own capabilities, motivation and determination in achieving the goal: attaining a sustainable and healthy rural economy and environment in order to ensure a high quality of life for individuals, families and communities.

Rural Entrepreneurship

Many examples of successful rural entrepreneurship can already be found in literature. Diversification into non-agricultural uses of available resources such as catering for tourists, blacksmithing, carpentry, spinning, etc. as well as diversification into activities other than those solely related to agricultural usage, for example, the use of resources other than land such as water, woodlands, buildings, available skills and local features, all fit into rural entrepreneurship.

The entrepreneurial combinations of these resources are, for example: tourism, sport and recreation facilities, professional and technical training, retailing and wholesaling, industrial applications, servicing, value added and the possibility of off-farm work. Equally entrepreneurial, are new uses of land that enable a reduction in the intensity of agricultural production, for example, organic production. Dynamic rural entrepreneurs can also be found. They are expanding their activities and markets and they find new markets for their products and services beyond the local boundaries.

To leave general examples of rural entrepreneurship behind, let us look at the real cases. All illustrating entrepreneurial initiatives, individuals and local communities from Great Britain. The names of entrepreneurs I have chosen to present here are not globally known but are no less important because of that.

They are very well known to the communities to which they belong and their initiatives are highly appreciated by the community members. One of them is Graham-Probin owner of a 110 acre farm in Malpas, Cheshire, England. By converting a two-storey building into four workshop units, he created employment opportunities within the community. Another one is John Anderson from Kirkwhelpington, who created employment opportunities in the local area by restoring traditional stables into business premises and renting them out to a blacksmith who shoes horses and does light engineering work for farmers.

Another is the McNamara family from Canaston Bridge. They responded to the dairy quotas imposed by the Government by diversification of their land for non-agricultural usage. The family converted 80 acres of land into an adventure and leisure complex. After three years of investment, amounting to £800 000, the adventure and leisure facilities were opened in 1987, boasting a range of attractions entirely unconnected with agriculture, such as: a bobsleigh run, a miniature railway, a pitch and putt golf course, a natural history centre, go-kart tracks, assault courses, a restaurant and various shops.

This entrepreneurial venture is an example of a straightforward entrepreneurship and not so much an example of on-farm diversification. It is an example of how seeing and seizing the opportunity are vital ingredients of entrepren eurial success. Let me turn now to illustrations related to social entrepreneurship, to examples of when people have changed things, acting in the interest of their communities while playing the same role as an individual entrepreneur. East Cleveland Training and Enterprise Group from Loftus, Small Industries Groups in Somerset and Antur Teifi from West Wales, are all real examples of social entrepreneurship.

The East Cleveland Training and Enterprise Group began as a group of four people in Loftus who were angry and frustrated at the lack of action by statutory bodies to tackle the area's unemployment. The Group developed a large programme of activities, such as employment training, youth training, initiating the establishment of a training and enterprise centre, improving environmental and property acquisition to benefit the community. The Small Industries Group Somerset, West Somerset, started with the objective of helping to create local jobs.

The founding group consisted of a dairy farmer, a sub-postmaster, an insurance broker, a lecturer, a youth worker and the manager of a field studies centre. For ten years the Group greatly fostered the development of the community and contributed to the change of attitudes of farmers as well as local communities, to favour self employment and business expansion.

Antur Teifi, from the Teifi Valley, the enterprise agency, was started by a group of local volunteers who were concerned with the high level of unemployment and unbalanced structure of the local population. The group set the objectives as follows: to identify and support community initiatives, to establish new permanent jobs and to initiate activities to prevent the area's economic and cultural decline. The group has more than achieved these objectives. Among the case studies presented here, there is no woman's name. Although the evidence shows that there are many activities in rural areas pursued by female entrepreneurs such as: trade, food processing, handicrafts, production of basic consumer articles, catering, running tourist establishments, and bed and breakfast arrangements.

However, compared to male entrepreneurs, female entrepreneurs in rural areas still tend to be limited to what have traditionally been viewed as women's activities. Also the scale of their entrepreneurial operation tends to be smaller when compared with male entrepreneurs. Although agriculture today still provides income to rural communities, rural development is increasingly linked to enterprise development. Since national economies are more and more globalized and competition is intensifying at an unprecedented pace, affecting not only industry but any economic activity including agriculture, it is not surprising that rural entrepreneurship is gaining in its importance as a force of economic change that must take place if many rural communities are to survive. However, entrepreneurship demands an enabling environment in order to flourish.

Environment Conducive to Entrepreneurship

Behind each of the success stories of rural entrepreneurship there is usually some sort of institutional support. Besides individual or group entrepreneurial initiative the enabling environment supporting these initiatives is of utmost importance.

The creation of such an environment starts already at the national level with the foundation policies for macro-economic stability and for well-defined property rights as well as international orientation. Protection of the domestic economy hinders instead of fosters entrepreneurship. National agricultural policies such as price subsidies to guarantee minimum farm incomes and the keeping of land in production when over-production already exists are definitely counter-productive to entrepreneurship.

The long run solution for sustainable agricultural development is only one, *i.e.*' competitive agriculture. While prices can set the direction, entrepreneurs who will meet the challenge of increasingly demanding international markets and who will find profitable alternative uses of land, alternative business opportunities and so on are needed.

Therefore, policies and programmes targeted more specifically at the development and channelling of entrepreneurial talent, are needed. Policies to increase the supply of entrepreneurs, policies developing the market for other inputs into successful entrepreneurship, policies for increasing the effectiveness of entrepreneurs and policies for increasing demand for entrepreneurship can significantly speed up entrepreneurial activities at national, regional and community levels. The policies and programmes targeted specifically to the development of entrepreneurship do not differ much with respect to location.

From the perspective of the process of entrepreneurship, whether the location is urban, semi-rural or rural, is not important in itself. For example, the needs of a would be entrepreneur or an existing small business do not differ much from those in an urban area. To realise their entrepreneurial ideas or to grow and sustain in business, they all need access to capital, labour, markets and good management skills.

What differs is the availability of markets for other inputs. The inputs into an entrepreneurial process, capital, management, technology, buildings, communications and transportation infrastructure, distribution channels and skilled labour, tend to be easier to find in urban areas. Professional advice is also hard to come by. Consequently, entrepreneurial behaviour, the ability to spot unconventional market opportunities, is most lacking in those rural areas where it is most needed *i.e.*, where the scarcity of 'these other inputs' is the highest.

These are the reasons why rural entrepreneurship is more likely to flourish in those rural areas where the two approaches to rural development, the 'bottom up. and the 'top down', complement each other. Developing entrepreneurs requires a much more complex approach to rural development than is many times the case in practice. It requires not only the development of local entrepreneurial capabilities but also a coherent regional/local strategy. Evidence shows that where this is the case, individual and social entrepreneurship play an important role in rural economic, social and community development.

The top down approach gains effectiveness when it is tailored to the local environment that it intends to support. The second prerequisite for its success is that ownership of the initiative remains in the hands of members of the local community. The regional development agencies that fit both criteria can contribute much to rural development through entrepreneurship. Other institutions that can make a difference to rural development based on entrepreneurship are agricultural extension services.

However, to be able to act in this direction, they too must be entrepreneurially minded. They must see agricultural activities as one of many possible activities that contribute to rural development. They must seek new entrepreneurial uses of land and support local initiative in this respect. While tradition is important it is nevertheless dangerous to be over-occupied with the past, otherwise the rural community may turn into a nostalgia-driven society.

Networking between different agencies involved in the promotion of rural development through entrepreneurship, by pooling together different sources and skills, by reaching a greater number of would be entrepreneurs and by assisting a greater number of local entrepreneurial initiatives, can have a much more positive effect on rural development than when each agency is working on its own. Entrepreneurship in rural areas can benefit a lot from the so called strategic development alliances, *i.e.*, partnership among governments or nonprofit seeking organizations, universities and the private sector.

To summarise, policy implications for rural entrepreneurship development are:

- Sound national economic policy with respect to agriculture, including recognition of the vital contribution of entrepreneurship to rural economic development;
- Policies and special programmes for the development and channelling of entrepreneurial talent;
- Entrepreneurial thinking about rural development, not only by farmers but also by everyone and every rural development organization; and
- Institutions supporting the development of rural entrepreneurship as well as strategic development alliances.

Women Entrepreneurs

Is there still a need to talk specifically about women entrepreneurs. on top of everything that has been already said'? Yes and no. No, because all that has been said about entrepreneurship is directly applicable to women, the concept, characteristics, sources' etc. Women entrepreneurs, as research demonstrates, may do things differently. For example, in comparison to male entrepreneurs, women tend to work more in teams, are less self-centred and personal ego to them is less important than success of the organization or business idea they are pursuing.

However, there is no difference in characteristics such as achievement, autonomy, aggression, independence and benevolence between female and male entrepreneurs. Also, no differences were found in risk taking propensity of male and female entrepreneurs. However, we do need to talk explicitly about women entrepreneurs. It should be stressed that rural women can encounter many constraints when trying to take part in the transformation process. Rural areas tend to be more traditional in regard to the gender issue.

In rural areas, the gender issue is usually a much stronger hindering factor to potential female entrepreneurs than it is in urban areas, their self-esteem and managerial skills being lower when compared to urban women and access to external financial resources more difficult than in urban areas. Therefore, special programmes of assistance to overcome these constraints should be developed and designed to meet the needs of rural women in order to be able to take an active part in entrepreneurial restructuring of their communities, to start to develop their own ventures, to expand their already existing businesses, or to function as social entrepreneurs since their number today is still below the potential one.

To this end, based on my own experience as well as on the experiences of so many entrepreneurial women I have met across the world in my profession and in business, I very much agree with Juliana Schwager-Jebbink's comment: "Nowadays, reflecting on the phenomenon of the successful female manager read entrepreneur), it is the individuality which must stand out and there are no general recipes to be presented. After my years as President of the Swiss Federation of Business and Professional Women, going all over the country and abroad to speak on development programmes for women, I firmly believe that quotas, positive discrimination and equal opportunity' politics do not help the female manager: it is she herself who must do the managing of her life.

This is true for all of Europe... " This belief is the one for which we as trainers are responsible to bring to rural women in addition to trying to put in place all factors crucial for rural women to enter into entrepreneurial activities. Without it, entrepreneurial opportunities will not be seen, they will be lost and then the role of women in rural development will be much below their potential.

ENTREPRENEURSHIP AND ECONOMIC GROWTH

The idea that entrepreneurship and economic growth are very closely and positively linked together has undoubtedly made its way since the early works of Schumpeter. An increase in the number of entrepreneurs leads to an increase in economic growth. This effect is a result of the concrete expression of their skills, and more precisely, their propensity to innovate.

Schumpeter has already described this innovative activity,"the carrying out of new combinations", by distinguishing five cases:"

1. The introduction of a new good - that is one with which consumers are not yet familiar - or of a new quality of a good.
2. The introduction of a new method of production, that is one not yet tested by experience in the branch of manufacture concerned, which need by no means be founded upon a discovery scientifically new, and can also exist in a new way of handling a commodity commercially.
3. The opening of a new market, that is a market into which the particular branch of manufacture of the country in question has not previously entered, whether or not this market has existed before.
4. The conquest of a new source of supply of raw materials or halfmanufactured goods, again irrespective of whether this source already exists or whether it has first to be created.
5. The carrying out of the new organisation of any industry, like the creation of a monopoly position or the breaking up of a monopoly position".

Through his innovative activity, the Schumpeterian entrepreneur seeks to create new profit opportunities. These opportunities can result from productivity increases, in which case, their relationship to economic growth appears quite clearly. Moreover, the disequilibrium created by the entrepreneur can be propitious for additional innovations and profit opportunities.

Therefore, more entrepreneurs means more growth, which in turn leads to more entrepreneurs... The phenomena seem to be self-feeding. Although in some way relatively limited in regards to the interaction between entrepreneurship and economic growth, economic theory is not without enlightening arguments on the subject. As suggested, use some of these arguments in our examination of two fundamental questions, which have already received some treatment in the economic literature.

The first of these questions is the assessment, by means of a non-formalised discussion, of the interdependent nature of entrepreneurship and growth. This assessment will permit us to set certain limits on this relationship. As suggested, grant special attention to particular concepts, as well as to the description of entrepreneurial supply, by referring to individual decisions to undertake economic activities.

These decisions can appear as the result of an arbitrage between different professional occupations based on relative expected rewards just as to the specific abilities of the agent. As suggested, then suggest the endogenous relationship between entrepreneurship and growth and how labour market reactions operate to create some boundaries on their symbiotic interactions. The second question that is examined is in fact threefold.

It deals with the types of activities to which the entrepreneur directs his talents. These activities will be distinguished just as to the social productivity of their character. As suggested, introduce, at this time, rent-seeking behaviour, followed by an examination of factors explaining the allocation of entrepreneurial skill. Finally, respective to this allocation, as suggested, see that an assessment of its impact in terms of economic growth must be appreciated not only in a static framework - the importance of positive effects for the society as a whole depends upon the proportion of productive projects -, but must also take into account the interactions between entrepreneurship and rent-seeking behaviour.

OCCUPATIONAL ARBITRAGE AND ECONOMIC GROWTH

This part is articulated as follows: first, as suggested, reappraise, from the introduction, the relationship between entrepreneurship and economic growth by going a step further into conceptualisation. As suggested, point out skills that are generally associated with the entrepreneur. The individual arbitrage between different professional occupations will then be sketched. An entrepreneurial supply will be defined. Finally, taking into account the aggregated impact of individual choices on expected pay-offs, will allow us to underscore the endogeneity of growth and entrepreneurial decisions.

Innovative Entrepreneurship and Economic Growth

Among the possible sources of economic growth and development, innovation has received a special treatment in the economic literature because it has been more or less linked with the figure of the individual entrepreneur. Relatively to this question, the early Schumpeter appears to be particularly original and pervasive.

Since the beginning of the twentieth century however, the way in which economic theory brings together economic and innovative processes through entrepreneurship, must certainly be revised. In fact, this has been in that economic analysis has undoubtedly reduced the"noise" between the articulation of simple concepts and recent observations. Schumpeter himself predicted that, due to irresistible trend of concentration in the capitalist system, innovation could no longer be the realm of the entrepreneur, but would in fact primarily be the job of innovation professionals and laboratories controlled by big companies, themselves being directed by managers.

If indeed there still remains a place for innovative entrepreneurship, embodied by the action of individuals, it can no longer be seen as the sole vector of innovation. In a recent and comprehensive survey of the literature,

Wennekers and Thurik emphasise the decomposition of the concept of entrepreneurship in order to gain a better understanding of the links between entrepreneurship and economic growth. Although their"pragmatic distinctions" are formulated for operational and not theoretical purposes, they remain helpful in grasping the question at hand.

Table. Three Type of Entrepreneurs

Self-employed	Employee
Entrepreneurial	Schumpeterian
Intrapreneurs	
	Entrepreneurs
Managerial	Managerial business
Executive managers	owners

Associating, on the one hand, entrepreneurial with"the manifest ability and willingness of individuals, on their own, in teams, within and outside existing organisations, to perceive and create new economic opportunities and to introduce their ideas in the market, in the face of uncertainty and other obstacles, by making decisions on location, form and the use of resources and institutions", and, on the other hand, managerial with"organising and coordinating", Wennekers and Thurik cross these definitions with the distinction between self-employed and employee.

Thus, the authors are able to define four different types of situations. Three of these are types of entrepreneurs: Schumpeterian entrepreneurs (entrepreneurial and self- employed), entrepreneurs (entrepreneurial and employee) and managerial business owners (managerial and self-employed).

Both Schumpeterian entrepreneurs and intrapreneurs contribute actively to feed a creative destruction process. Although managerial business owners play an important role in the economy for the achievement of production and trade, and can even reveal themselves as entrepreneurial and develop innovative projects, their activities are more closely tied to routine work. So,"(t)hey include many franchisees, shopkeepers and people in professional occupations" and generally represent the great majority of the self-employed.

By introducing new ideas, new processes, new products and services, Schumpeterian entrepreneurs and intrapreneurs affect and ultimately renew the economic activities: the activities not only of the firms and industries, but also those of the region in which they are situated. When these entrepreneurial initiatives are aggregated and evaluated in terms of economic impacts at a territorial level, it could mean economic growth.

This process tends to be a diverse one."At the aggregate level of industries, regions and national economies, the many individual entrepreneurial actions compose a mosaic of new experiments. In evolutionary terms this can be called variety. A process of competition between these various ideas and initiatives takes place continuously, leading to the selection of the most viable firms and industries. Variety, competition, selection and also imitation (...) expand and transform the productive potential of a regional or national economy (by replacement or displacement of obsolete firms, by higher productivity and by expansion of new niches and industries)".

Greater productivity, as well as firm exits, allow for the possibility of resource reallocation into new combinations. When particular to a given territory, this greater productivity could mean an increase in competitive advantages and localised economic growth.

However, this process should be globally followed by a positive net effect. In other words, the competition case that we describe is not a zero-sum game. From entrepreneurial initiatives to economic growth, a number of conditions and multiple effects, at different levels, ultimately determine the impact of one phenomenon in regards to another. However, a working assumption will be: the larger the share of innovative entrepreneurs in the workforce, the more elevated the rhythm of economic growth.

Towards the Definition of an Entrepreneurial Supply

A simple approach in determining the share of innovative entrepreneurs in the active population is to begin by considering each individual as a potential entrepreneur, characterised by the specific capacity to become one. That is, we recognise the heterogeneity of the population. These individuals are then confronted with heterogeneous career opportunities (different projects) with different expected pay-offs.

The individual choice is finally an arbitrage between pairs of project and pay-offs, for given skill sets. These projects include the choice of a career as an employee. What then, briefly, are the individual characteristics that determine the entrepreneurial potentialities? Knight introduces a distinction between risk and uncertainty. Risk enters into computations with known probabilities.

On the contrary, uncertainty although it takes into account the notion of risk, refers also to non-foreseeable events. In other words, events whose probabilities are at this time unknown. Estimating the degree, to which a particular event is weighted with uncertainty, depends upon individual judgement expressed in terms of subjective probabilities.

This understood, an entrepreneurial candidate is the one who, taking into account his judgement, would accept to bear the uncertainty of production and trade. Expected profits would be payment for this specific activity. We note, by the way, that, within a Schumpeterian framework, what characterises an entrepreneur is not a particular ability to bear the consequences of unforeseeable events.

The capitalist plays this role. Undertaking economic activities and innovating require skills that make the entrepreneur a person of exception. One of his motives continues to be profit-seeking. Lucas, Murphy, Shleifer and Vishny, Jovanovic come closer to a Schumpeterian concept of entrepreneurship in the sense that, in their models, individuals are not different in their attitude towards risk, but in their competence, intelligence, creative capacities... It is in fact possible to see in the enumeration, a wide range of skills that are corresponding to "talents", valuable traits in an entrepreneurial project.

A synthesis of the different approaches runs through the tight definition of an entrepreneur offer curve. This offer sums up, amongst other arguments, the previously evoked traits of the working population. It meets an entrepreneurial demand that represents a variety of profit opportunities. What can be considered as the advantageous aspects of the offer-demand synthesis, at the same time comprises some of its weaknesses.

The general framework on which it is based, can disguise heterogeneous situations that each previous model translates, although only in part. We must recognise that what is following an individual arbitrage is in fact rather coming out of a black box.

More Entrepreneurs, more Growth, more Entrepreneurs

We can consider an individual's career as a chain of individual arbitrages between pairs of project and pay-offs given individual abilities. Aggregating individual situations at a given time t, reveals the share of entrepreneurs in the working population. However, for the purposes of assessing more carefully the links between entrepreneurship and economic growth, this is not a sufficient result.

Time must be reintroduced as a period, allowing in that case interactions between each term By fostering economic growth, entrepreneurship affects the whole economy. Particularly hard to ignore are its effects on labour markets. More growth might, on one hand, signify an increase in profit opportunities for potential entrepreneurs. On the other hand, it could lead to inflationary pressures on wages.

It must be noted that raises in wage cannot necessarily be derived as the result of disequilibrium on the labour markets. In fact, raises in wage may indeed be the consequence of the application of profit-sharing schemes within the firms. It follows that growth in turn can seriously affect the individual arbitrage that we have discussed. So, appears the problem of endogeneity by way of markets and pay-offs adjustments.

ENTREPRENEURSHIP VERSUS RENT-SEEKING

Different rhythms of growth between nations, that have been theoretically associated with entrepreneurship, are not fully explained by different entrepreneurial supply, measured in quantitative terms. The allocation of this supply between more and less socially productive projects must also be taken into account. This question introduces the idea of rent-seeking behaviour. After having briefly defined the general framework and the employed concepts, as suggested, discuss the allocation of entrepreneurs between different types of economic projects, as well as the explicative factors of this allocation. A dynamic set-up will follow, where as suggested, examine interactions between project categories and their relations to growth.

Definitions

To this point, the individual arbitrage between different remunerative occupations ended up, in all cases, in the development of socially productive activities. Therefore, the described economy has been a strict income economy. Individuals were exploiting, as best they could, their skills entrepreneurial or otherwise and given the exercised occupations, private interests and social benefits were successfully coinciding.

As suggested, introduce another type of activity, which is remunerated by transfers. We may note that, by definition, transfers do not imply a productive counterpart. This assumption will result in the possibility that a distortion between private and collective interests may occur. This distortion becomes undoubtedly effective when rent-seeking is involved. The rent-seeking refers to "the socially costly pursuit of wealth transfers". In other words, rent-seeking is manifested when the bottom-line of its social consequences is negative.

The fact that this definition allows for an expression of the social opportunity cost that represents a diversion of resources towards this type of activity should be emphasised. Examples of rentseeking are: corruption, stealing, bribery, as well as seeking abusive judicial compensation or protection-seeking with the express purpose of limiting economic competition and promoting particular interest... Rent-seeking can originate both from the public or private sector.

In regards to the connection between entrepreneurship and growth, the occurrence of unproductive but yet remunerated activities means not only that projects with socially positive or negative impacts are in competition, but also that there is a direct potential diversion of entrepreneurial talents. For this diversion to take place, we need indeed to assume that the skills and abilities required by entrepreneurship and by rent-seeking correspond. Following these considerations, at least two remarks can be formulated. The first one refers to public services.

These are generally financed by transfers, but are not included in rent-seeking, given their productive contribution. We note furthermore that discussing the redistribution role of the state is outside the framework. This is different, however, as soon as we look at legal institutions that organise productive activities, as they might, by limiting competition for example, create rent-seeking situations. The second remark concerns the entrepreneurial initiatives. Through innovation, the entrepreneur seeks to create a monopoly position, from which he will assume overprofit. In the Schumpeterian model, this position is necessary fore it motivates the innovation activity.

It is however temporary, as competition will quickly reduce this position to zero in favour of a new monopoly position created by a new innovation... The institutional framework, that of competition, is then of primary importance. In this case, a dynamic assessment of events will justify the existence of an abnormal profit, as it will distinguish its positive net contribution to the social benefit. Rent-seeking behaviour thus being defined, as suggested, address in the remaining discussion the allocation of talents and its links to growth.

Explaining the Allocation of Talents

The allocation of talents between socially productive and unproductive projects and its impact on economic growth have already been subject to theoretical studies.

The static results of these studies scarcely elicit further commentary, when we take into account the preceding arguments. Indeed it appears quite easily that the diversion of entrepreneurial talents towards unproductive activities will have a negative impact on growth rate.

However, the explicative factors of the allocation deserve greater consideration. Attempting to explain the allocation of talents implies both reconsidering the arguments that have been exposed with regard to the individual arbitrage between remunerative activities and considering the non-pecuniary factors that may also have some impact. Murphy, Shleifer and Vishny, the point is the following: "talent goes into activities with the highest private returns, which need not have the highest social returns". These authors assume increasing returns on talent.

In other words, the greater the ability of an individual, the greater his private benefits will be. Because the exercise of talent is physically limited, talented individuals tend to invest themselves and their abilities into reward maximising occupations. It follows that their occupational choice will be determined by the size of the market, the compensation contract and the technology.

Furthermore, the allocation of talent can be linked both with institutional context, as well as non-pecuniary explicative factors. The legal framework and its effective use define a propitious environment for entrepreneurship and, contrarily, for rent-seeking behaviour. Property rights, the conditions of their application, and the respect of these rights, appear to be crucial factors. They contribute particularly and decisively to precise the compensation circumstances that have already been quoted, as well as the fiscal organisation.

Information is also important as it determines the efficiency of allocation and the possibility of linking the application of talent and its results. Social esteem might play a role. The question becomes therefore how much entrepreneurship is socially valuable and valorised, over another less socially productive occupation. Finally, entrepreneurs or rent-seekers might influence, by voting or lobbying, political organisation and political decisions. The idea is that the political equilibrium, replying to one or another group's interests, will make decisions that favour its maintenance.

Entrepreneurship and Rent-seeking in Motion

The interaction between entrepreneurship and rent-seeking is without doubt an interesting question to examine. Formalised models show that multiple equilibria – an equilibrium being defined by an entrepreneur share in the population and a rate of growth – may exist. As suggested, not insist on model developments.

The interested reader may consult the references we provide. However, briefly, we note that the results are grounded on the specification of two functions, both with negative slopes, and consequently a potential for multiple intersections. Because it places burdens on entrepreneurial rewards, rent-seeking negatively affects entrepreneurship. Moreover, given competition in the rent-seeking sector itself, rent-seeking rewards will depend negatively on the number of rent-seekers.

Baland and Francois formalise as well the effect of entrepreneurial activities on rent-seeking. Their model can apply to an economy with import license. The production of direct substitutes by local entrepreneurs tends to turn off the rents obtained by importers. Here also, results suggest the existence of multiple equilibria.

Murphy, Shleifer and Vishny deal with rent-seeking affecting the innovation sector. The rent-seeking, whether from private or public origins, can undoubtedly burden the profits of established productive sectors. The innovation sector, however, might be described the reserved hunting ground, for the most part, of public rent-seeking. Their arguments rely particularly on the nature of innovation. In his project developments, the innovative entrepreneur is confronted with legal and environmental constraints. Innovation can imply indeed production permits, licenses, dispensations, as well as amending the local zoning regulations.

This results in demand for government intervention and it provides opportunities for corruption. Moreover, the socially unproductive transfers that corruption implies, might have some inhibitive effects on innovation activity, given that innovators may not have equal lobbying power compared to that of established firms, or the same financial resources to pay bribes. Important funds may then be consumed instead of being invested, to avoid expropriation.

The ex post existence of rent-seeking should raise the project risk and effective cost. The authors mention, following these arguments, that the negative effects of rent-seeking could be limited if the rent-seeker himself becomes a stakeholder in the innovation project. In the long run, he would find his interest in such an involvement.

We note moreover that this idea can be generalised as: rent-seeking, by burdening current entrepreneurial profits, limits its future transfer opportunities. Thus, the interaction between entrepreneurship and rent-seeking can generate multiple equilibria that correspond to an allocation of talents and an economic growth rate.

Starting from a dynamic extension of his basic model, Acemoglu discusses the history dependence of an economy. Past and current allocations of talents influence the future structure of rewards. Given historical circumstances, the economy can be locked in low or high steady state equilibrium. Under these circumstances, only a shock will have any positive and sustainable effect.

FACTORS EFFECTING ENTREPRENEURIAL GROWTH

Following are the factors of environment affecting entrepreneurial growth. These conditions are grouped under two categories:

1. Economic conditions
2. Non-economic conditions

ECONOMIC FACTORS (STUDY OF CLASS)

Economic conditions includes the capital, labour, raw material and market.

Capital

It is the essence of enterprise. Availability of capital facilitates mobility of land, material etc., is required to produce goods. Therefore, capital is a lubricant which smoothens the working of vehicle called enterprise. Increases capital investment, capital output ratio results in profit, which ultimately goes up to capital formation.

Labour

Quality and quantity of labour influence the entrepreneurship mobility, dexterity and immobility. Low cost labour and capital intensive technology oriented enterprises influence entrepreneurship.

Raw Material

Availability of raw material, nature of industrial establishment, technology innovation and mobility of raw material encourages or curbs the development of entrepreneurship.

Market

The potential of the market constitutes the major department of probable rewards from entrepreneurial function. The size and composition of market monopoly in a particular product influence entrepreneurship.

NON-ECONOMIC FACTORS (WITH REFERENCE TO CLASS STUDY)

Non-economic conditions are as follows: social conditions, psychological conditions and political or governmental action. Sociologists and psychologists view that the influence of economic factors on entrepreneurial emergence largely depend upon the existence of non-economic factors.

Social conditions are as follow:

- Socio-cultural norms and values
- Degree of approval or disapproval of entrepreneurial behaviour.
- Family background, standard of education, technical knowledge and information.
- Financial stability, caste and religious affiliation.

Psychological conditions are as follow:

- David Mcdellond's theory of need achievement—A constellation of personality characteristics, and high need achievement is the major determinant of entrepreneurship.
- Individual works in the society but remains different.
- Impact of achievement motivation and training programmes influence development of entrepreneurship.

GOVERNMENT ACTIONS:- (WITH REFERENCE TO SPECIAL LEGISLATIONS AND COURT CASES)

- Government encourage entrepreneurship by creating basic facilities, utilities and services and by providing incentives and concessions.
- Government provides the prospective entrepreneurships a facilitative socio-economic setting.
- Entrepreneurship development is based on the government interest in economic development of the society.

The emergence of entrepreneurship. These factors are interlocking, mutually dependent and mutually reinforcing.

ENTREPRENEURIAL MOTIVATION—MEANING

It is often said that a person cannot win a game that they do not play. In the context of entrepreneurship, this statement suggests that success depends on people's willingness to become entrepreneurs.

Moreover, because the pursuit of entrepreneurial opportunity is an evolutionary process in which people select out at many steps along the way, decisions made after the discovery of opportunities—to positively evaluate opportunities, to pursue resources, and to design the mechanisms of exploitation—also depend on the willingness of people to "play" the game.

We argue that human motivations influence these decisions, and that variance across people in these motivations will influence who pursues entrepreneurial opportunities, who assembles resources, and how people undertake the entrepreneurial process. In recent years, entrepreneurship research has focused largely on the environmental characteristics influencing firm foundings and the characteristics of entrepreneurial opportunities. Although this focus has greatly enhanced our understanding of the entrepreneurial phenomenon, it ignores the role of human agency. Entrepreneurship depends on the decisions that people make about how to undertake that process.

We argue that the attributes of people making decisions about the entrepreneurial process influence the decisions that they make. Although previous researchers have rightly criticized much of the existing empirical research on the role of human motivation in entrepreneurship, we argue that inadequate empirical work does not negate the importance of understanding the role of human motivation in the entrepreneurial process.

In fact, even sociologists who have argued strongly against the usefulness of trait-based research in entrepreneurship implicitly acknowledge that motivation must matter to this process. Aldrich and Zimmer, for example, write, entrepreneurial activity "can be conceptualized as a function of opportunity structures and motivated entrepreneurs with access to resources". We also believe that these criticisms have resulted in insufficient consideration of the role of the human motivation in the entrepreneurial process in recent entrepreneurship research.

Consequently, we are left with theories of entrepreneurship that do not consider variation in the motivations of different people. We believe that such an omission is problematic because, as Baumol eloquently argued, the study of entrepreneurship that does not explicitly consider entrepreneurs is like the analysis of Shakespeare in which "the Prince of Denmark has been expunged from the discussion of Hamlet."

We identify several human motivations that influence the entrepreneurial process. In our arguments, we explicitly assume that all human action is the result of both motivational and cognitive factors, the latter including ability, intelligence, and skills. We also assume that entrepreneurship is not solely the result of human action; external factors also play a role. However, environmental factors being held constant, we argue that human motivation plays a critical role in the entrepreneurial process.

To this end, we suggest ways that researchers could develop more realistic explanations for how human motivation influences the entrepreneurial process than is the norm in the literature to date. We believe that this approach could overcome many of the criticisms of prior research on person-centric explanations for entrepreneurship. Finally, we offer suggestions on how empirical researchers should test these arguments in ways that overcome many of the criticisms of extant research on this topic. Our object proceeds as follows: We define entrepreneurship and present several arguments for why the study of entrepreneurship in general and consideration of the role of human motivation in the process in particular are important.

We discuss opposing views of how opportunities may affect the relationship between motivation and entrepreneurship. We summarize the major mechanisms by which previous researchers believe motivation influences entrepreneurship. We identify what we believe are the major problems with prior research on motivation and entrepreneurship. We provide some recommendations for researchers conducting empirical research in this area.

WHAT IS ENTREPRENEURSHIP AND WHY STUDY IT FROM THE POINT OF VIEW OF HUMAN MOTIVATION?

We believe that the study of the entrepreneurial process is important for several reasons. First, entrepreneurship drives innovation and technical change, and therefore generates economic growth. Second, as the Austrian economists have explained, entrepreneurial action is the process through which supply and demand are equilibrated. Third, entrepreneurship is an important process by which new knowledge is converted into products and services.

Fourth, entrepreneurship has become an important vocation and we need to understand its role in the development of human and intellectual capital. We adopt Shane and Venkataraman's definition of entrepreneurship as the process by which "opportunities to create future goods and services are discovered, evaluated, and exploited." As these authors have explained, this definition does not require viewing entrepreneurs as the founders of new organizations.

An options trader can be an entrepreneur, as can a corporate salesman who discovers and pursues opportunities for the creation of new products. Moreover, this definition shows that entrepreneurship is a creative process. By rearranging resources in a new way, entrepreneurs engage in creative activity. However, the degree of creativity involved in entrepreneurship varies across the types of resource recombination that occurs. For example, the creation of business to undertake space tourism may be more creative than the creation of a new restaurant in a strip mall. Entrepreneurship involves human agency.

The entrepreneurial process occurs because people act to pursue opportunities. People differ in their willingness and abilities to act on these opportunities because they are different from each other. We argue that the variation among people in their willingness and ability to act has important effects on the entrepreneurial process. Recent research has been relatively accepting of arguments that people vary in their willingness and ability to engage in the entrepreneurial process because of nonmotivational individual differences. Researchers have shown that the willingness of people to pursue entrepreneurial opportunities depends on such things as their opportunity cost, their stocks of financial capital, their social ties to investors, and their career experience.

We argue that motivational differences also influence the entrepreneurial process. For example, such things as variation across people in their perceptions of risk and opportunity influence entrepreneurial decisions. People vary in how they view the risk of expending resources before knowing the distribution of outcomes. Similarly, the probability of success at the entrepreneurial process is low, and those people who are willing to proceed despite these odds might be more optimistic or higher in self-efficacy than people deterred by these odds. We consider the incorporation of this individual-level variation in motivation to be important to the entrepreneurial process.

To isolate the effects of entrepreneurial motivation, other factors that could have a causal effect on the process and outcome of entrepreneurship need to be controlled. One category of control variables is the external environment.

These would include such things as:

- Political factors (*e.g.*, legal restrictions, quality of law enforcement, political stability, and currency stability);
- Market forces (*e.g.*, structure of the industry, technology regime, potential barriers to entry, market size, and population demographics);
- Resources (*e.g.*, availability of investment capital, labour market including skill availability, transportation infrastructure, and complementary technology).

Most researchers either explicitly or implicitly agree that these categories of factors influence the entrepreneurial process and need to be controlled to measure the effect of motivations on the entrepreneurial process. While it is clear why the factors need to be controlled if we are to fully understand how motivation is related to entrepreneurship, it is less clear how opportunities affect this relationship. Because the first two authors were unable to agree on the concept of opportunities, we present two versions of the relationship between opportunities and motivation. First, as suggested, present the view shared by Shane and Collins, then as suggested, present Locke's view.

ENTREPRENEURS, OPPORTUNITIES, AND THE EFFECTS OF MOTIVATION

Opportunities are aspects of the environment that represent potentialities for profit making. We follow Shane and Venkataraman to define entrepreneurial opportunities as "situations in which new goods, services, raw materials, and organizing methods can be introduced and sold at greater than the cost of their production." Since potentialities are not yet actual, measuring them objectively and prospectively at the level of an individual entrepreneur poses daunting challenges.

Entrepreneurs can pursue opportunities in any industry at any time. For example, some entrepreneurs build successful new companies by contributing to the founding of a new industry, such as Robert Swanson in biotechnology. Other entrepreneurs build new companies in old and mature industries such as Sam Walton in retailing. Aggregate statistics show us that the general category of opportunities to which Sam Walton and Bob Swanson responded was not equal.

The average value of new businesses created in retail is lower than the average value of new businesses created in biotechnology. Because human motivations are likely widely distributed across industry categories at the aggregate level, statistically significant differences in the mean value of businesses created in different industry categories suggest that the value of opportunities varies across industry.

This does not mean that entrepreneurs cannot successfully pursue opportunities in lowopportunity industries. Rather it means that the opportunities in these industries are simply less attractive to the average person.

The value of opportunities also varies within industries. Because the opportunities that entrepreneurs identify and pursue have different economic value, the opportunities themselves influence entrepreneurial behaviour. We believe that it is important for behaviourally oriented entrepreneurship researchers to consider and measure the economic value of these opportunities in research about the motivations of entrepreneurs. For example, in the early 1970s, Butler Lampson and Chuck Thacker, researchers at Xerox Parc, invented the Alto—the first personal computer.

However, their design would have cost over US$10,000 to build. When Steve Jobs and Steve Wozniak came up with the design for the Apple computer, their design cost less than US$3000 to build. Because the number of people who would pay more than US$10,000 for a PC was much smaller than number of people who would pay US$3000, the financial value of the Jobs and Wozniak opportunity was greater than the value of the Xerox opportunity.

One would expect that differences in the estimates of the value of the PC opportunity that resulted from the different solutions influenced the decisions of the different parties about their opportunities. Of course, although it is possible that Jobs and Wozniak possessed more of the relevant motives to pursue entrepreneurial opportunities than did Lampson and Thacker, researchers can only estimate the effect of these motives if they account for the differences in the two opportunities. Although we argue that opportunities influence entrepreneurial behaviour, we do not argue that opportunities fully determine the process. Entrepreneurs are people and may make different decisions when confronted with similar opportunities. In addition to being influenced by the opportunity that Steve Jobs pursued at the time of founding, the development of Apple was likely influenced by Steve Jobs' motivations. Empirically, the objective and subjective parts of opportunity are difficult to separate.

The mechanism for actualizing an opportunity often initially exists mainly in the entrepreneur's mind, making the entrepreneur's idea for how to exploit the opportunity a personal interpretation of the opportunity. This idea is basically what we would call vision.

Such judgements may be mistaken; entrepreneurs sometimes believe that they have identified valuable opportunities when, in fact, no valuable opportunities actually existed, at least in the form in which they were conceptualized. Also, entrepreneurs may differ in how they interpret opportunities. For example, the development of the Internet has allowed entrepreneurs to develop new organizing methods, such as "e-tailing," that were never before possible. Although a wide variety of entrepreneurs have responded to the opportunities to develop new organizing methods that the Internet has generated, these entrepreneurs have developed approaches of different value in response to this organizing opportunity.

Some entrepreneurs have developed opportunities to compete with established retailers through e-tailing, while others have sought only to design web sites. Even though the way that opportunities are manifested in the entrepreneur's plans for exploitation are personal, the variance in their estimated value likely influences the decisions that people make in the entrepreneurial process and can confound attempts to measure the effects of motivation on this process.

This is true even if the value is partially a function of the other decisions that the entrepreneur has made and partially a function of external forces.

MOTIVATION AND ENTREPRENEURSHIP: IMPORTANT MOTIVATIONAL CONCEPTS FROM PRIOR QUANTITATIVE RESEARCH

Previous research has explored several motivations and their effects on entrepreneurship. We discuss several of these concepts. However, we do not provide a complete review of prior empirical research for two reasons. First, the definitions of entrepreneurship used in previous empirical research on motivation and entrepreneurship are inconsistent with our definition, making it impossible to draw direct implications of prior work for research using our definition. Second, prior research has suffered from significant methodological problems, making prior findings suggestive rather than conclusive, even for research that employs the same definition of entrepreneurship as was used in those studies. Therefore, we discuss empirical research only to show the ways in which motivation can influence different aspects of the entrepreneurial process.

Need for Achievement

Within the research domain of personality traits and entrepreneurship, the concept of need for achievement has received much attention. McClelland argued that individuals who are high in nAch are more likely than those who are low in nAch to engage in activities or tasks that have a high degree of individual responsibility for outcomes, require individual skill and effort, have a moderate degree of risk, and include clear feedback on performance.

Further, McClelland argued that entrepreneurial roles are characterized as having a greater degree of these task attributes than other careers; thus, it is likely that people high in nAch will be more likely to pursue entrepreneurial jobs than other types of roles. Johnson conducted a traditional review of 23 studies, which varied regarding samples, measurement of nAch,, and definitions of entrepreneurship.

Based on this group of studies, Johnson concluded that there is a relationship between nAch and entrepreneurial activity—in this case, nAch distinguished firm founders from other members of society. In a similar review of 19 studies, Fineman concluded that both projective and questionnaire measures of nAch significantly predict firm founding. Collins, Locke, and Hanges conducted the first and only meta-analysis of nAch and entrepreneurship studies, examining 63 nAch and entrepreneurship studies.

The overall finding of the meta-analysis is that nAch is significantly related to founding a company. The nAch both differentiated between entrepreneurs and others and predicted the performance of the founders' firms.

Further, they found no significant differences in the predictive validity of three different measures of nAch. Moreover, Collins found that the relationship between nAch and entrepreneurial activity was moderated by several factors. First, nAch was a more robust predictor of group-level effects (*e.g.*, mean differences between firm founders and another profession, mean differences between high-performing and low-performing founders) than individuallevel effects (*e.g.*, predicting the performance of individuals). Second, they found that while nAch is a strong differentiator between firm founders and nonmanagerial employees, it is not a strong differentiator between firm founders and managers.

Based on these results, Collins concluded that nAch is an effective tool for differentiating between firm founders and the general population but less so for differentiating between firm founders and managers. Further, they concluded that nAch might be particularly effective at differentiating between successful and unsuccessful groups of firm founders. Thus, nAch could play a very useful role in explaining entrepreneurial activity.

Risk Taking

Risk-taking propensity is another motivation of interest, which emerged from McClelland's original research on entrepreneurs. McClelland claimed that individuals with high achievement needs would have moderate propensities to take risk. This claim by McClelland is especially interesting for entrepreneurship research because the entrepreneurial process involves acting in the face of uncertainty. Liles argued that entrepreneurs often must accept uncertainty with respect to financial well-being, psychic well-being, career security, and family relations.

Moreover, several theories of entrepreneurship view the entrepreneur as bearing residual uncertainty. Atkinson argued that individuals who have higher achievement motivation should prefer activities of intermediate risk because these types of activities will provide a challenge, yet appear to be attainable.

On the other hand, individuals who score high on the motive to avoid failure will avoid intermediate risks. Instead, they will prefer easy and safe under- takings or extremely difficult and risky ones. Following the lead of Atkinson, risk-taking propensity has been defined in the entrepreneurship literature as the willingness to take moderate risks.

Despite these theoretical claims, previous research suggests that firm owners do not differ significantly from managers or even the general population in risk taking. For example, Litzinger failed to find any difference between motel owners and motel managers on risk preference. Kogan and Wallach found that firm founders clustered around the mean risk-taking score of the general population.

In comparisons of firm founders and managers, neither Babb and Babb nor Palich and Bagby found significant differences between the two groups in terms of risk-taking propensity. However, moderate, or high risk-takers. Only Brockhaus tested for the actual level of risk taking, and he found that firm founders did prefer moderate risk but did not differ from managers in this regard.

Only one study found a difference between firm founders and managers in this motivation. In a study of 239 New England business executives, Begley found that risk-taking propensity was the only trait on which founders and nonfounders differed. Begley failed to identify whether the level of entrepreneurial risk taking was low, moderate, or high.

While these empirical findings suggest that risk taking may or may not be an entrepreneurial motivation, self-efficacy may be confounding the findings. Several recent evaluative studies using interviews and expert evaluations showed that firm founders objectively have a higher propensity for risk than do members of the general population, but that firm founders do not perceive their actions as risky. Similarly, Sarasvathy, Simon, and Lave found that when expert firm founders were asked to evaluate the same entrepreneurial simulations as bankers, the firm founders saw opportunities in information that the bankers thought indicated risk. Thus, the measurement of risk-taking propensity may be confounded with high self-efficacy.

Tolerance for Ambiguity

Schere argued that tolerance for ambiguity is an important trait for entrepreneurs because the challenges and potential for success associated with business start-ups are by nature unpredictable. Budner defined tolerance for ambiguity as the propensity to view situations without clear outcomes as attractive rather than threatening. Because entrepreneurs continually face more uncertainty in their everyday environment than do managers of established organizations, entrepreneurs who remain in their jobs are likely to score high on tests for this trait than would managers. There is mixed support for this prediction. Begley and Boyd found that firm founders scored significantly higher in tolerance for ambiguity than did managers, defined as nonfounders working in business.

In smaller sample studies, both Schere and Miller and Drodge found that firm founders were significantly higher in tolerance for ambiguity than were managers. Finally, based on a review of four additional studies, Sexton and Bowman identified tolerance for ambiguity as a distinguishing psychological characteristic between firm founders and managers. However, several studies did not match these findings.

Babb and Babb found no significant difference in tolerance for ambiguity between founders and nonfounders of rural businesses in Northern Florida. Similarly, Begley found no significant differences between New England firm founders and managers on their tolerance for ambiguity. This inconsistency in findings and potential methodological problems in the research that provides support for the tolerance of ambiguity proposition suggests that we do not yet know if tolerance of ambiguity is a motivation that affects any part of the entrepreneurial process.

Locus of Control

Another motivational trait that has received attention is locus of control—the belief in the extent to which individuals believe that their actions or personal characteristics affect outcomes. Individuals who have an external locus of control believe that the outcome of an extent is out of their control, whereas individuals with an internal locus of control believe that their personal actions directly affect the outcome of an event. As McClelland discussed earlier, individuals who are high in nAch prefer situations in which they feel that they have direct control over outcomes or in which they feel that they can directly see how their effort affects outcomes of a given event. This point was extended by Rotter who argued that individuals with an internal locus of control would be likely to seek entrepreneurial roles because they desire positions in which their actions have a direct impact on results. The research on locus of control suggests that firm founders differ from the general population in terms of locus of control.

Shapero found that firm founders from Texas and Italy were more "internal" than other groups of professions reported by Rotter. This same pattern holds with female firm founders versus the general female population and with Black firm founders versus the general Black population. While locus of control orientation differs between firm founders and the general public, most studies have not found a difference between firm founders and managers on locus of control, a result similar to the situation with studies on nAch.

For example, Babb and Babb found no differences in locus of control between founders and managers in small businesses in Northern Florida. Similarly, Brockhaus found that managers and owners of new businesses did not differ on locus of control. In a longitudinal study of students, Hull, Bosley, and Udell found that locus of control did not differentiate between students who went on to work in managerial positions and those who started their own business.

Finally, in the studies of New England entrepreneurs, Begley and Begley and Boyd found that locus of control did not distinguish between founders and managers. We suspect that one reason for the difference between firm founder and the general population, but not between founders and managers, is the similarity between founding a company and managing.

Defining entrepreneurial situations as starting a company rather than working for others might not capture the real differences between entrepreneurial and nonentrepreneurial situations. For example, serving as a manager in a rapidly growing high-technology company might demand greater entrepreneurial motivations than starting a corner grocery store.

Self-efficacy

Self-efficacy is the belief in one's ability to muster and implement the necessary personal resources, skills, and competencies to attain a certain level of achievement on a given task. In other words, self-efficacy can be seen as task-specific self-confidence. Self-efficacy for a specific task has been shown to be a robust predictor of an individual's performance in that task and helps to explain why people of equal ability can perform differently. An individual with high self-efficacy for a given task will exert more effort for a greater length of time, persist through set backs, set and accept higher goals, and develop better plans and strategies for the task.

A person with high self-efficacy will also take negative feedback in a more positive manner and use that feedback to improve their performance. These attributes of self-efficacy may be important to the entrepreneurial process because these situations are often ambiguous ones in which effort, persistence, and planning are important. One study directly assessed the effect of self-efficacy on some dimension of the entrepreneurial process.

Baum assessed firm founders in the architectural woodworking industry on a number of variables including general traits and motives, specific skills and competencies, situation-specific motivation, vision, and strategic action. In a LISREL model, Baum found that self-efficacy had a strong positive relationship with realised growth. In fact, it was the single best predictor in the entire array of variables.

Goal Setting

Tracy, Locke, and Renard conducted a study of the owners of small printing firms. Both concurrent and longitudinal measures of four aspects of performance were obtained: financial performance, growth, and innovation. The quantitative goals the entrepreneurs had for each outcome were significantly related to their corresponding outcomes, both concurrently and longitudinally.

Baum, Locke, and Smith also found that growth goals were significantly related to the subsequent growth of architectural woodworking firms. Although there have been other studies of entrepreneurial goals, to our knowledge, only these two have related quantitative measures of goal difficulty to performance.

PROBLEMS WITH PREVIOUS RESEARCH ON HUMAN MOTIVATION AND ENTREPRENEURSHIP AND SUGGESTED SOLUTIONS TO THESE PROBLEMS

Despite the importance of including individual-level factors in a comprehensive explanation for the entrepreneurial process, previous studies of entrepreneurial motivation have often led to disappointing results. However, we believe that researchers should not conclude from this failure that human motivation is irrelevant to the entrepreneurial process. Rather, we suggest that there are specific reasons for the limited results obtained in previous research.

Controls for Opportunities

Previous research has suffered from a lack of control for the variation in the opportunities that different entrepreneurs pursue. To accurately measure the effects of motivation on entrepreneurial decisions, researchers need to control the effects of opportunities. As Venkataraman argued, a valuable opportunity for an individual is one that generates a level of profit that exceeds the entrepreneur's opportunity cost, a premium for the illiquidity of money, time, and effort expended, and a premium for bearing risk and uncertainty.

Because some opportunities will exceed this threshold by a greater amount than will others, the nature of the opportunity will influence entrepreneurial decisions. Researchers need to know the magnitude of the force exerted by the opportunities themselves to accurately estimate the effect of the individual motivations on entrepreneurial decisions. In the absence of such controls, one cannot know if the effects observed represent the effects of individual motivations or are artifacts of unobserved correlation between the opportunities and the people who pursue them.

Prior research has generally failed to control the effect of opportunities by examining entrepreneurs pursuing different opportunities without explicitly modeling the value of the different opportunities pursued. In addition, prior studies have generally compared managers with firm founders. However, human motivations can influence the tendency of people to engage in entrepreneurial activities only if those activities are possible.

If people have not discovered entrepreneurial opportunities or have discovered opportunities but cannot act on those discoveries, it is impossible to determine if their individual motivations make them more or less likely than others to act on entrepreneurial opportunities. Therefore, one cannot tell from studies that compare managers to firm founders whether certain motivations influence people to make entrepreneurial decisions unless researchers have ensured that the managers have discovered opportunities and have measured the value of those opportunities.

Otherwise, researchers might only capture the fact that some managers have all of the right motivations, but no opportunities in which to use them. We offer four suggestions to researchers interested in examining the effect of motivations on entrepreneurial decisions about how to deal with variation in opportunities.

First, researchers could explore settings in which potential entrepreneurs pursue reasonably identical opportunities. For example, every year, many potential entrepreneurs evaluate and pursue opportunities to purchase McDonald's franchises. When a person applies to be a McDonald's franchisee or company-owned outlet manager, one applies only to be part of the system rather than to select a particular outlet.

Therefore, the opportunities to which people respond in this setting are identical. By comparing the motivations of a sample of people seek to be McDonald's franchisees with people who seek to be McDonald's company-owned outlet managers, researchers can determine the contributions of particular motivations on the decision to entrepreneur. Second, as a variety of researchers are beginning to do, scholars could employ experimental designs in which potential entrepreneurs are asked to make a series of entrepreneurial decisions in a controlled simulation.

By measuring the motivations of potential entrepreneurs and examining the correlation between the motivations and the decisions made in these simulations, researchers could determine how motivations influence entrepreneurial decisions. Third, the most obvious means of controlling opportunity are to use a sample of entrepreneurs within the same industry and country and to measure aspects of the environment that might vary within industry and region.

We recommend these approaches to limiting other sources of variance than motivations from studies of motivation and entrepreneurship. Fourth, as some researchers are beginning to do, scholars could employ third parties to code the value of potential opportunities. For example, researchers could explore the propensity of inventors to found companies based on their inventions.

Because all inventors are at risk of exploiting their inventions through firm formation, this setting provides a useful context in which to explore the decision to entrepreneur. By partialing out the externally evaluated value of the opportunities, researchers could determine whether motivations influence the decision to entrepreneur, net of the effects of the value of the opportunity.

Entrepreneurship as a Process

Much of the prior research has looked at entrepreneurship as a profession that certain types of people adopt, rather than as a process that occurs over time. This approach is problematic because the appropriate conceptual lens through which to look at entrepreneurship is as a dynamic process. Because entrepreneurship is episodic and much entrepreneurial action is not long lasting, it is unrealistic to model motivation as dividing entrepreneurs and other members of society into two groups.

In fact, relatively little of the motivation research on entrepreneurship has considered the effects of motivation on specific steps in the entrepreneurial process. Most studies on motivation and entrepreneurship adopt static designs that seek to determine if firm founders are different from each other, managers, or the general population at the moment the two groups are measured. This approach makes two problematic assumptions.

First, it assumes that a given motivation influences all steps in the entrepreneurial process equally, and that the effects of a given motivation do not select out some people at earlier stages in the process. Second, it assumes that, at the moment in which the founders are compared to the others, the founders who are still in charge of the organizations that they founded represent the population of people who engage in entrepreneurial activity.

Because entrepreneurship is a process, with tremendous selection at each step, we believe that these assumptions are quite faulty. The motivations that allow progression from opportunity recognition to resource assembly might not lead from financial assembly to first sales. For example, to assemble resources, a person might need to be highly confident. Those people lacking sufficient overconfidence to assemble resources are selected out of the entrepreneurial process. If there is very little variation in overconfidence among the people who have resources and seek to reach first sales, overconfidence will have no effect on achieving first sales.

For these reasons, we believe that it may not be possible to examine the direct effects of a lead entrepreneur's motivations on the financial performance of a new company that the individual founds. The effects of motivation might be captured by the intervening variables in any causal model of the effects of motivation on firm performance. For example, those higher in nAch might be more likely to obtain venture capital financing. However, once venture capital financing is measured, there is no effect of nAch on firm performance.

We offer several specific suggestions for how researchers could better think about how motivations influence the entrepreneurial process. First, researchers could incorporate motivations into a dynamic evolutionary perspective on entrepreneurship by using motivations to distinguish those individuals who select out at different steps in the entrepreneurial process. For example, motivations could separate those individuals who positively evaluate opportunities from those who do not, those who obtain outside funding from those who do not, those who continue to pursue opportunities from those who abandon the effort, or those who pursue rapid rather than slow growth.

The pursuit of opportunity provides a good example. As Aldrich and Zimmer explain, "opportunities are irrelevant unless taken advantage of, and people vary widely in their ability to seize opportunities". We agree, but would argue that people also differ widely in their motivation to seize opportunities. It would be interesting to know if certain motivations predispose people to take action in response to the discovery of opportunities.

One might argue, for example, that people higher in self-efficacy will be more likely to seek financing to exploit opportunities than will people lower in self-efficacy. Because the process of financing exposes a person's entrepreneurial ideas to the scrutiny of skeptical others, those people willing to expose their ideas to scrutiny might have to be more confident than those who will not.

Second, researchers could theorize more deeply about how motivation might impact entrepreneurial decisions. Rather than falling back on the stock idea that firm founders must be fundamentally different types of people from other members of society, we suggest researchers consider how motivations might influence some people to make different decisions from others in the entrepreneurial process.

For example, inventors higher in selfefficacy might found firms to exploit their inventions while inventors lower in self-efficacy might license their technology to others. Similarly, entrepreneurs with a greater need for independence might self-finance new firms, whereas those with a lesser need for independence might seek venture capital.

We also suggest that it is not necessarily important for entrepreneurship researchers to show that specific motivations influence the financial performance of new firms. If financial performance of a new firm is conditional on the ability of an entrepreneur to create the firm, and that act of creation depends heavily on human motivation, then human motivation matters to entrepreneurship even if motivation has no direct effect on the performance of the newly founded firm.

In fact, we would expect that the more significant a firm that an entrepreneur founds, the less their motivations influence the firm formation process. For example, the more significant the new firm that an entrepreneur builds, the less influence they will have personally on day-to-day operations, and the less that we would expect the financial performance of the firm to be affected by their personal motivations.

Meta-analysis

The third criticism of previous research is the failure to use meta-analysis. The ability to combine the results of scores or hundreds of individual studies into a single statistic was not always available to researchers.

This sometimes led people who conducted narrative reviews to underestimate the effect of the variable being considered; for example, nonsignificant results in single studies may be due to sampling error rather than invalidity. Although metaanalytic results are not available for all the motivations we discuss, such data, where available, throw new light on some motivations.

Wrong Motives

A fourth criticism of extant research is its tendency to study the wrong motives. Some motives are more relevant to entrepreneurial activity than others. For example, risk-taking propensity as measured by self-perception and tolerance for ambiguity has long been assumed to be an entrepreneurial motive, but the evidence so far is only equivocal.

Regarding risk, perhaps the problem has been that people cannot perceive the riskiness of their own actions, or that what is risky to one person is not risky to another. For example, several recent studies using interviews and expert evaluations showed that entrepreneurs objectively have a higher propensity for risk than either entrepreneurs or the general population but that entrepreneurs do not perceive their actions as risky. Thus, the effects of risk-taking propensity may be confounded with the high self-efficacy of entrepreneurs.

We suggest that researchers better define the motives that they think are important and focus on more precise measures of them. One way to do that would be for researchers to go back to the underlying psychological literature and examine how researchers have dealt with the nuances of theorizing about and measuring the same motives in other settings. If psychologists have figured a way around the problems of using self-perceptions in the measurement of risky behaviour, like drug usage, those same techniques can be brought to bear on the measurement of risky behaviour in entrepreneurial settings. We believe that another important step for research on motivation and entrepreneurship would be for researchers to develop more complete models of the entrepreneurial process before examining the effects of particular motives on particular activities.

A fuller understanding of the role of motivations in the overall process would require consideration of factors other than motives. We suggest that researchers develop explanations that include the variety of such influences.

Indirect Effects

A fifth criticism has been the failure to look for indirect effects of motivational traits. Most, though not all, researchers have assumed that traits and motives have direct effects on outcomes and this may be true to some extent. However, an increasing body of literature is revealing that traits affect action indirectly through other mechanisms.

For example, in the general realm of work, conscientiousness is a reliable predictor of performance, but there is considerable evidence that the effects of conscientiousness on work performance are mediated by situation-specific factors such as goal setting and goal commitment. Similarly, Bandura has argued that locus of control is not a strong, direct predictor of performance in a task; and studies have shown that the effects of self-efficacy mediate the effects of locus of control when self-efficacy is added to the equation.

Therefore, locus of control effects reported in the entrepreneurship literature might be proxying unobserved self-efficacy. One recent study to have taken the approach of considering indirect effects of motivation in the setting of entrepreneurial action is that of Baum, who studied the growth of small companies in the architectural woodworking industry. They included variables from five separate domains: traits and motives, skills and abilities, situation-specific motivation, business strategies, and environmental factors.

They combined the measures within each domain into single indexes and related these indexes to each other and to venture growth. All the domains played a role in venture growth but the effects of motives were all indirect. Motives worked through skills, situation-specific motivation, and strategies to affect growth. Given the indirect effects observed in this study, we suggest that researchers consider such indirect patterns in their explanations for the effect of motivation on entrepreneurial action.

Definitions

A sixth criticism has stemmed from a lack of consistent definitions of entrepreneurship. In general, the definition of what constitutes entrepreneurial activity varies significantly across studies. For example, McClelland viewed managerial positions of certain types such as sales as one that demanded entrepreneurial skills, whereas much of the recent work in the applied field of management has sought to compare entrepreneurs to managers. Therefore, it is unclear if the samples from these different studies are comparable, or even represent entrepreneurship in a meaningful way.

This point, of course, brings us back to the importance of a common definition of entrepreneurship. As we indicated earlier, we advocate the definition proposed by Shane and Venkataraman. Whether researchers adopt this particular definition, however, is less important than the existence of a common definition. Without a common definition, it will not be possible to accumulate findings that are comparable from study to study.

HOW MOTIVATIONS INFLUENCE ENTREPRENEURSHIP

We suggest how human motivations might influence the entrepreneurial process. We offer this example to help future researchers design empirical tests of the role of motivation in entrepreneurship. Our example is shown graphically in Fig.

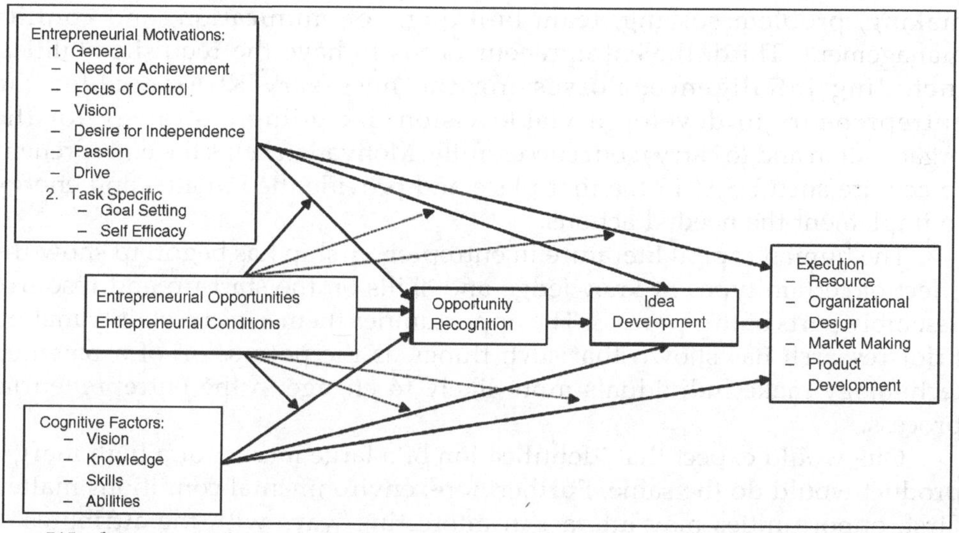

We begin with the set of human motivations that psychologists have shown to influence many aspects of human behaviour. These include the motivations that we described earlier in the study, in particular, nAch, locus of control, desire for independence, passion, and drive.

We propose that entrepreneurship is a process that begins with the recognition of an entrepreneurial opportunity and is followed by the development of an idea for how to pursue that opportunity, the evaluation of the feasibility of the opportunity, the development of the product or service that will be provided to customers, assembly of human and financial resources, organizational design, and the pursuit of customers. We suggest that some or all of the motivations influence the transition of individuals from one stage of the entrepreneurial process to another. In some cases, all of the motivations might matter. In other cases, only some of the motivations might matter.

The relative magnitudes of how much each motivation matters will likely vary, depending on the part of the process under investigation. In fact, it is quite plausible that motivations that influence one part of the process have all of their effects at that stage in the process and have no effects on later stages in the process. In this example, motivations are not the only things that influence these transitions. Cognitive factors, including knowledge, skills, and abilities, certainly matter. All action is the result of the combination or integration of motivation and cognition. First, the entrepreneurs need to have some knowledge, especially of the industry and of any relevant technology that is critical to success.

They can hire people with certain specialized skills that they lack, but they must possess enough expertise to know that they are doing the right thing. Second, the entrepreneur must have skills.

The necessary skills will depend on the circumstances, but they may include such factors as selling and bargaining, leadership, planning, decision making, problem solving, team building, communication, and conflict management. Third, the entrepreneur needs to have the requisite abilities, including intelligence. Possessing the necessary KSAs enables the entrepreneurs to develop a viable vision, including a strategy for the organization and to carry it out successfully. Motivation helps the entrepreneur to acquire such KSAs in the first place and provide the impetus and energy to implement the needed actions.

The human capital literature in entrepreneurship has begun to show the effect of certain types of knowledge and skills on the start-up and resource assembly parts of this process. The opportunities themselves certainly matter. Prior research has shown that such things as the possession of a patented technology make individuals more likely to engage in the entrepreneurial process.

One would expect that identification of a large market or a high margin product would do the same. Furthermore, environmental conditions matter. First, opportunities may interact in interesting ways with the attributes of people. Second, as much of the macrolevel research has shown, the willingness to engage in entrepreneurial activities depends on such things as the legal system of the country in which the entrepreneur operates, the age of the industry, the availability of capital in the economy, the condition of capital markets, and the state of the overall economy.

We believe that these factors are important, but that it might also be interesting to know whether motivations of particular people lead to different types of entrepreneurial action under different environmental conditions. Motivations might be more or less stronger than these other factors in the degree that they influence particular transition points. In addition, there might be important and interesting interaction effects between motivations and opportunities, KSAs, and environmental factors.

The relative importance of different categories of factors, their independent and combined effects, and their relative importance at different stages of the entrepreneurial process are clearly important theoretical and empirical questions that remain largely unexplored. We hope that researchers will begin to explore them because they appear to us to be central issues in the field of entrepreneurship.

MOTIVATION FACTORS AND THEORIES

MOTIVATION FACTORS

When we look at the psychology of human behaviour we can begin to understand certain baseline motivations which draw adults to on line social networks. Abraham Maslow published his theory of human motivation in 1943.

Its popularity continues unabated. Like his colleague Carl Rogers, Maslow believed that actualization was the driving force of human personality, a concept he captures in his 1954 book, Motivation and PersonalityMaslow's great insight was to place actualization into a hierarchy of motivation. Self actualization, as he called it, is the highest drive, but before a person can turn to it, he or she must satisfy other, lower motivations like hunger, safety and belonging.

The hierarchy has five levels:

1. Physiological (hunger, thirst, shelter, sex, etc.)
2. Safety (security, protection from physical and emotional harm)
3. Social (affection, belonging, acceptance, friendship)
4. Esteem (also called ego). The internal ones are self respect, autonomy, achievement and the external ones are status, recognition, and attention.
5. Self actualization (doing things)

Maslow points out that the hierarchy is dynamic; the dominant need is always shifting. The hierarchy does not exist by itself, but is affected by the situation and the general culture. Satisfaction is relative.

Douglas McGregor makes it the building block for his Theory X and Theory Y. Mihalyi Csikszentmihalyi continues the tradition in his concept of"flow."

A 1990s example of self actualization may be surfing the Internet. Empirical research has confirmed the first three levels, but has not done so for the fourth and fifth levels of esteem and self actualization. Some have noted that Maslow's hierarchy follows the life cycle. A newborn baby's needs are almost entirely physiological.

As the baby grows, it needs safety, then love. Toddlers are eager for social interaction. Teenagers are anxious about social needs; young adults are concerned with esteem and only more mature people transcend the first four levels to spend much time self actualizing. Based on the observations across numerous networking platforms and reflect on the past definitions of human motivation we can see that social networks on line provide a primary motivation for adults in the category of self actualization, or doing things. Maslow defines self actualization as growth-motivated rather than deficiency-motivated.

What Things are Adults doing within Social Networks than Enhance Individual Growth

Based on observations and interview as suggested, provide a general categorization of the factors that enhance individual growth for adults participating in on line social networks.

The Learning Factor

With all the hype, craze and media coverage of social networking platforms, *i.e.*, Facebook and Linkedin, many adults are drawn to the medium to learn what the hype is all about.

The Connection Factor

Once adults enter networks and learn the"tools of the trade" many are amazed to find the presence of other adults they know and many they don't already engaged with the medium.

The Affinity Factor

Adults begin to find association with groups, causes, forums, media and other affinities which relate to their interest both personally and professionally. The predominant business segment using social networks today is employment recruiters. However, as the medium and adult participation has grown there is an exponential growth of business opportunities that adults are learning to facilitate using social networks as the medium.

The Creative Factor

Adults, and their businesses, are applying creative ways to use the technology behind social computing to extend its value to both personal and professional needs.

The Expectation Factor

When you consider the creative possibilities of social networks adults expect to the formation of some economic and social value to be derived from their participation whether currently or in the future. The expectation of individual growth and satisfaction is high.These factors combined with the media hype over social networking are the motivating issues which are driving millions of adults to the medium at annual growth rates of 70% and more. The opportunity to capitalize economically is emerging quickly. Word of mouth will fuel growth rates faster than any other technological medium in our past. The growth and related factors will usher in The Relationship Economy.

THEORIES OF MOTIVATION

Contribution of Robert Owen

Though Owen is considered to be paternalistic in his view, his contribution is of a considerable significance in the theories of Motivation. During the early years of the nineteenth century, Owen's textile mill at New Lanark in Scotland was the scene of some novel ways of treating people. His view was that people were similar to machines.

A machine that is looked after properly, cared for and maintained well, performs efficiently, reliably and lastingly, similarly people are likely to be more efficient if they are taken care of. Robert Owen practiced what he preached and introduced such things as employee housing and company shop. His ideas on this and other matters were considered to be too revolutionary for that time.

Jeremy Bentham's "The Carrot and the Stick Approach"

Possibly the essence of the traditional view of people at work can be best appreciated by a brief look at the work of this English philosopher, whose ideas were also developed in the early years of the Industrial Revolution, around 1800.

Bentham's view was that all people are self-interested and are motivated by the desire to avoid pain and find pleasure. Any worker will work only if the reward is big enough, or the punishment sufficiently unpleasant. This view - the 'carrot and stick' approach - was built into the philosophies of the age and is still to be found, especially in the older, more traditional sectors of industry.

The various leading theories of motivation and motivators seldom make reference to the carrot and the stick. This metaphor relates, of course, to the use of rewards and penalties in order to induce desired behaviour. It comes from the old story that to make a donkey move, one must put a carrot in front of him or dab him with a stick from behind.

Despite all the research on the theories of motivation, reward and punishment are still considered strong motivators. For centuries, however, they were too often thought of as the only forces that could motivate people. At the same time, in all theories of motivation, the inducements of some kind of 'carrot' are recognized. Often this is money in the form of pay or bonuses. Even though money is not the only motivating force, it has been and will continue to be an important one.

The trouble with the money 'carrot' approach is that too often everyone gets a carrot, regardless of performance through such practices as salary increase and promotion by seniority, automatic 'merit' increases, and executive bonuses not based on individual manager performance. It is as simple as this: If a person put a donkey in a pen full of carrots and then stood outside with a carrot, would the donkey be encouraged to come out of the pen? The 'stick', in the form of fear–fear of loss of job, loss of income, reduction of bonus, demotion, or some other penalty–has been and continues to be a strong motivator.

Yet it is admittedly not the best kind. It often gives rise to defensive or retaliatory behaviour, such as union organization, poor-quality work, executive indifference, failure of a manager to take any risks in decision making or even dishonesty. But fear of penalty cannot be overlooked. Whether managers are first-level supervisors or chief executives, the power of their position to give or with hold rewards or impose penalties of various kinds gives them an ability to control, to a very great extent, the economic and social well-being of their subordinates.

Abraham Maslow's "Need Hierarchy Theory"

One of the most widely theories of motivation is the hierarchy of needs theory put forth by psychologist Abraham Maslow. Maslow saw human needs in the form of a hierarchy, ascending from the lowest to the highest, and he concluded that when one set of needs is satisfied, this kind of need ceases to be a motivator. As per his theory this needs are:

Physiological Needs

These are important needs for sustaining the human life. Food, water, warmth, shelter, sleep, medicine and education are the basic physiological needs which fall in the primary list of need satisfaction. Maslow was of an opinion that until these needs were satisfied to a degree to maintain life, no other motivating factors can work.

Security or Safety Needs

These are the needs to be free of physical danger and of the fear of losing a job, property, food or shelter. It also includes protection against any emotional harm.

Social Needs

Since people are social beings, they need to belong and be accepted by others. People try to satisfy their need for affection, acceptance and friendship.

Esteem Needs

Maslow, once people begin to satisfy their need to belong, they tend to want to be held in esteem both by themselves and by others. This kind of need produces such satisfaction as power, prestige status and self-confidence. It includes both internal esteem factors like self-respect, autonomy and achievements and external esteem factors such as states, recognition and attention.

Need for Self-actualization

Maslow regards this as the highest need in his hierarchy. It is the drive to become what one is capable of becoming, it includes growth, achieving one's potential and self-fulfillment. It is to maximize one's potential and to accomplish something.

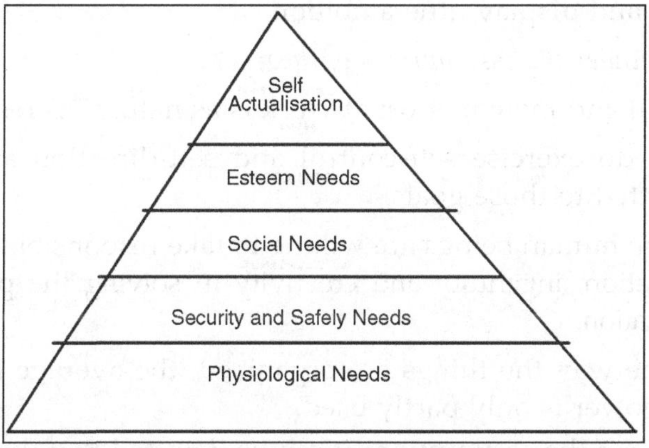

As each of these needs are substantially satisfied, the next need becomes dominant. From the standpoint of motivation, the theory would say that although no need is ever fully gratified, a substantially satisfied need no longer motivates.

So if you want to motivate someone, you need to understand what level of the hierarchy that person is on and focus on satisfying those needs or needs above that level. Maslow's need theory has received wide recognition, particularly among practicing managers.

This can be attributed to the theory's intuitive logic and ease of understanding. However, research does not validate these theory. Maslow provided no empirical evidence and other several studies that sought to validate the theory found no support for it.

"Theory X and Theory Y" of Douglas McGregor

McGregor, "The Human side of Enterprise" states that people inside the organization can be managed in two ways.

The first is basically negative, which falls under the category X and the other is basically positive, which falls under the category Y. After viewing the way in which the manager dealt with employees, McGregor concluded that a manager's view of the nature of human beings is based on a certain grouping of assumptions and that he or she tends to mold his or her behaviour towards subordinates just as to these assumptions.

Under the assumptions of theory X:

- Employees inherently do not like work and whenever possible, will attempt to avoid it.
- Because employees dislike work, they have to be forced, coerced or threatened with punishment to achieve goals.
- Employees avoid responsibilities and do not work fill formal directions are issued.
- Most workers place a greater importance on security over all other factors and display little ambition.

In contrast under the assumptions of theory Y:

- Physical and mental effort at work is as natural as rest or play.
- People do exercise self-control and self-direction and if they are committed to those goals.
- Average human beings are willing to take responsibility and exercise imagination, ingenuity and creativity in solving the problems of the organization.
- That the way the things are organized, the average human being's brain power is only partly used.

On analysis of the assumptions it can be detected that theory X assumes that lower-order needs dominate individuals and theory Y assumes that higher-order needs dominate individuals. An organization that is run on Theory X lines tends to be authoritarian in nature, the word "authoritarian" suggests such ideas as the "power to enforce obedience" and the "right to command."

In contrast Theory Y organizations can be described as "participative", where the aims of the organization and of the individuals in it are integrated; individuals can achieve their own goals best by directing their efforts towards the success of the organization.

However, this theory has been criticized widely for generalization of work and human behaviour.

Contribution of Rensis Likert

Likert developed a refined classification, breaking down organizations into four management systems.

- 1st System – Primitive authoritarian
- 2nd System – Benevolent authoritarian

- 3rd System – Consultative
- 4th System – Participative

As per the opinion of Likert, the 4th system is the best, not only for profit organizations, but also for non-profit firms.

Frederick Herzberg's Motivation-hygiene Theory

Frederick has tried to modify Maslow's need Hierarchy theory. His theory is also known as two-factor theory or Hygiene theory. He stated that there are certain satisfiers and dissatisfiers for employees at work. Intrinsic factors are related to job satisfaction, while extrinsic factors are associated with dissatisfaction.

He devised his theory on the question: "What do people want from their jobs ?" From the responses that he received, he concluded that opposite of satisfaction is not dissatisfaction. Removing dissatisfying characteristics from a job does not necessarily make the job satisfying.

He states that presence of certain factors in the organization is natural and the presence of the same does not lead to motivation. However, their nonpresence leads to demotivation. In similar manner there are certain factors, the absence of which causes no dissatisfaction, but their presence has motivational impact.

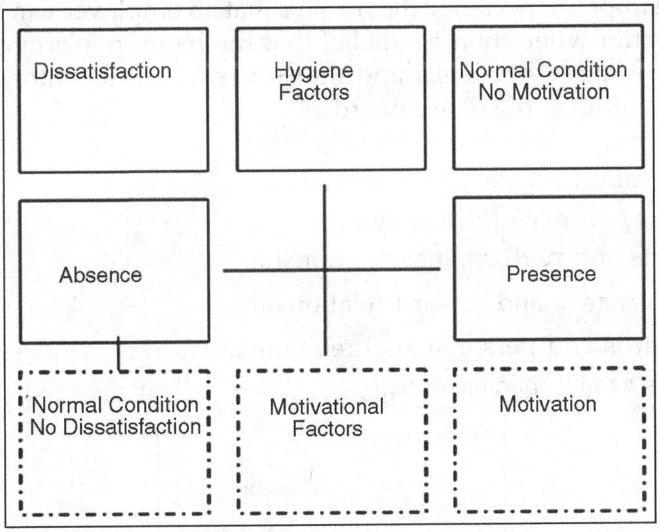

Examples of Hygiene factors are:

- Security, status, relationship with subordinates, personal life, salary, work conditions, relationship with supervisor and company policy and administration.

Examples of Motivational factors are:

- Growth prospectus job advancement, responsibility, challenges, recognition and achievements.

Contributions of Elton Mayo

The work of Elton Mayo is famously known as "Hawthorne Experiments." He conducted behavioural experiments at the Hawthorne Works of the American Western Electric Company in Chicago. He made some illumination experiments, introduced breaks in between the work performance and also introduced refreshments during the pause's. It was not only about pay, work condition and morale but also included psychological and social factors.

Although this research has been criticized from many angles:

- People are motivated by more than pay and conditions.
- The need for recognition and a sense of belonging are very important.
- Attitudes towards work are strongly influenced by the group.

Vroom's Valence x Expectancy Theory

The most widely accepted explanations of motivation has been propounded by Victor Vroom. His theory is commonly known as expectancy theory. The theory argues that the strength of a tendency to act in a specific way depends on the strength of an expectation that the act will be followed by a given outcome and on the attractiveness of that outcome to the individual to make this simple, expectancy theory says that an employee can be motivated to perform better when their is a belief that the better performance will lead to good performance appraisal and that this shall result into realisation of personal goal in form of some reward.

Therefore an employee is:

- Motivation = Valence x Expectancy.

The theory focuses on three things:

- Efforts and performance relationship
- Performance and reward relationship
- Rewards and personal goal relationship

This leads us to a conclusion that:

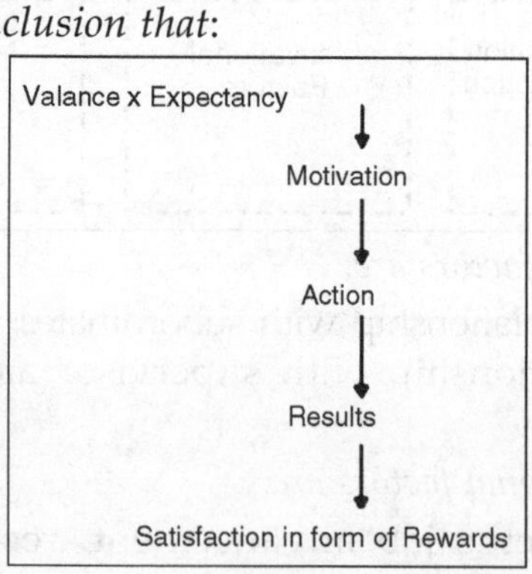

The Porter and Lawler Model

Lyman W. Porter and Edward E. Lawler developed a more complete version of motivation depending upon expectancy theory.

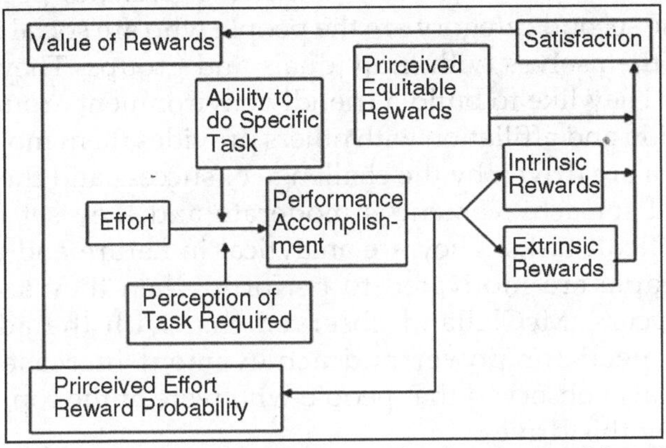

Actual performance in a job is primarily determined by the effort spent. But it is also affected by the person's ability to do the job and also by individual's perception of what the required task is. So performance is the responsible factor that leads to intrinsic as well as extrinsic rewards. These rewards, along with the equity of individual leads to satisfaction. Hence, satisfaction of the individual depends upon the fairness of the reward.

Clayton Alderfer's ERG Theory

Alderfer has tried to rebuild the hierarchy of needs of Maslow into another model named ERG *i.e.* Existence – Relatedness – Growth.

The existence group is concerned mainly with providing basic material existence. The second group is the individuals need to maintain interpersonal relationship with other members in the group. The final group is the intrinsic desire to grow and develop personally.

The major of this theory are:

- In an individual, more than one need may be operative at the same time.
- If a higher need goes unsatisfied than the desire to satisfy a lower need intensifies.
- It also contains the frustration-regression dimension.

McClelland's Theory of Needs

David McClelland has developed a theory on three types of motivating needs:

1. Need for Power
2. Need for Affiliation
3. Need for Achievement

Basically people for high need for power are inclined towards influence and control. They like to be at the centre and are good orators. They are demanding in nature, forceful in manners and ambitious in life.

They can be motivated to perform if they are given key positions or power positions. In the second category are the people who are social in nature. They try to affiliate themselves with individuals and groups. They are driven by love and faith. They like to build a friendly environment around themselves. Social recognition and affiliation with others provides them motivation. People in the third area are driven by the challenge of success and the fear of failure.

Their need for achievement is moderate and they set for themselves moderately difficult tasks. They are analytical in nature and take calculated risks. Such people are motivated to perform when they see atleast some chances of success. McClelland observed that with the advancement in hierarchy the need for power and achievement increased rather than Affiliation. He also observed that people who were at the top, later ceased to be motivated by this drives.

Equity Theory

As per the equity theory of J. Stacey Adams, people are motivated by their beliefs about the reward structure as being fair or unfair, relative to the inputs. People have a tendency to use subjective judgment to balance the outcomes and inputs in the relationship for comparisons between different individuals. Accordingly:

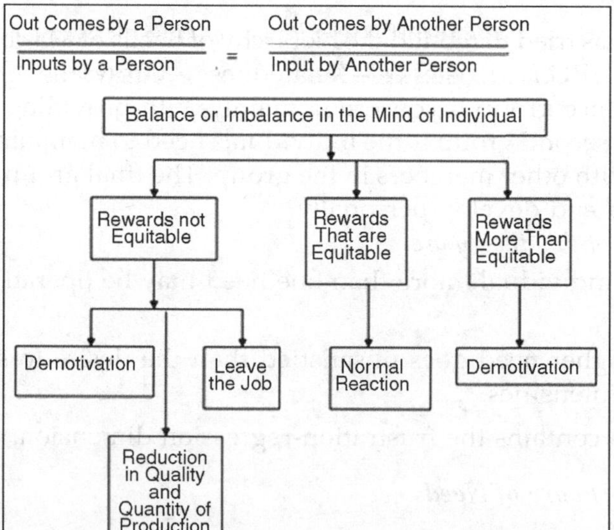

If people feel that they are not equally rewarded they either reduce the quantity or quality of work or migrate to some other organization. However, if people perceive that they are rewarded higher, they may be motivated to work harder.

Reinforcement Theory

B.F. Skinner, who propounded the reinforcement theory, holds that by designing the environment properly, individuals can be motivated. Instead of considering internal factors like impressions, feelings, attitudes and other cognitive behaviour, individuals are directed by what happens in the environment external to them.

Skinner states that work environment should be made suitable to the individuals and that punishments actually leads to frustration and de-motivation. Hence, the only way to motivate is to keep on making positive changes in the external environment of the organization.

Goal Setting Theory of Edwin Locke

Instead of giving vague tasks to people, specific and pronounced objectives, help in achieving them faster. As the clarity is high, a goal orientation also avoids any misunderstandings in the work of the employees. The goal setting theory states that when the goals to be achieved are set at a higher standard than in that case employees are motivated to perform better and put in maximum effort. It revolves around the concept of "Self-efficacy" *i.e.* individual's belief that he or she is capable of performing a hard task.

Cognitive Evaluation Theory

As per this theory a shift from external rewards to internal rewards results into motivation. It believes that even after the stoppage of external stimulus, internal stimulus survives. It relates to the pay structure in the organization. Instead of treating external factors like pay, incentives, promotion etc and internal factors like interests, drives, responsibility etc, separately, they should be treated as contemporary to each other. The cognition is to be such that even when external motivators are not there the internal motivation continues. However, practically extrinsic rewards are given much more weightage.

OBJECTIVES AND ACHIEVEMENTS OF MOTIVATION

MAIN OBJECTIVES OF MOTIVATION

Self preservation, whether this is pointed directly to survivial or towards our image of ourselves painted by our beliefs and ideals. What I mean by this is that we have in our mind a view point of who we are and we trive to accomplish this in either advancement or a continuation of our currant state. This personal view point might look down upon theft, and so seeing a theft we might feel "motivated" to call police, in order to up keep our currant view of what kind of person we see ourselves as.

ACHIEVEMENT

Over the years, behavioural scientists have noticed that some people have an intense desire to achieve something, while others may not seem that concerned about their achievements. This phenomenon has attracted a lot of discussions and debates.

Scientists have observed that people with a high level of achievement motivation exhibit certain characteristics. Achievement motivation is the tendency to endeavor for success and to choose goal oriented success or failure activities. Achievement motivation forms to be the basic for a good life. People who are oriented towards achievement, in general, enjoy life and feel in control. Being motivated keeps people dynamic and gives them self-respect. They set moderately difficult but easily achievable targets, which help them, achieve their objectives. They do not set up extremely difficult or extremely easy targets. By doing this they ensure that they only undertake tasks that can be achieved by them.

Achievement motivated people prefer to work on a problem rather than leaving the outcome to chance. It is also seen that achievement motivated people seem to be more concerned with their personal achievement rather than the rewards of success.

It is generally seen that achievement motivated people evidenced a significantly higher rate of advancement in their company compared to others. Programmes and courses designed, involves seven "training inputs." The first step refers to the process through which achievement motivation thinking is taught to the person.

The second step helps participants understand their own individuality and goals. The third assist participants in practicing achievement-related actions in cases, role-plays, and real life. A fourth refers to practicing of achievement-related actions in business and other games. A fifth input encourages participants to relate the achievement behaviour model to their own behaviour, self-image, and goals. The sixth programme facilitates participants to develop a personal plan of action. Finally, the course provides participants with feedback on their progress towards achieving objectives and targets. Achievement motivation as a branch of study has greatly established its prominence. A number of companies are now training their employees in the same.

ENTREPRENEURIAL COMPETENCIES—MEANING

Every career draws on the competencies of an individual. Some of these competencies may be general and some peculiar to the chosen career. You may understand competencies to mean abilities and skills. However, we would desist from calling these as personality traits as such a conceptualization only reinforces the mistaken belief that entrepreneurs are born rather than made.

We believe that recognition of these competencies as abilities and skills makes entrepreneurship as a teachable and learnable behaviour. We orient you towards a set of entrepreneurial competencies developed by the Entrepreneurship Development Institute of India Ahemdabad. These competencies were identified by a thorough research procedure based on critical analysis of the case studies of the successful entrepreneurs.

ENTREPRENEURIAL COMPETENCIES IDENTIFIED BY THE EDI

- *Initiative*: Acting out of choice rather than compulsion, taking the lead rather than waiting for others to start.
- *Sees and Acts on Opportunities*: A mindset where one is trained to look for business opportunities from everyday experiences.
- *Persistence*: A 'never say die' attitude, not giving up easily, striving Information seeking continuously until success is achieved.
- *Knowing*: Knowing who knows, consulting experts, reading relevant material and an overall openness to ideas and information.
- *Concern for High Quality of Work*: Attention to details and observance of established standards and norms.
- *Commitment to Work Contract*: Taking personal pains to complete a task as scheduled.
- *Efficiency Orientation*: Concern for conservation of time, money and effort.
- *Systematic Planning*: Breaking up the complex whole into parts, close examination of the parts and inferring about the whole; *e.g.* simultaneously attending to production, marketing and financial aspects (parts) of the overall business strategy (the whole).
- *Problem solving*: Observing the symptoms, diagnosing and curing.
- *Self-confidence*: Not being afraid of the risks associated with business and relying on one's capabilities to successfully manage these.
- *Assertiveness*: Conveying emphatically one's vision and convincing others of its value.
- *Persuasion*: Eliciting support of others in the venture.
- *Use of Influence Strategies*: Providing leadership.
- *Monitoring*: Ensuring the progress of the venture as planned.
- *Concern for Employee Welfare*: Believing in employee well being as the key to competitiveness and success and initiating programmes of employee welfare.

These competencies matter in entrepreneurial success. EDI estimates that development of these competencies can substantially bring down incidence of business failures/industrial sickness.

DEVELOPING COMPETENCIES

'Awareness,' they say, is the first step towards 'improvement' and 'success.' Now that you are aware of the critical competencies for entrepreneurial success and also have a measure of your scores on these, it is appropriate that you also think in terms of how to improve your scores. Suppose, you find yourself lacking in the competency- 'opportunity spotting,' you may start practicing to think like an entrepreneur. With just a little change in perspective, the world changes for you. Similarly you may work on the other competencies as well.

2

Entrepreneurship and Market Dynamics

UNDERSTANDING THE MARKET

A market is any one of a variety of systems, institutions, procedures, social relations and infrastructures whereby businesses sell their goods, services and labour to people in exchange for money. Goods and services are sold using a legal tender such as fiat money. This activity forms part of the economy. It is an arrangement that allows buyers and sellers to exchange goods. Competition is essential in markets, and separates market from trade.

Two people may trade, but it takes at least three persons to have a market, so that there is competition on at least one of its two sides. Markets vary in size, range, geographic scale, location, types and variety of human communities, as well as the types of goods and services traded.

Some examples include local farmers' markets held in town squares or parking lots, shopping centres and shopping malls, international currency and commodity markets, legally created markets such as for pollution permits, and illegal markets such as the market for illicit drugs. In mainstream economics, the concept of a market is any structure that allows buyers and sellers to exchange any type of goods, services and information.

The exchange of goods or services for money is a transaction. Market participants consist of all the buyers and sellers of a good who influence its price. This influence is a major study of economics and has given rise to several theories and models concerning the basic market forces of supply and demand. There are two roles in markets, buyers and sellers.

The market facilitates trade and enables the distribution and allocation of resources in a society. Markets allow any tradable item to be evaluated and priced.

A market emerges more or less spontaneously or is constructed deliberately by human interaction in order to enable the exchange of rights of services and goods. Historically, markets originated in physical marketplaces which would often develop into — or from — small communities, towns and cities.

TYPES OF MARKETS

Although many markets exist in the traditional sense — such as a marketplace — there are various other types of markets and various organizational structures to assist their functions. The nature of business transactions could define markets.

Financial markets

Financial markets facilitate the exchange of liquid assets. Most investors prefer investing in two markets, the stock markets and the bond markets. NYSE, AMEX, and the NASDAQ are the most common stock markets in the US. Futures markets, where contracts are exchanged regarding the future delivery of goods are often an outgrowth of general commodity markets. Currency markets are used to trade one currency for another, and are often used for speculation on currency exchange rates. The money market is the name for the global market for lending and borrowing.

Prediction Markets

Prediction markets are a type of speculative market in which the goods exchanged are futures on the occurrence of certain events. They apply the market dynamics to facilitate information aggregation.

ORGANIZATION OF MARKETS

A market can be organized as an auction, as a private electronic market, as a commodity wholesale market, as a shopping centre, as a complex institution such as a stock market, and as an informal discussion between two individuals. Markets of varying types can spontaneously arise whenever a party has interest in a good or service that some other party can provide.

Hence there can be a market for cigarettes in correctional facilities, another for chewing gum in a playground, and yet another for contracts for the future delivery of a commodity. There can be black markets, where a good is exchanged illegally and virtual markets, such as eBay, in which buyers and sellers do not physically interact during negotiation. There can also be markets for goods under a command economy despite pressure to repress them.

MECHANISMS OF MARKETS

In economics, a market that runs under laissez-faire policies is a free market. It is "free" in the sense that the government makes no attempt to intervene through taxes, subsidies, minimum wages, price ceilings, etc. Market prices may be distorted by a seller or sellers with monopoly power, or a buyer with monopsony power. Such price distortions can have an adverse effect on market participant's welfare and reduce the efficiency of market outcomes. Also, the relative level of organization and negotiating power of buyers and sellers markedly affects the functioning of the market. Markets where price negotiations meet equilibrium though still do not arrive at desired outcomes for both sides are said to experience market failure.

STUDY OF MARKETS

The study of actual existing markets made up of persons interacting in space and place in diverse ways is widely seen as an antidote to abstract and all-encompassing concepts of"the market" and has historical precedent in the works of Fernand Braudel and Karl Polanyi. The latter term is now generally used in two ways.

First, to denote the abstract mechanisms whereby supply and demand confront each other and deals are made. In its place, reference to markets reflects ordinary experience and the places, processes and institutions in which exchanges occurs.

Second, the market is often used to signify an integrated, all-encompassing and cohesive capitalist world economy. A widespread trend in economic history and sociology is skeptical of the idea that it is possible to develop a theory to capture an essence or unifying thread to markets. For economic geographers, reference to regional, local, or commodity specific markets can serve to undermine assumptions of global integration, and highlight geographic variations in the structures, institutions, histories, path dependencies, forms of interaction and modes of self-understanding of agents in different spheres of market exchange.

Reference to actual markets can show capitalism not as a totalizing force or completely encompassing mode of economic activity, but rather as"a set of economic practices scattered over a landscape, rather than a systemic concentration of power". C. B. Macpherson identifies an underlying model of the market underlying Anglo-American liberal-democratic political economy and philosophy in the seventeenth and eighteenth centuries: Persons are cast as self-interested individuals, who enter into contractual relations with other such individuals, concerning the exchange of goods or personal capacities cast as commodities, with the motive of maximizing pecuniary interest.

The state and its governance systems are cast as outside of this framework. This model came to dominant economic thinking in the later nineteenth century, as economists such as Ricardo, Mill, Jevons, Walras and later neo-classical economics shifted from reference to geographically located marketplaces to an abstract"market".

This tradition is continued in contemporary neoliberalism, where the market is held up as optimal for wealth creation and human freedom, and the states' role imagined as minimal, reduced to that of upholding and keeping stable property rights, contract, and money supply. This allowed for boilerplate economic and institutional restructuring under structural adjustment and post-Communist reconstruction. Similar formalism occurs in a wide variety of social democratic and Marxist discourses that situate political action as antagonistic to the market. In particular, commodification theorists such as Georg Lukács insist that market relations necessarily lead to undue exploitation of labour and so need to be opposed in toto.

Pierre Bourdieu has suggested the market model is becoming self-realising, in virtue of its wide acceptance in national and international institutions through the 1990s. The formalist conception faces a number of insuperable difficulties, concerning the putatively global scope of the market to cover the entire Earth, in terms of penetration of particular economies, and in terms of whether particular claims about the subjects (individuals with pecuniary interest), objects (commodities), and modes of exchange (transactions) apply to any actually existing markets.

A central theme of empirical analyses is the variation and proliferation of types of markets since the rise of capitalism and global scale economies. The Regulation School stresses the ways in which developed capitalist countries have implemented varying degrees and types of environmental, economic, and social regulation, taxation and public spending, fiscal policy and government provisioning of goods, all of which have transformed markets in uneven and geographical varied ways and created a variety of mixed economies.

Drawing on concepts of institutional variance and path dependency, varieties of capitalism theorists (such as Hall and Soskice) identify two dominant modes of economic ordering in the developed capitalist countries,"coordinated market economies" such as Germany and Japan, and an Anglo-American"liberal market economies".

However, such approaches imply that the Anglo-American liberal market economies in fact operate in a matter close to the abstract notion of"the market". While Anglo-American countries have seen increasing introduction of neo-liberal forms of economic ordering, this has not lead to simple convergence, but rather a variety of hybrid institutional orderings. Rather, a variety of new markets have emerged, such as for carbon trading or rights to pollute. In some cases, such as emerging markets for water, different forms of privatization of different aspects of previously state run infrastructure have created hybrid private-public formations and graded degrees of commodification, commercialization and privatization.

Problematic for market formalism is the relationship between formal capitalist economic processes and a variety of alternative forms, ranging from semi-feudal and peasant economies widely operative in many developing economies, to informal markets, barter systems, worker cooperatives, or illegal trades that occur in most developed countries. Practices of incorporation of non-Western peoples into global markets in the nineteenth and twentieth century did not merely result in the quashing of former social economic institutions.

Rather, various modes of articulation arose between transformed and hybridized local traditions and social practices and the emergence world economy. So called capitalist markets in fact include and depend on a wide range of geographically situated economic practices that do not follow the market model.

Economies are thus hybrids of market and non-market elements. Helpful here is J. K. Gibson-Graham's complex topology of the diversity of contemporary market economies describing different types of transactions, labour, and economic agents.

Transactions can occur in underground markets (such as for marijuana) or be artificially protected (such as for patents). They can cover the sale of public goods under privatization schemes to co-operative exchanges and occur under varying degrees of monopoly power and state regulation. Likewise, there are a wide variety of economic agents, which engage in different types of transactions on different terms: One cannot assume the practices of a religious kindergarten, multinational corporation, state enterprise, or community-based cooperative can be subsumed under the same logic of calculability.

This emphasis on proliferation can also be contrasted with continuing scholarly attempts to show underlying cohesive and structural similarities to different markets. A prominent entry point for challenging the market model's applicability concerns exchange transactions and the homo economicus assumption of self-interest maximization.

There are now a number of streams of economic sociological analysis of markets focusing on the role of the social in transactions, and the ways transactions involve social networks and relations of trust, cooperation and other bonds. Economic geographers in turn draw attention to the ways in exchange transactions occur against the backdrop of institutional, social and geographic processes, including class relations, uneven development, and historically contingent path dependencies. A useful schema is provided by Michel Callon's concept of framing: Each economic act or transaction occurs against, incorporates and also re-performs a geographically and cultural specific complex of social histories, institutional arrangements, rules and connections.

These network relations are simultaneously bracketed, so that persons and transactions may be disentangled from thick social bonds. The character of calculability is imposed upon agents as they come to work in markets and are"formatted" as calculative agencies.

Market exchanges contain a history of struggle and contestation that produced actors predisposed to exchange under c An emerging theme worthy of further study is the interrelationship, interpenetrability and variations of concepts of persons, commodities, and modes of exchange under particular market formations. This is most pronounced in recent movement towards post-structuralist theorizing that draws on Foucault and Actor Network Theory and stress relational aspects of personhood, and dependence and integration into networks and practical systems. Commodity network approaches further both deconstruct and show alternatives to the market models concept of commodities.

Here, both researchers and market actors are understood as reframing commodities in terms of processes and social and ecological relationships. Rather than a mere objectification of things traded, the complex network relationships of exchange in different markets calls on agents to alternatively deconstruct or"get with" the fetish of commodities.

Gibson-Graham thus read a variety of alternative markets, for fair trade and organic foods, or those using Local Exchange Trading Systems as not only contributing to proliferation, but also forging new modes of ethical exchange and economic subjectivities. Most markets are regulated by state wide laws and regulations.

While barter markets exist, most markets use currency or some other form of money.Any investments made in markets should be carefully analysed and read through before investing if the market crashes value of stock may go down leading to heavy losses

SIZE PARAMETERS

Market size can be given in terms of the number of buyers and sellers in a particular market or in terms of the total exchange of money in the market, generally annually (per year). When given in terms of money, market size is often termed market value, but in a distinguished sense than the market value of individual products. For one and the same goods, there may be different (and generally increasing) market values at the production level, the wholesale level and the retail level.

For example, the value of the global illicit drug market for the year 2003 was estimated by the United Nations to be US$13 billion at the production level, $94 billion at the wholesale level (taking seizures into account), and US$322 billion at the retail level (based on retail prices and taking seizures and other losses into account).

COMPETITIVE ANALYSIS OF MARKET

In formulating business strategy, managers must consider the strategies of the firm's competitors. While in highly fragmented commodity industries the moves of any single competitor may be less important, in concentrated industries competitor analysis becomes a vital part of strategic planning.

Competitor analysis has two primary activities:

1. Obtaining information about important competitors,
2. Using that information to predict competitor behaviour.

The goal of competitor analysis is to understand:

- With which competitors to compete,
- Competitors' strategies and planned actions,

- How competitors might react to a firm's actions,
- How to influence competitor behaviour to the firm's own advantage.

Casual knowledge about competitors usually is insufficient in competitor analysis. Rather, competitors should be analysed systematically; using organized competitor intelligence-gathering to compile a wide array of information so that well informed strategy decisions can be made.

COMPETITOR ANALYSIS FRAMEWORK

Michael Porter presented a framework for analysing competitors.

This framework is based on the following four key aspects of a competitor:

1. Competitor's objectives
2. Competitor's assumptions
3. Competitor's strategy
4. Competitor's capabilities

Objectives and assumptions are what drive the competitor, and strategy and capabilities are what the competitor is doing or is capable of doing. These components can be depicted as shown in the following diagram.

A competitor analysis should include the more important existing competitors as well as potential competitors such as those firms that might enter the industry, for example, by extending their present strategy or by vertically integrating.

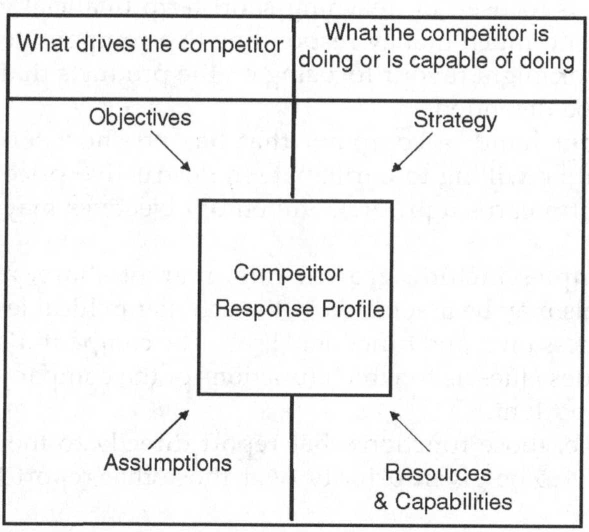

Fig. Competitor Analysis Components

COMPETITOR'S CURRENT STRATEGY

The two main sources of information about a competitor's strategy is what the competitor says and what it does.

What a competitor is saying about its strategy is revealed in:

- Annual shareholder reports
- 10K reports
- Interviews with analysts
- Statements by managers
- Press releases

However, this stated strategy often differs from what the competitor actually is doing. What the competitor is doing is evident in where its cash flow is directed, such as in the following tangible actions:

- Hiring activity
- R & D projects
- Capital investments
- Promotional campaigns
- Strategic partnerships
- Mergers and acquisitions

COMPETITOR'S OBJECTIVES

Knowledge of a competitor's objectives facilitates a better prediction of the competitor's reaction to different competitive moves. For example, a competitor that is focused on reaching short-term financial goals might not be willing to spend much money responding to a competitive attack. Rather, such a competitor might favour focusing on the products that hold positions that better can be defended.

On the other hand, a company that has no short term profitability objectives might be willing to participate in destructive price competition in which neither firm earns a profit. Competitor objectives may be financial or other types.

Some examples include growth rate, market share, and technology leadership. Goals may be associated with each hierarchical level of strategy - corporate, business unit, and functional level. The competitor's organizational structure provides clues as to which functions of the company are deemed to be the more important.

For example, those functions that report directly to the chief executive officer are likely to be given priority over those that report to a senior vice president.

Other aspects of the competitor that serve as indicators of its objectives include risk tolerance, management incentives, backgrounds of the executives, composition of the board of directors, legal or contractual restrictions, and any additional corporate-level goals that may influence the competing business unit. Whether the competitor is meeting its objectives provides an indication of how likely it is to change its strategy.

COMPETITOR'S ASSUMPTIONS

The assumptions that a competitor's managers hold about their firm and their industry help to define the moves that they will consider. For example, if in the past the industry introduced a new type of product that failed, the industry executives may assume that there is no market for the product.

Such assumptions are not always accurate and if incorrect may present opportunities. For example, new entrants may have the opportunity to introduce a product similar to a previously unsuccessful one without retaliation because incumbant firms may not take their threat seriously. Honda was able to enter the U.S. motorcycle market with a small motorbike because U.S. manufacturers had assumed that there was no market for small bikes based on their past experience.

A competitor's assumptions may be based on a number of factors, including any of the following:

- Beliefs about its competitive position
- Past experience with a product
- Regional factors
- Industry trends
- Rules of thumb

A thorough competitor analysis also would include assumptions that a competitor makes about its own competitors, and whether that assessment is accurate.

COMPETITOR'S RESOURCES AND CAPABILITIES

Knowledge of the competitor's assumptions, objectives, and current strategy is useful in understanding how the competitor might want to respond to a competitive attack. However, its resources and capabilities determine its ability to respond effectively. A competitor's capabilities can be analysed just as to its strengths and weaknesses in various functional areas, as is done in a SWOT analysis.

The competitor's strengths define its capabilities. The analysis can be taken further to evaluate the competitor's ability to increase its capabilities in certain areas. A financial analysis can be performed to reveal its sustainable growth rate.

Finally, since the competitive environment is dynamic, the competitor's ability to react swiftly to change should be evaluated. Some firms have heavy momentum and may continue for many years in the same direction before adapting.

Others are able to mobilize and adapt very quickly. Factors that slow a company down include low cash reserves, large investments in fixed assets, and an organizational structure that hinders quick action.

COMPETITOR RESPONSE PROFILE

Information from an analysis of the competitor's objectives, assumptions, strategy, and capabilities can be compiled into a response profile of possible moves that might be made by the competitor. This profile includes both potential offensive and defensive moves. The specific moves and their expected strength can be estimated using information gleaned from the analysis. The result of the competitor analysis should be an improved ability to predict the competitor's behaviour and even to influence that behaviour to the firm's advantage.

PATENTS, TRADEMARK AND COPYRIGHT

PATENT

A patent is a set of exclusive rights granted by a state (national government) to an inventor or their assignee for a limited period of time in exchange for a public disclosure of an invention. The procedure for granting patents, the requirements placed on the patentee, and the extent of the exclusive rights vary widely between countries just as to national laws and international agreements.

Typically, however, a patent application must include one or more claims defining the invention which must be new, non-obvious, and useful or industrially applicable. In many countries, certain subject areas are excluded from patents, such as business methods and mental acts. The exclusive right granted to a patentee in most countries is the right to prevent others from making, using, selling, or distributing the patented invention without permission. It is just a right to prevent others' use. A patent does not give the proprietor of the patent the right to use the patented invention, should it fall within the scope of an earlier patent.

Under the World Trade Organization's (WTO) Agreement on Trade-Related Aspects of Intellectual Property Rights, patents should be available in WTO member states for any inventions, in all fields of technology, and the term of protection available should be the minimum twenty years. Different types of patents may have varying patent terms (*i.e.*, durations).

Definition

The term patent usually refers to a right granted to anyone who invents or discovers any new and useful process, machine, article of manufacture, or composition of matter, or any new and useful improvement thereof. The additional qualification utility patent is used in the United States to distinguish it from other types of patents (*e.g.* design patents) but should not be confused with utility models granted by other countries. Examples of particular species of patents for inventions include biological patents, business method patents, chemical patents and software patents.

Some other types of intellectual property rights are referred to as patents in some jurisdictions: industrial design rights are called design patents in some jurisdictions (they protect the visual design of objects that are not purely utilitarian), plant breeders' rights are sometimes called plant patents, and utility models or Gebrauchsmuster are sometimes called petty patents or innovation patents. This object relates primarily to the patent for an invention, although so-called petty patents and utility models may also be granted for inventions.

Certain grants made by the monarch in pursuance of the royal prerogative were sometimes called letters patent, which was a government notice to the public of a grant of an exclusive right to ownership and possession. These were often grants of a patent-like monopoly and predate the modern origins of the patent system. For other uses of the term patent see notably land patents, which were land grants by early state governments in the USA, and printing patent, a precursor of modern copyright. These meanings reflect the original meaning of letters patent that had a broader scope than current usage.

History

In 500 BC, in the Greek city of Sybaris (located in what is now southern Italy),"encouragement was held out to all who should discover any new refinement in luxury, the profits arising from which were secured to the inventor by patent for the space of a year."

The Florentine architect Filippo Brunelleschi received a three-year patent for a barge with hoisting gear, that carried marble along the Arno River in 1421. In 1449, King Henry VI granted the first patent with a license of 20 years to John of Utynam for introducing the making of coloured glass to England. Patents in the modern sense originated in 1474, when the Republic of Venice enacted a decree that new and inventive devices, once put into practice, had to be communicated to the Republic to obtain the right to prevent others from using them.

England followed with the Statute of Monopolies in 1623 under King James I, which declared that patents could only be granted for"projects of new invention." During the reign of Queen Anne (1702-14), the lawyers of the English Court developed the requirement that a written description of the invention must be submitted. The patent system in many other countries, including Australia, is based on British law and can be traced back to the Statute of Monopolies.

In France, patents were granted by the monarchy and by other institutions like the"Maison du Roi". The Academy examined novelty. Examinations were generally done in secret with no requirement to publish a description of the invention. Actual use of the invention was deemed adequate disclosure to the public. The modern French patent system was created during the Revolution in 1791. Patents were granted without examination since inventor's right was considered as a natural one. In the United States, during the so-called colonial period and Articles of Confederation years (1778-89), several states adopted patent systems of their own. The first Congress adopted a Patent Act, in 1790, and the first patent was issued under this Act on July 31, 1790.

Law

Effects

A patent is not a right to practice or use the invention. Rather, a patent provides the right to exclude others from making, using, selling, offering for sale, or importing the patented invention for the term of the patent, which is usually 20 years from the filing date subject to the payment of maintenance fees. A patent is, in effect, a limited property right that the government offers to inventors in exchange for their agreement to share the details of their inventions with the public. Like any other property right, it may be sold, licensed, mortgaged, assigned or transferred, given away, or simply abandoned.

The rights conveyed by a patent vary country-by-country. For example, in the United States, a patent covers research, except"purely philosophical" inquiry. A U.S. patent is infringed by any"making" of the invention, even a making that goes towards development of a new invention-which may itself become subject of a patent. A patent being an exclusionary right does not, however, necessarily give the owner of the patent the right to exploit the patent.

For example, many inventions are improvements of prior inventions that may still be covered by someone else's patent. If an inventor takes an existing, patented mouse trap design, adds a new feature to make an improved mouse trap, and obtains a patent on the improvement, he or she can only legally build his or her improved mouse trap with permission from the patent holder of the original mouse trap, assuming the original patent is still in force. On the other hand, the owner of the improved mouse trap can exclude the original patent owner from using the improvement.

Some countries have"working provisions" that require the invention be exploited in the jurisdiction it covers. Consequences of not working an invention vary from one country to another, ranging from revocation of the patent rights to the awarding of a compulsory license awarded by the courts to a party wishing to exploit a patented invention. The patentee has the opportunity to challenge the revocation or license, but is usually required to provide evidence that the reasonable requirements of the public have been met by the working of invention.

Enforcement

Patents can generally only be enforced through civil lawsuits (for example, for a U.S. patent, by an action for patent infringement in a United States federal court), although some countries (such as France and Austria) have criminal penalties for wanton infringement. Typically, the patent owner will seek monetary compensation for past infringement, and will seek an injunction prohibiting the defendant from engaging in future acts of infringement. To prove infringement, the patent owner must establish that the accused infringer practices all the requirements of at least one of the claims of the patent.

(In many jurisdictions the scope of the patent may not be limited to what is literally stated in the claims, for example due to the"doctrine of equivalents"). An important limitation on the ability of a patent owner to successfully assert the patent in civil litigation is the accused infringer's right to challenge the validity of that patent. Civil courts hearing patent cases can and often do declare patents not valid.

A patent can be found invalid on grounds that are set out in the relevant patent legislation that vary between countries. Often, the grounds are a subset of requirements for patentability in the relevant country. Although an infringer is generally free to rely on any available ground of invalidity (such as a prior publication, for example), some countries have sanctions to prevent the same validity questions being relitigated. An example is the UK Certificate of contested validity.

The vast majority of patent rights, however, are not determined through litigation, but are resolved privately through patent licensing. Patent licensing agreements are effectively contracts in which the patent owner (the licensor) agrees to forgo their right to sue the licensee for infringement of the licensor's patent rights, usually in return for a royalty or other compensation. It is common for companies engaged in complex technical fields to enter into dozens of license agreements associated with the production of a single product.

Moreover, it is equally common for competitors in such fields to license patents to each other under cross-licensing agreements in order to share the benefits of using each other's patented inventions.

Ownership

In most countries, both natural persons and corporate entities may apply for a patent. In the United States, however, only the inventor(s) may apply for a patent although it may be assigned to a corporate entity subsequently and inventors may be required to assign inventions to their employers under a contract of employment.

In most European countries, ownership of an invention may pass from the inventor to their employer by rule of law if the invention was made in the course of the inventor's normal or specifically assigned employment duties, where an invention might reasonably be expected to result from carrying out those duties, or if the inventor had a special obligation to further the interests of the employer's company. The inventors, their successors or their assignees become the proprietors of the patent when and if it is granted. If a patent is granted to more than one proprietor, the laws of the country in question and any agreement between the proprietors may affect the extent to which each proprietor can exploit the patent.

For example, in some countries, each proprietor may freely license or assign their rights in the patent to another person while the law in other countries prohibits such actions without the permission of the other proprietor(s).

The ability to assign ownership rights increases the liquidity of a patent as property. Inventors can obtain patents and then sell them to third parties. The third parties then own the patents and have the same rights to prevent others from exploiting the claimed inventions, as if they had originally made the inventions themselves.

Governing Laws

The grant and enforcement of patents are governed by national laws, and also by international treaties, where those treaties have been given effect in national laws. Patents are, therefore, territorial in nature. Commonly, a nation forms a patent office with responsibility for operating that nation's patent system, within the relevant patent laws. The patent office generally has responsibility for the grant of patents, with infringement being the remit of national courts.

There is a trend towards global harmonization of patent laws, with the World Trade Organization (WTO) being particularly active in this area. The TRIPs Agreement has been largely successful in providing a forum for nations to agree on an aligned set of patent laws. Conformity with the TRIPs agreement is a requirement of admission to the WTO and so compliance is seen by many nations as important.

This has also led to many developing nations, which may historically have developed different laws to aid their development, enforcing patents laws in line with global practice. A key international convention relating to patents is the Paris Convention for the Protection of Industrial Property, initially signed in 1883.

The Paris Convention sets out a range of basic rules relating to patents, and although the convention does not have direct legal effect in all national jurisdictions, the principles of the convention are incorporated into all notable current patent systems. The most significant aspect of the convention is the provision of the right to claim priority: filing an application in any one member state of the Paris Convention preserves the right for one year to file in any other member state, and receive the benefit of the original filing date.

Because the right to a patent is intensely date-driven, this right is fundamental to modern patent usage. The authority for patent statutes in different countries varies. In the UK, substantive patent law is contained in the Patents Act 1977 as amended. In the United States, the Constitution empowers Congress to make laws to"promote the Progress of Science and useful Arts..." The laws Congress passed are codified in Title 35 of the United States Code and created the United States Patent and Trademark Office.

In addition, there are international treaty procedures, such as the procedures under the European Patent Convention (EPC), and the Patent Cooperation Treaty (PCT) (administered by WIPO and covering more than 140 countries), that centralize some portion of the filing and examination procedure.

Similar arrangements exist among the member states of ARIPO and OAPI, the analogous treaties among African countries, and the nine CIS member states that have formed the Eurasian Patent Organization.

Application and Prosecution

A patent is requested by filing a written application at the relevant patent office. The person or company filing the application is referred to as"the applicant".

The applicant may be the inventor or its assignee. The application contains a description of how to make and use the invention that must provide sufficient detail for a person skilled in the art (*i.e.,* the relevant area of technology) to make and use the invention. In some countries there are requirements for providing specific information such as the usefulness of the invention, the best mode of performing the invention known to the inventor, or the technical problem or problems solved by the invention. Drawings illustrating the invention may also be provided.

The application also includes one or more claims, although it is not always a requirement to submit these when first filing the application. The claims set out what the applicant is seeking to protect in that they define what the patent owner has a right to exclude others from making, using, or selling, as the case may be.

In other words, the claims define what a patent covers or the"scope of protection". After filing, an application is often referred to as"patent pending". While this term does not confer legal protection, and a patent cannot be enforced until granted, it serves to provide warning to potential infringers that if the patent is issued, they may be liable for damages.

For a patent to be granted, that is to take legal effect in a particular country, the patent application must meet the patentability requirements of that country. Most patent offices examine the application for compliance with these requirements. If the application does not comply, objections are communicated to the applicant or their patent agent or attorney and one or more opportunities to respond to the objections to bring the application into compliance are usually provided.

Once granted the patent is subject in most countries to renewal fees to keep the patent in force. These fees are generally payable on a yearly basis, although the US is a notable exception. Some countries or regional patent offices (*e.g.* the European Patent Office) also require annual renewal fees to be paid for a patent application before it is granted.

Economics

Rationale

There are four primary incentives embodied in the patent system: to invent in the first place; to disclose the invention once made; to invest the sums necessary to experiment, produce and market the invention; and to design around and improve upon earlier patents.

- Patents provide incentives for economically efficient research and development (R&D). A study conducted annually by the IPTS shows that the 2,000 largest global companies invested more than 430 billion euros in 2008 in their R&D departments. If the investments can be considered as inputs of R&D, patents are the outputs. Based on these groups, a project named Corporate Invention Board, had measured and analysed the patent portfolios to produce an original picture of their technological profiles. Without patents, R&D spending would be significantly less or eliminated altogether, limiting the possibility of technological advances or breakthroughs.Corporations would be much more conservative about the R&D investments they made, as third parties would be free to exploit any developments. This second justification is closely related to the basic ideas underlying traditional property rights.
- In accordance with the original definition of the term"patent," patents facilitate and encourage disclosure of innovations into the public domain for the common good. If inventors did not have the legal protection of patents, in many cases, they would prefer or tend to keep their inventions secret. Awarding patents generally makes the details of new technology publicly available, for exploitation by anyone after the patent expires, or for further improvement by other inventors. Furthermore, when a patent's term has expired, the public record ensures that the patentee's idea is not lost to humanity.
- In many industries (especially those with high fixed costs and either low marginal costs or low reverse engineering costs - computer processors, software, and pharmaceuticals for example), once an invention exists, the cost of commercialization (testing, tooling up a factory, developing a market, etc.) is far more than the initial conception cost. (For example, the internal"rule of thumb" at several computer companies in the 1980s was that post-R&D costs were 7-

to-1). Unless there is some way to prevent copies from competing at the marginal cost of production, companies will not make that productization investment.

One effect of modern patent usage is that a small-time inventor can use the exclusive right status to become a licensor. This allows the inventor to accumulate capital from licensing the invention and may allow innovation to occur because he or she may choose to not manage a manufacturing buildup for the invention.

Thus the inventor's time and energy can be spent on pure innovation, allowing others to concentrate on manufacturability. Another effect of modern patent usage is to cause competitors to design around each other's patents. This promotes healthy competition among manufacturers, resulting in gradual improvements of the technology base. This may help augment national economies and confer better living standards to the citizens.

Costs

Some of the costs to society associated with the granting of a patent are: the immediate costs associated with preparing the patent; patent office work; legal costs associated with prosecuting alleged infringements; business costs associated with those legal actions; increasing the cost of determining whether a method is covered by an existing patent, and reduced certainty in the result; restrictions on the use of the patented method (particularly in cases where the method is redeveloped independently).

The costs of preparing and filing a patent application, prosecuting it until grant and maintaining the patent vary from one jurisdiction to another, and may also be dependent upon the type and complexity of the invention, and on the type of patent. The European Patent Office estimated in 2005 that the average cost of obtaining a European patent (via a Euro-direct application, *i.e.* not based on a PCT application) and maintaining the patent for a 10 year term was around 32 000 Euro. Since the London Agreement entered into force on May 1, 2008, this estimation is however no longer up-to-date, since fewer translations are required.

In the United States, direct legal costs of patent litigation are on average in the order of a million dollars per case, not including associated business costs, based on an American Intellectual Property Law Association (AIPLA) survey of patent lawyers (2005), and court documents for a sample of 89 court cases where one side was ordered to pay the other side's legal fees.

Criticism

Patents have been criticized both in principle and in implementation. In principle, patents have been criticized as a restraint of trade, for conferring a negative right upon a patent owner, permitting them to exclude competitors from using or exploiting the invention, even if the competitor subsequently develops the same invention independently.

This may be subsequent to the date of invention, or to the priority date, depending upon the relevant patent law. As state-granted monopolies, patents have been criticized as inconsistent with free trade.

On that basis, in 1869 the Netherlands abolished patents, and did not reintroduce them until 1912. In implementation, patents have been criticized for being granted on already-known inventions.

In 1938, R. Buckminster Fuller wrote of the patent application process in the United States:

- At present, the files, are so extraordinarily complex and the items so multitudinous that a veritable army of governmental servants is required to attend them and sort them into some order of distinguishable categories to which reference may be made when corresponding with patent applicants for the purposes of examiner citation of"prior art" disclosure. This complexity makes it inevitable that the human-equation involved in government servants relative to carelessness or mechanical limitations should occasion the granting of multitudes of"probably" invalid patent claims.

Patents may hinder innovation as well in the case of"troll" entities. A holding company, pejoratively known as a"patent troll", owns a portfolio of patents, and sues others for infringement of these patents while doing little to develop the technology itself. Other commentators suggest that patent trolls are not bad for the patent system at all but instead realign market participant incentives, make patents more liquid, and clear the patent market.

Another theoretical problem with patent rights was proposed by law professors Michael Heller and Rebecca Sue Eisenberg. Based on Heller's theory of the tragedy of the anticommons, the authors argued that intellectual property rights may become so fragmented that, effectively, no one can take advantage of them as to do so would require an agreement between the owners of all of the fragments.

Pharmaceutical patents prevent generic alternatives to enter the market until the patents expire, and thus maintains high prices for medication. This can have significant effects in the developing world, as those who are most in need of basic essential medicines are unable to afford such high priced pharmaceuticals. Critics also question the rationale that exclusive patent rights and the resulting high prices are required for pharmaceutical companies to recoup the large investments needed for research and development. One study concluded that marketing expenditures for new drugs often doubled the amount that was allocated for research and development. Other objects shed light on the problems of today's medical research. It sets wrong priorities in research and pricing, and pushes the state-run healthcare systems even of rich nations to their limits.

In one response to these criticisms, one review concluded that less than 5 per cent of medicines on the World Health Organization's list of essential drugs are under patent. Also, the pharmaceutical industry has contributed US$2 billion for healthcare in developing countries, providing HIV/AIDS drugs at lower cost or even free of charge in certain countries, and has used differential pricing and parallel imports to provide medication to the poor.

Other groups are investigating how social inclusion and equitable distribution of research and development findings can be obtained within the existing intellectual property framework, although these efforts have received less exposure.

Brazil filed a proposal in 2010 with the WIPO Standing Committee on the Law of Patents about the imbalance of rights between IP title holders and the society as a whole with emphasis on the imbalance of benefits from strong IP rights between the few developed countries and the majority of member states.

Such imbalance is also recognized between freedom rights and exclusion rights by the computing profession. Concerns of a similar order have also been documented elsewhere, showing that public campaigns have had a concern for"preventing the over-reach" of IP protection including patent protection, and"to retain a public balance in property rights" of this kind.

The same source also noted the shift that had taken place away from the historical classification of such rights as"grants of privilege", towards referring to them in terms of property and rights; a change that encouraged a change of view of the relation of sovereign governments towards them, away from something that the government"may grant" towards a"duty to uphold them".

TRADEMARK

A trademark or trade mark or trade-mark is a distinctive sign or indicator used by an individual, business organization, or other legal entity to identify that the products or services to consumers with which the trademark appears originate from a unique source, and to distinguish its products or services from those of other entities.

A trademark is designated by the following symbols:

- ™ (for an unregistered trade mark, that is, a mark used to promote or brand goods)
- ℠ (for an unregistered service mark, that is, a mark used to promote or brand services)
- ® (for a registered trademark)

A trademark is typically a name, word, phrase, logo, symbol, design, image, or a combination of these elements. There is also a range of non-conventional trademarks comprising marks which do not fall into these standard categories, such as those based on colour, smell, or sound.

The owner of a registered trademark may commence legal proceedings for trademark infringement to prevent unauthorized use of that trademark.

However, registration is not required. The owner of a common law trademark may also file suit, but an unregistered mark may be protectable only within the geographical area within which it has been used or in geographical areas into which it may be reasonably expected to expand.

The term trademark is also used informally to refer to any distinguishing attribute by which an individual is readily identified, such as the well known characteristics of celebrities. When a trademark is used in relation to services rather than products, it may sometimes be called a service mark, particularly in the United States.

Fundamental Concepts

The essential function of a trademark is to exclusively identify the commercial source or origin of products or services, such that a trademark, properly called, indicates source or serves as a badge of origin. In other words, trademarks serve to identify a particular business as the source of goods or services.

The use of a trademark in this way is known as trademark use. Certain exclusive rights attach to a registered mark, which can be enforced by way of an action for trademark infringement, while unregistered trademark rights may be enforced pursuant to the common law tort of passing off.

It should be noted that trademark rights generally arise out of the use or to maintain exclusive rights over that sign in relation to certain products or services, assuming there are no other trademark objections. Different goods and services have been classified by the International (Nice) Classification of Goods and Services into 45 Trademark Classes (1 to 34 cover goods, and 35 to 45 services).

The idea of this system is to specify and limit the extension of the intellectual property right by determining which goods or services are covered by the mark, and to unify classification systems around the world.

History

In trademark treatises it is usually reported that blacksmiths who made swords in the Roman Empire are thought of as being the first users of trademarks. Other notable trademarks that have been used for a long time include Löwenbräu, which claims use since 1383, and Stella Artois, which claims use since 1366.

Registered trademarks involve registering the trademark with the government.

The oldest registered trademarks in various countries include:

- *United Kingdom*: 1876 - The Bass Red Triangle was the first trademark to be registered under the Trade Mark Registration Act 1875.
- *United States*: Picture of Samson wrestling a lion, to Samson Rope in 1884.

Symbols

The two symbols associated with U.S. trademarks ™ (the trademark symbol) and ® (the registered trademark symbol) represent the status of a mark and accordingly its level of protection. While ™ can be used with any common law usage of a mark, ® may only be used by the owner of a mark following registration with the relevant national authority, such as the U.S. Patent and Trademark Office (USPTO or PTO). The proper manner to display either symbol is immediately following the mark in superscript style.

Terminology

Terms such as"mark","brand" and"logo" are sometimes used interchangeably with"trademark"."Trademark", however, also includes any device, brand, label, name, signature, word, letter, numerical, shape of goods, packaging, colour or combination of colours, smell, sound, movement or any combination thereof which is capable of distinguishing goods and services of one business from those of others. It must be capable of graphical representation and must be applied to goods or services for which it is registered.

Specialized types of trademark include certification marks, collective trademarks and defensive trademarks. A trademark which is popularly used to describe a product or service (rather than to distinguish the product or services from those of third parties) is sometimes known as a genericized trademark. If such a mark becomes synonymous with that product or service to the extent that the trademark owner can no longer enforce its proprietary rights, the mark becomes generic.

Registration

The law considers a trademark to be a form of property. Proprietary rights in relation to a trademark may be established through actual use in the marketplace, or through registration of the mark with the trademarks office (or"trademarks registry") of a particular jurisdiction. In some jurisdictions, trademark rights can be established through either or both means. Certain jurisdictions generally do not recognize trademarks rights arising through use.

If trademark owners do not hold registrations for their marks in such jurisdictions, the extent to which they will be able to enforce their rights through trademark infringement proceedings will therefore be limited. In cases of dispute, this disparity of rights is often referred to as"first to file" as opposed to"first to use." Other countries such as Germany offer a limited amount of common law rights for unregistered marks where to gain protection, the goods or services must occupy a highly significant position in the marketplace - where this could be 40% or more market share for sales in the particular class of goods or services.

In the United States the registration process entails several steps prior to a trademark receiving its Certificate of Registration. First, an Applicant, the individual or entity applying for the registration, files an application to register the respective trademark.

The application is then placed in line in the order it was received to be examined by an examining attorney for the U.S. Patent and Trademark Office. Second, following a period of anywhere from three to six months the application is reviewed by an examining attorney to make sure that it complies with all requirements in order to be entitled to registration.

This review includes procedural matters such as making sure the applicant's goods or services are identified properly. It also includes more substantive matters such as making sure the applicant's mark is not merely descriptive or likely to cause confusion with a pre-existing applied-for or registered mark. If the application runs afoul of any requirement, the examining attorney will issue an office action requiring the applicant to address certain issues or refusals prior to registration of the mark.

Third, and after the examination of the mark has concluded with no issues to be addressed or an applicant has responded adequately to an examining attorney's concerns, the application will be published for opposition. During this 30-day period third-parties who may be affected by the registration of the trademark may step forward to file an Opposition Proceeding to stop the registration of the mark. If an Opposition proceeding is filed it institutes a case before the Trademark Trial and Appeal Board to determine both the validity of the grounds for the opposition as well as the ability of the applicant to register the mark at issue.

Fourth, provided that no third-party opposes the registration of the mark during the opposition period or the opposition is ultimately decided in the applicant's favour the mark will be registered in due course. Outside of the United States the registration process is substantially similar to that found in the U.S. save for one notable exception in many countries: registration occurs prior to the opposition proceeding.

In short, once an application is reviewed by an examiner and found to be entitled to registration a registration certificate is issued subject to the mark being open to opposition for a period of typically 6 months from the date of registration. A registered trademark confers a bundle of exclusive rights upon the registered owner, including the right to exclusive use of the mark in relation to the products or services for which it is registered.

The law in most jurisdictions also allows the owner of a registered trademark to prevent unauthorized use of the mark in relation to products or services which are identical or"colourfully" similar to the"registered" products or services, and in certain cases, prevent use in relation to entirely dissimilar products or services. The test is always whether a consumer of the goods or services will be confused as to the identity of the source or origin. An example may be a very large multinational brand such as"Sony" where a non-electronic product such as a pair of sunglasses might be assumed to have come from Sony Corporation of Japan despite not being a class of goods that Sony has rights in.

Once trademark rights are established in a particular jurisdiction, these rights are generally only enforceable in that jurisdiction, a quality which is sometimes known as territoriality. However, there is a range of international trademark laws and systems which facilitate the protection of trademarks in more than one jurisdiction.

Search

The USPTO maintains a database of registered trademarks. The database is open to the public; however a licensed attorney may be required to interpret the search results. Furthermore as trademarks are governed by federal law, state law, and common law, a thorough search as to the availability of a mark is very important. In the United States, obtaining a trademark search and relying upon the results of an opinion issued by an attorney may insulate a trademark user from being required to pay treble damages and attorney's fees in a trademark infringement case as it demonstrates that the trademark user performed due diligence and was using the mark in good faith.

Trademarks may also be searched on third-party databases, such as LexisNexis, Dialog and Compu-Mark. In Europe and if a community trademark has to be filed, searches have to be conducted with the OHIM (Community Trademark Office) and with the various national offices. An alternative solution is to conduct a trademark search within private databases.

Ability to Register

In most systems, a trademark can be registered if it is able to distinguish the goods or services of a party, will not confuse consumers about the relationship between one party and another, and will not otherwise deceive consumers with respect to the qualities of the product.

Maintaining Rights

Trademarks rights must be maintained through actual lawful use of the trademark. These rights will cease if a mark is not actively used for a period of time, normally 5 years in most jurisdictions. In the case of a trademark registration, failure to actively use the mark in the lawful course of trade, or to enforce the registration in the event of infringement, may also expose the registration itself to become liable for an application for the removal from the register after a certain period of time on the grounds of"non-use". It is not necessary for a trademark owner to take enforcement action against all infringement if it can be shown that the owner perceived the infringement to be minor and inconsequential.

This is designed to prevent owners from continually being tied up in litigation for fear of cancellation. An owner can at any time commence action for infringement against a third party as long as it had not previously notified the third party of its discontent following third party use and then failed to take action within a reasonable period of time (called acquiescence).

The owner can always reserve the right to take legal action until a court decides that the third party had gained notoriety which the owner'must' have been aware of. It will be for the third party to prove their use of the mark is substantial as it is the onus of a company using a mark to check they are not infringing previously registered rights. In the US, owing to the overwhelming number of unregistered rights, trademark applicants are advised to perform searches not just of the trademark register but of local business directories and relevant trade press. Specialized search companies perform such tasks prior to application.

All jurisdictions with a mature trademark registration system provide a mechanism for removal in the event of such non use, which is usually a period of either three or five years. The intention to use a trademark can be proven by a wide range of acts as shown in the"Wooly Bull" and"Ashton v Harlee" cases.

In the U.S., failure to use a trademark for this period of time, aside from the corresponding impact on product quality, will result in abandonment of the mark, whereby any party may use the mark. An abandoned mark is not irrevocably in the public domain, but may instead be re-registered by any party which has re-established exclusive and active use, and must be associated or linked with the original mark owner. If a court rules that a trademark has become"generic" through common use (such that the mark no longer performs the essential trademark function and the average consumer no longer considers that exclusive rights attach to it), the corresponding registration may also be ruled invalid.

Unlike other forms of intellectual property (*e.g.*, patents and copyrights) a registered trademark can, theoretically, last forever. So long as a trademark's use is continuous a trademark holder may keep the mark registered with the U.S. Patent and Trademark Office by filing Section 8 Affidavit(s) of Continuous Use as well as Section 9 Applications for renewal, as required. Specifically, once registered with the U.S. Patent and Trademark Office the owner of a trademark is required to file a Section 8 Affidavit of Continuous Use to maintain the registration between the 5th and 6th year anniversaries of the registration of the mark or during the 6-month grace period following the 6th-year anniversary of the registration.

Note, if the Section 8 Affidavit is filed during the 6-month grace period additional fees to file the Affidavit with the U.S. Patent and Trademark Office will apply. In U.S. trademark registrations are also required to be renewed on or about every 10-year anniversary of the registration of the trademark.

The procedure for 10-year renewals is somewhat different from that for the 5th-6th year renewal. In brief, registrants are required to file both a Section 8 Affidavit of Continuous Use as well as a Section 9 Application for Renewal every ten years to maintain their registration.

Enforcing Rights

The extent to which a trademark owner may prevent unauthorized use of trademarks which are the same as or similar to its trademark depends on various factors such as whether its trademark is registered, the similarity of the trademarks involved, the similarity of the products or services involved, and whether the owner's trademark is well known or, under U.S. law relating to trademark dilution, famous.

If a trademark has not been registered, some jurisdictions (especially Common Law countries) offer protection for the business reputation or goodwill which attaches to unregistered trademarks through the tort of passing off. Passing off may provide a remedy in a scenario where a business has been trading under an unregistered trademark for many years, and a rival business starts using the same or a similar mark.

If a trademark has been registered, then it is much easier for the trademark owner to demonstrate its trademark rights and to enforce these rights through an infringement action. Unauthorized use of a registered trademark need not be intentional in order for infringement to occur, although damages in an infringement lawsuit will generally be greater if there was an intention to deceive.

For trademarks which are considered to be well known, infringing use may occur where the use occurs in relation to products or services which are not the same as or similar to the products or services in relation to which the owner's mark is registered. A growing area of law relating to the enforcement of trademark rights is secondary liability, which allows for the imputation of liability to one who has not acted directly to infringe a trademark but whose legal responsibility may arise under the doctrines of either contributory or vicarious liability.

Limits and Defences to Claims of Infringement

Trademark is subject to various defences, such as abandonment, limitations on geographic scope, and fair use. In the United States, the fair use defence protects many of the interests in free expression related to those protected by the First Amendment.

Fair use may be asserted on two grounds, either that the alleged infringer is using the mark to describe accurately an aspect of its products, or that the alleged infringer is using the mark to identify the mark owner. One of the most visible proofs that trademarks provide a limited right in the U.S. comes from the comparative advertising that is seen throughout U.S. media. An example of the first type is that although Maytag owns the trademark"Whisper Quiet", makers of other products may describe their goods as being"whisper quiet" so long as these competitors are not using the phrase as a trademark. An example of the second type is that Audi can run advertisements saying that a trade publication has rated an Audi model higher than a BMW model, since they are only using"BMW" to identify the competitor. In a related sense, an auto mechanic can truthfully advertise that he services Cadillacs, and a former Playboy Playmate of the Year can identify herself.

Wrongful or Groundless Threats of Infringement

Various jurisdictions have laws which are designed to prevent trademark owners from making wrongful threats of trademark infringement action against other parties. These laws are intended to prevent large or powerful companies from intimidating or harassing smaller companies.

Where one party makes a threat to sue another for trademark infringement, but does not have a genuine basis or intention to carry out that threat, or does not carry out the threat at all within a certain period, the threat may itself become a basis for legal action. In this situation, the party receiving such a threat may seek from the Court a declaratory judgment; also known as a declaratory ruling.

Other Aspects

Public Policy

Trademark law is designed to fulfill the public policy objective of consumer protection, by preventing the public from being misled as to the origin or quality of a product or service. By identifying the commercial source of products and services, trademarks facilitate identification of products and services which meet the expectations of consumers as to quality and other characteristics.

Trademarks may also serve as an incentive for manufacturers, providers or suppliers to consistently provide quality products or services to maintain their business reputation. Furthermore, if a trademark owner does not maintain quality control and adequate supervision in relation to the manufacture and provision of products or services supplied by a licensee, such"naked licensing" will eventually adversely affect the owner's rights in the trademark.

This proposition has, however, been watered down by the judgment of the House of Lords in the case of Scandecor Development AB v. Scandecor Marketing AB *et al.* UKHL 21; wherein it has been held that the mere fact that a bare license (equivalent of the United States concept of a naked license) has been granted did not automatically mean that a trademark was liable to mislead.

By the same token, trademark holders must be cautious in the sale of their mark for similar reasons as apply to licensing. When assigning an interest in a trademark, if the associated product or service is not transferred with it, then this may be an"assignment-in-gross" and could lead to a loss of rights in the trademark.

It is still possible to make significant changes to the underlying goods or services during a sale without jeopardizing the trademark, but companies will often contract with the sellers to help transition the mark and goods or services to the new owners to ensure continuity of the trademark.

Comparison with Patents, Designs and Copyright

While trademark law seeks to protect indications of the commercial source of products or services, patent law generally seeks to protect new and useful inventions, and registered designs law generally seeks to protect the look or appearance of a manufactured object.

Trademarks, patents and designs collectively form a subset of intellectual property known as industrial property because they are often created and used in an industrial or commercial context.

By comparison, copyright law generally seeks to protect original literary, artistic and other creative works. Continued active use and re-registration can make a trademark perpetual, whereas copyright usually lasts for the duration of the author's lifespan plus 70 years for works by individuals, and some limited time after creation for works by bodies corporate. This can lead to confusion in cases where a work passes into the public domain but the character in question remains a registered trademark.

Although intellectual property laws such as these are theoretically distinct. For example, the particular design of a bottle may qualify for copyright protection as a non-utilitarian, or for trademark protection based on its shape, or the'trade dress' appearance of the bottle as a whole may be protectable. Titles and character names from books or movies may also be protectable as trademarks while the works from which they are drawn may qualify for copyright protection as a whole.

Drawing these distinctions is necessary, but often challenging for the courts and lawyers, especially in jurisdictions where patents and copyrights pass into the public domain, depending on the jurisdiction. Unlike patents and copyrights, which in theory, are granted for one-off fixed terms, trademarks remain valid as long as the owner actively uses and defends them and maintains their registrations with the competent authorities. This often involves payment of a periodic renewal fee.

As a trademark must be used to maintain rights in relation to that mark, a trademark can be'abandoned' or its registration can be cancelled or revoked if the mark is not continuously used. By comparison, patents and copyrights cannot be'abandoned' and a patent holder or copyright owner can generally enforce their rights without taking any particular action to maintain the patent or copyright. Additionally, patent holders and copyright owners may not necessarily need to actively police their rights. However, a failure to bring a timely infringement suit or action against a known infringer may give the defendant a defence of implied consent or estoppel when suit is finally brought.

Dilution

A trademark is diluted when the use of similar or identical trademarks in other non-competing markets means that the trademark in and of itself will lose its capacity to signify a single source. In other words, unlike ordinary trademark law, dilution protection extends to trademark uses that do not confuse consumers regarding who has made a product.

Instead, dilution protection law aims to protect sufficiently strong trademarks from losing their singular association in the public mind with a particular product, perhaps imagined if the trademark were to be encountered independently of any product (*e.g.*, just the word Pepsi spoken, or on a billboard).

Under trademark law, dilution occurs either when unauthorized use of a mark"blurs" the"distinctive nature of the mark" or"tarnishes it." Likelihood of confusion is not required. 15 U.S.C §§ 1127, 1125(c).

Sale, Transfer and Licensing

In various jurisdictions a trademark may be sold with or without the underlying goodwill which subsists in the business associated with the mark. However, this is not the case in the United States, where the courts have held that this would"be a fraud upon the public". In the U.S., trademark registration can therefore only be sold and assigned if accompanied by the sale of an underlying asset.

Examples of assets whose sale would ordinarily support the assignment of a mark include the sale of the machinery used to produce the goods that bear the mark, or the sale of the corporation (or subsidiary) that produces the trademarked goods.

Most jurisdictions provide for the use of trademarks to be licensed to third parties. The licensor (usually the trademark owner) must monitor the quality of the goods being produced by the licensee to avoid the risk of trademark being deemed abandoned by the courts. A trademark license should therefore include appropriate provisions dealing with quality control, whereby the licensee provides warranties as to quality and the licensor has rights to inspection and monitoring.

Domain Names

The advent of the domain name system has led to attempts by trademark holders to enforce their rights over domain names that are similar or identical to their existing trademarks, particularly by seeking control over the domain names at issue. As with dilution protection, enforcing trademark rights over domain name owners involves protecting a trademark outside the obvious context of its consumer market, because domain names are global and not limited by goods or service.

This conflict was more easily resolved when the domain name user actually used to compete with the trademark owner. Cybersquatting, however, involves no such competition, but instead an unlicensed user registering the trademark as a domain name to pressure a payoff (or other benefit) from the lawful mark owner.

Typosquatters-those registering common misspellings of trademarks as domain names-have also been targeted successfully in trademark infringement suits. Other types of domain name disputes include the so-called"gripe site," which use a registered trademark in a domain." There are also disputes arising from the subdomain, when a third party uses a protected mark in a web address.

This clash of the new technology with preexisting trademark rights resulted in several high profile decisions as the courts of many countries tried to coherently address the issue (and not always successfully) within the framework of existing trademark law. There was no actual consumer confusion, and so initial interest confusion was a concept applied instead. Initial interest confusion refers to customer confusion that creates an initial interest in a competitor's"product". Even though initial interest confusion is dispelled by the time any actual sales occur, it allows a trademark infringer to capitalize on the goodwill associated with the original mark.

Several cases have wrestled with the concept of initial interest confusion. In Brookfield Commc'ns v. West Coast Ent'mt the court found initial interest confusion could occur when a competitor's trademarked terms were used in the HTML metatags of resulting in that site appearing in the search results when a user searches on the trademarked term.

In Playboy v. Netscape, the court found initial interest confusion when users typed in Playboy's trademarks into a search engine, resulting in the display of search results alongside unlabeled banner ads, triggered by keywords that included Playboy's marks, that would take users to Playboy's competitors.

Though users might ultimately realise upon clicking on the banner ads that they were not Playboy-affiliated, the court found that the competitor advertisers could have gained customers by appropriating Playboy's goodwill since users may be perfectly happy to browse the competitor's site instead of returning the search results to find the Playboy sites. In Lamparello v. Falwell, however, the court clarified that a finding of initial interest confusion is contingent on financial profit from said confusion, such that, if a domain name confusing similar to a registered trademark is used for a non-trademark related, the site owner will not be found to have infringed where he does not seek to capitalize on the mark's goodwill for his own commercial enterprises.

In addition, courts have upheld the rights of trademark owners with regard to commercial use of domain names, even in cases where goods sold there legitimately bear the mark. In the landmark decision Creative Gifts, Inc. v. UFO, 235 F.3d 540, defendants had registered the domain name"Levitron.com" to sell goods bearing the trademark"Levitron" under an at-will license from the trademark owner. The 10th Circuit affirmed the rights of the trademark owner with regard to said domain name, despite arguments of promissory estoppel.

Most courts particularly frowned on cybersquatting, and found that it was itself a sufficiently commercial use (*i.e.,*"trafficking" in trademarks) to reach into the area of trademark infringement.

Most jurisdictions have since amended their trademark laws to address domain names specifically, and to provide explicit remedies against cybersquatters. In the US, the legal situation was clarified by the Anticybersquatting Consumer Protection Act, an amendment to the Lanham Act, which explicitly prohibited cybersquatting. It defines cybersquatting as"(occurring) when a person other than the trademark holder registers the domain name of a well known trademark and then attempts to profit from this by either ransoming the domain name back to the trademark holder or using the domain name to divert business from the trademark holder to the domain name holder".

The provision states that"[a] person shall be liable in a civil action by the owner of the mark... if, without regard to the goods or services of the person, that person (i) had a bad faith intent to profit from the mark...; and registers, traffics in, or uses domain name [that is confusingly similar to another's mark or dilutes another's mark]".

This international legal change has also led to the creation of ICANN Uniform Domain-Name Dispute-Resolution Policy (UDRP) and other dispute policies for specific countries (such as Nominet UK's DRS) which attempt to streamline the process of resolving who should own a domain name (without dealing with other infringement issues such as damages). This is particularly desirable to trademark owners when the domain name registrant may be in another country or even anonymous. Registrants of domain names also sometimes wish to register the domain names themselves as trademarks for perceived advantages, such as an extra bulwark against their domain being hijacked, and to avail themselves of such remedies as confusion or passing off against other domain holders with confusingly similar or intentionally misspelled domain names.

As with other trademarks, the domain name will not be subject to registration unless the proposed mark is actually used to identify the registrant's goods or services to the public, rather than simply being the location on the Internet where the applicant's web site appears. Terms which are not protectable by themselves, such as a generic term or a merely descriptive term that has not acquired secondary meaning, may become registrable when a Top-Level Domain Name (*e.g.* dot-COM) is appended to it. An example of such a domain name ineligible for trademark or service mark protection as a generic term, but which currently has a registered U.S. service mark.

Among trademark practitioners there remains a great deal of debate around trademark protection under ICANN's proposed generic top-level domain name space expansion. World Trademark Review has been reporting on the at times fiery discussion between trademark owners and domainers.

International Law

It is important to note that although there are systems which facilitate the filing, registration or enforcement of trademark rights in more than one jurisdiction on a regional or global basis, it is currently not possible to file and obtain a single trademark registration which will automatically apply around the world. Like any national law, trademark laws apply only in their applicable country or jurisdiction, a quality which is sometimes known as"territoriality".

Territorial Application

The inherent limitations of the territorial application of trademark laws have been mitigated by various intellectual property treaties, foremost amongst which is the WTO Agreement on Trade-Related Aspects of Intellectual Property Rights. TRIPS establishes legal compatibility between member jurisdictions by requiring the harmonization of applicable laws. For example, Article 15(1) of TRIPS provides a definition for"sign" which is used as or forms part of the definition of"trademark" in the trademark legislation of many jurisdictions around the world.

Madrid System

The major international system for facilitating the registration of trademarks in multiple jurisdictions is commonly known as the"Madrid system". Madrid provides a centrally administered system for securing trademark registrations in member jurisdictions by extending the protection of an"international registration" obtained through the World Intellectual Property Organization. This international registration is in turn based upon an application or registration obtained by a trade mark applicant in its home jurisdiction.

The primary advantage of the Madrid system is that it allows a trademark owner to obtain trademark protection in many jurisdictions by filing one application in one jurisdiction with one set of fees, and make any changes (*e.g.* changes of name or address) and renew registration across all applicable jurisdictions through a single administrative process. Furthermore, the"coverage" of the international registration may be extended to additional member jurisdictions at any time.

Trademark Law Treaty

The Trademark Law Treaty establishes a system pursuant to which member jurisdictions agree to standardize procedural aspects of the trademark registration process. It is not necessarily respective of rules within individual countries.

Community Trade Mark system

The Community Trade Mark system is the trademark system which applies in the European Union, whereby registration of a trademark with the Office for Harmonization in the Internal Market (Trade Marks and Designs) (*i.e.* OHIM, the trademarks office of the European Union), leads to a registration which is effective throughout the EU as a whole. The CTM system is therefore said to be unitary in character, in that a CTM registration applies indivisibly across all European Union member states. However, the CTM system did not replace the national trademark registration systems; the CTM system and the national systems continue to operate in parallel to each other.

If you reside outside the EU, you must have professional representative to the procedures before the OHIM. If you are a European resident, you don't have to have professional representation to file an opposition, however, it is strongly recommended by the OHIM.

One of the tasks of a CTM owner is the monitoring of the later applications whether any of those is similar to his/her earlier trademark. Monitoring is not easy and usually requires professional expertise. To conduct a monitoring there is the so-called Trademark Watching service where it can be checked if someone tries to get registered marks that are similar to the existing marks.

Oppositions should be filed on the standard opposition form in any official language of the European Union, however, the substantive part of the opposition (*e.g.* the argumentations) can be submitted only in the language of the opposed application, that is one of the working languages of the OHIM, *e.g.* English, Spanish, German. Worth noting that in most of the cases the opponents file their oppositions in English.

Well-known Status

Well-known trade mark status is commonly granted to famous international trade marks in less-developed legal jurisdictions.

Pursuant to Article 6 bis of the Paris Convention, countries are empowered to grant this status to marks that the relevant authority considers are'well known'. In addition to the standard grounds for trade mark infringement (same/similar mark applied same/similar goods or services, and a likelihood of confusion), if the mark is deemed well known it is an infringement to apply the same or a similar mark to dissimilar goods/services where there is confusion, including where it takes unfair advantage of the well-known mark or causing detriment to it.

A well-known trademark does not have to be registered in the jurisdiction to bring a trade mark infringement action (equivalent to bringing a passing off claim without having to show goodwill and having a lesser burden of proof).

COPYRIGHT

Copyright is a set of exclusive rights granted by the law of a jurisdiction to the author or creator of an original work, including the right to copy, distribute and adapt the work. Exceptions and limitations to these rights strive to balance the public interest in the wide distribution of the material produced and to encourage creativity. Exceptions include fair dealing and fair use, and such use does not require the permission of the copyright owner. All other uses require permission and copyright owners can license or permanently transfer or assign their exclusive rights to others.

Copyright does not protect ideas, only their expression or fixation. In most jurisdictions, copyright arises upon fixation and does not need to be registered. Copyright protection applies for a specific period of time, after which the work is said to enter the public domain. The first copyright statute was the British Statute of Anne of 1709, the full title of which was:"An Act for the Encouragement of Learning, by vesting the Copies of Printed Books in the Authors or purchasers of such Copies". Copyright laws are partially standardized through international and regional agreements such as the Berne Convention and the European copyright directives.

Although there are consistencies among nations' copyright laws, each jurisdiction has separate and distinct laws and regulations covering copyright. National copyright laws on licensing, transfer and assignment of copyright still vary greatly between countries and copyrighted works are licensed on a territorial basis. Some jurisdictions also recognize moral rights of creators, such as the right to be credited for the work.

Initially copyright only applied to published books, but over time copyright was extended to other uses, such as translations and derivative works. Copyright now covers a wide range of works, including maps, dramatic works, paintings, photographs, sound recordings, motion pictures, and computer programmes.

Justification

The British Statute of Anne was the first act to directly protect the rights of authors. Under US copyright law, the justification appears in Article I, Section 8 Clause 8 of the Constitution, known as the Copyright Clause. It empowers the United States Congress"To promote the Progress of Science and useful Arts, by securing for limited Times to Authors and Inventors the exclusive Right to their respective Writings and Discoveries."

The World Intellectual Property Organisation the purpose of copyright is twofold:

- "To encourage a dynamic culture, while returning value to creators so that they can lead a dignified economic existence, and to provide widespread, affordable access to content for the public."

History

Early European Printers' Monopoly

The origin of copyright law in most European countries lies in efforts by the church and governments to regulate and control printing, which was widely established in the 15th and 16th centuries. Before the invention of the printing press a writing, once created, could only be physically multiplied by the highly laborious and error-prone process of manual copying by scribes. Printing allowed for multiple exact copies of a work, leading to a more rapid and widespread circulation of ideas and information. While governments and church encouraged printing in many ways, which allowed the dissemination of Bibles and government information, works of dissent and criticism could also circulate rapidly.

As a consequence, governments established controls over printers across Europe, requiring them to have official licences to trade and produce books. The licenses typically gave printers the exclusive right to print particular works for a fixed period of years, and enabled the printer to prevent others from printing or importing the same work during that period. The notion that the expression of dissent should be tolerated, not censured or punished by law, developed alongside the rise of printing and the press.

The Areopagitica, published in 1644 under the full title Areopagitica: A speech of Mr. John Milton for the liberty of unlicensed printing to the Parliament of England, was John Milton's response to the British parliament re-introducing government licensing of printers, hence publishers. In doing so, Milton articulated the main strands of future discussions about freedom of expression.

As the"menace" of printing spread, governments established centralised control mechanism and in 1557 the British Crown thought to stem the flow of seditious and heretical books by chartering the Stationers' Company. The right to print was limited to the members of that guild, and thirty years later the Star Chamber was chartered to curtail the"greate enormities and abuses" of"dyvers contentyous and disorderlye persons professinge the arte or mystere of pryntinge or selling of books." The right to print was restricted to two universities and to the 21 existing printers in the city of London, which had 53 printing presses. The French crown also repressed printing, and printer Etienne Dolet was burned at the stake in 1546. As the British took control of type founding in 1637, printers fled to the Netherlands. Confrontation with authority made printers radical and rebellious, with 800 authors, printers and book dealers being incarcerated in the Bastille before it was stormed in 1789.

Early British Copyright Law

In England the printers, known as stationers, formed a collective organisation, known as the Stationers' Company. In the 16th century the Stationers' Company was given the power to require all lawfully printed books to be entered into its register. Only members of the Stationers' Company could enter books into the register. This meant that the Stationers' Company achieved a dominant position over publishing in 17th century England (no equivalent arrangement formed in Scotland and Ireland). The monopoly came to an end in 1694, when the English Parliament did not renew the Stationers Company's power. The newly established Parliament of Great Britain passed the first copyright statute, the Statute of Anne, full title"An Act for the Encouragement of Learning, by vesting the Copies of Printed Books in the Authors or purchasers of such Copies".

The coming into force of the Statute of Anne in April 1710 marked a historic moment in the development of copyright law. As the world's first copyright statute it granted publishers of a book legal protection of 14 years with the commencement of the statute.

It also granted 21 years of protection for any book already in print. Unlike the monopoly granted to the Stationers' Company previously, the Statute of Anne was concerned with the reading public, the continued production of useful literature, and the advancement and spread of education. To encourage"learned men to compose and write useful books" the statute guaranteed the finite right to print and reprint those works.

It established a pragmatic bargain involving authors, the booksellers and the public. The Statute of Anne ended the old system whereby only literature that met the censorship standards administers by the booksellers could appear in print. The statute furthermore created a public domain for literature, as previously all literature belonged to the booksellers forever.

Common Law Copyright

When the statutory copyright term provided for by the Statute of Anne began to expire in 1731 London booksellers thought to defend their dominant position by seeking injunctions from the Court of Chancery for works by authors that fell outside the statute's protection. At the same time the London booksellers lobbied parliament to extend the copyright term provided by the Statute of Anne. Eventually, in a case known as Midwinter v. Hamilton (1743-

1748), the London booksellers turned to common law and starting a 30 year period known as the battle of the booksellers. The London booksellers argued that the Statute of Anne only supplemented and supported a pre-existing common law copyright.

The dispute was argued out in a number of notable cases, including Millar v Kincaid (1749-1751), Tonson v Collins (1761-1762), and Donaldson v Beckett (1774). Donaldson v Beckett eventually established that copyright was a"creature of statute", and that the rights and responsibilities in copyright were determined by legislation.

The Lords clearly voted against perpetual copyright and by confirming that the copyright term, that is the length of time of work is in copyright, did expire just as to statute the Lords also confirmed that a large number of works and books first published in Britain were in the public domain, either because the copyright term granted by statute had expired, or because they were first published before the Statute of Anne was enacted in 1709. This opened the market for cheap reprints of works from Shakespeare, John Milton and Geoffrey Chaucer, works now considered classics.

The expansion of the public domain in books broke the dominance of the London booksellers and allowed for competition, with the number of London booksellers and publishers rising threefold from 111 to 308 between 1772 and 1802.

Early French Copyright Law

In pre-revolutionary France all books needed to be approved by official censors and authors and publishers had to obtain a royal privilege before a book could be published. Royal privileges were exclusive and usually granted for six years, with the possibility of renewal. Over time it was established that the owner of a royal privilege has the sole right to obtain a renewal indefinitely. In 1761 the Royal Council awarded a royal privilege to the heirs of an author rather than the author's publisher, sparking a national debate on the nature of literary property similar to that taking place in Britain during the battle of the booksellers.

In 1777 a series of royal decrees reformed the royal privileges. The duration of privileges were set at a minimum duration of 10 years or the life of the author, which ever was longer. If the author obtained a privilege and did not transfer or sell it on, he could publish and sell copies of the book himself, and pass the privilege on to his heirs, who enjoyed an exclusive right into perpetuity.

If the privilege was sold to a publisher, the exclusive right would only last the specified duration. The royal degrees prohibited the renewal of privileges and once the privilege had expired anyone could obtain a"permission simple" to print or sell copies of the work. Hence the public domain in books whose privilege had expired was expressly recognised. After the French Revolution a dispute over Comédie-Française being granted the exclusive right to the public performance of all dramatic works erupted and in 1791 the National Assembly abolished the privilege. Anyone was allowed to establish a public theatre and the National Assembly declared that the works of any author who had died more than five years ago were public property. In the same degree the National Assembly granted authors the exclusive right to authorise the public performance of their works during their lifetime, and extended that right to the authors' heirs and assignees for five years after the author's death.

The National Assembly took the view that a published work was by its nature a public property, and that an author's rights are recognised as an exception to this principle, to compensate an author for his work. In 1793 a new law was passed giving authors, composers, and artists the exclusive right to sell and distribute their works, and the right was extended to their heirs and assigns for 10 years after the author's death.

The National Assembly placed this law firmly on a natural right footing, calling the law the"Declaration of the Rights of Genius" and so evoking the famous Declaration of the Rights of Man and of the Citizen. However, author's rights were subject to the condition of making depositing copies of the work with the Bibliothèque Nationale and 19th Century commentators characterised the 1793 law as utilitarian and"a charitable grant from society".

Early US Copyright Law

The Statute of Anne did not apply to the American colonies. The colonies' economy was largely agrarian, hence copyright law was not a priority, resulting in only three private copyright acts being passed in America prior to 1783. Two of the acts were limited to seven years, the other was limited to a term of five years.

In 1783 several authors' petitions persuaded the Continental Congress"that nothing is more properly a man's own than the fruit of his study, and that the protection and security of literary property would greatly tends to encourage genius and to promote useful discoveries." But under the Articles of Confederation, the Continental Congress had no authority to issue copyright, instead it passed a resolution encouraging the States to"secure to the authors or publishers of any new book not hitherto printed... the copy right of such books for a certain time not less than fourteen years from the first publication; and to secure to the said authors, the copy right of such books for another term of time no less than fourteen years.

Three states had already enacted copyright statutes in 1783 prior to the Continental Congress resolution, and in the subsequent three years all of the remaining states except Delaware passed a copyright statute. Seven of the States followed the Statute of Anne and the Continental Congress' resolution by providing two fourteen year terms. The five remaining States granted copyright for single terms of fourteen, twenty and twenty one years, with no right of renewal.

At the Constitutional Convention 1787 both James Madison of Virginia and Charles Pinckney of South Carolina submitted proposals that would allow Congress the power to grant copyright for a limited time. These proposals are the origin of the Copyright Clause in the United States Constitution, which allows the granting of copyright and patents for a limited time to serve a utilitarian function, namely"to promote the progress of science and useful arts". The first federal copyright act, the Copyright Act of 1790 granted copyright for a term of"fourteen years from the time of recording the title thereof", with a right of renewal for another fourteen years if the author survived to the end of the first term.

The act covered not only books, but also maps and charts. With exception of the provision on maps and charts the Copyright Act of 1790 is copied almost verbatim from the Statute of Anne.

At the time works only received protection under federal statutory copyright if the statutory formalities, such as a proper copyright notice, were satisfied. If this was not the case the work immediately entered into the public domain. In 1834 the Supreme Court ruled in Wheaton v. Peters, a case similar to the British Donaldson v Beckett of 1774, that although the author of an unpublished work had a common law right to control the first publication of that work, the author did not have a common law right to control reproduction following the first publication of the work.

Latin America

Latin American countries established national copyright laws following independence from the Spanish and Portuguese colonial powers. Latin American countries were among the first countries outside Europe to establish copyright law, with Brazil being the fourth country in the world to establish national copyright laws in 1804, after the UK, France and the United States.

The foundation of Brazilian copyright law was the French Civil Code. Copyright law was initially established in Mexico following a Spanish court order in 1820 and in 1832 Mexico passed its first copyright statute. Copyright statutes had been established in eight Latin American countries by the 1850s.

Africa, Asia, and the Pacific

Copyright law was introduced in African, Asian and Pacific countries in the late 19th Century by European colonial powers, especially Britain and France. After the 1884 Congress of Berlin European colonial powers imposed new laws and institutions in their colonies, including copyright laws.

The British Empire introduced copyright law in its African and Asian colonies though the Copyright Act 1911, also known as the Imperial Copyright Act of 1911. Similarly France applied its copyright law throughout its colonies and the French National Institute for Intellectual Property (INPI) acted as the colonial intellectual property authority. The introduction of copyright laws in colonies occurred in the context of colonial powers' desire to"civilize" their colonies and to protect the commercial interest of the colonial powers. While approaches varied, copyright laws were generally not adapted to fit local conditions.

International Copyright Law

Berne Convention for the Protection of Literary and Artistic Works

The Berne Convention was first established in 1886, and was subsequently re-negotiated in 1896 (Paris), 1908 (Berlin), 1928 (Rome), 1948 (Brussels), 1967 (Stockholm) and 1971 (Paris). The convention relates to literary and artistic works, which includes films, and the convention requires its member states to provide protection for every production in the literary, scientific and artistic domain. The Berne Convention has a number of core features, including the principle of national treatment, which holds that each member state to the Convention would give citizens of other member states the same rights of copyright that it gave to its own citizens (Article 3-5).

Another core feature is the establishment of minimum standards of national copyright legislation in that each member state agrees to certain basic rules which their national laws must contain, though member states can if they wish increase the amount of protection given to copyright owners. One important minimum rule was that the term of copyright was to be a minimum of the author's lifetime plus 50 years. Another important minimum rule established by the Berne Convention is that copyright arises with the creation of a work and does not depend upon any formality such as a system of public registration (Article 5(2)). At the time some countries did require registration of copyright, and when Britain implemented the Berne Convention in the Copyright Act 1911 it had to abolish its system of registration at Stationers' Hall.

The Berne Convention focuses on authors as the key figure in copyright law and the stated purpose of the convention is"the protection of the rights of authors in their literary and artistic works" (Article 1), rather than the protection of publishers and other actors in the process of disseminating works to the public. In the 1928 revision the concept of moral rights was introduced (Article 10bis), giving authors the right to be identified as a such and to object to derogatory treatment of their works. These rights, unlike economic rights such as preventing reproduction, could not be transferred to others.

The Berne Convention also enshrined limitations and exceptions to copyright, enabling the reproduction of literary and artistic works without the copyright owners prior permission. The detail of these exceptions was left to national copyright legislation, but the guiding principle is stated in Article 9 of the convention. The so called three-step test holds that an exception is only permitted"in certain special cases, provided that such reproduction does not conflict with a normal exploitation of the work and does not unreasonably prejudice the legitimate interests of the author". Free use of copyrighted work is expressly permitted in the case of quotations from lawfully published works, illustration for teaching purposes, and news reporting (Article 10).

European Copyright Law

In the 1980s the European Community started to regard copyright as an element in the creation of a single market. Since 1991 the EU has passed a number of directives on copyright, designed to harmonise copyright laws in member states in certain key areas, such as computer programmes, databases and the internet. The directives aimed to reduce obstacles to the free movement of goods and services within the European Union, such as for example in rental rights, satellite broadcasting, copyright term and resale rights. Key directives include the 1993 Copyright Duration Directive, the 2001 InfoSoc Directive, also known as Copyright Directive, and the 2004 Directive on the enforcement of intellectual property rights.

Agreement on Trade-Related Aspects of Intellectual Property Rights (TRIPS)

Important developments on copyright at international level in the 1990s include the 1994 Agreement on Trade-Related Aspects of Intellectual Property Rights, known as TRIPS Agreement. TRIPS was negotiated at the end of the Uruguay Round of the General Agreement on Tariffs and Trade (GATT) and contains a number of provisions on copyright. Compliance with the TRIPS Agreement is required of states wishing to be members of the World Trade Organisation (WTO).

States need to be signatory of the Berne Convention and comply with all its provisions, except for the provision on moral rights (Article 9(1)). States need to bring computer programmes and databases within the scope of works covered by copyright law (Article 10). States need to provide for rental rights in at least computer programmes and films (Article 11). Where copyright term, that is duration of copyright, is calculated other than by reference to the life of a natural person, States need to give a minimum term of 50 years calculated from either the date of authorised publication or the creation of the work.

Anti-Counterfeiting Trade Agreement

The Anti-Counterfeiting Trade Agreement (ACTA) is a proposed plurilateral trade agreement which is claimed by its proponents to be in response"to the increase in global trade of counterfeit goods and pirated copyright protected works." The scope of ACTA is broad, including counterfeit physical goods, as well as"internet distribution and information technology". In October 2007 the United States, the European Community, Switzerland and

Japan announced that they would negotiate ACTA. Furthermore the following countries have joined the negotiations: Australia, the Republic of Korea, New Zealand, Mexico, Jordan, Morocco, Singapore, the United Arab Emirates and Canada.

The ACTA negotiations have been largely conducted in secrecy, with very little information being officially disclosed. However, on 22 May 2008, a discussion about the proposed agreement was uploaded to Wikileaks, and newspaper reports about the secret negotiations quickly followed.

Copyright by Country

Copyright laws have been standardized to some extent through international conventions such as the Berne Convention. Although there are consistencies among nations' intellectual property laws, each jurisdiction has separate and distinct laws and regulations about copyright.

Obtaining Copyright

Copyright law is different from country to country, and a copyright notice is required in about 20 countries for a work to be protected under copyright. Before 1989, all published works in the US had to contain a copyright notice, the © symbol followed by the publication date and copyright owner's name, to be protected by copyright. This is no longer the case and use of a copyright notice is now optional in the US, though they are still used.

In all countries that are members of the Berne Convention, copyright is automatic and need not be obtained through official registration with any government office. Once an idea has been reduced to tangible form, for example by securing it in a fixed medium (such as a drawing, sheet music, photograph, a videotape, or a computer file), the copyright holder is entitled to enforce his or her exclusive rights.

However, while registration isn't needed to exercise copyright, in jurisdictions where the laws provide for registration, it serves as prima facie evidence of a valid copyright. The original copyright owner of the copyright may be the employer of the author rather than the author himself, if the work is a"work for hire".

Copyright Term

Copyright subsists for a variety of lengths in different jurisdictions. The length of the term can depend on several factors, including the type of work (*e.g.* musical composition or novel), whether the work has been published or not, and whether the work was created by an individual or a corporation. In most of the world, the default length of copyright is the life of the author plus either 50 or 70 years. In the United States, the term for most existing works is for a term ending 70 years after the death of the author. If the work was a work for hire (*e.g.*, those created by a corporation) then copyright persists for

120 years after creation or 95 years after publication, whichever is shorter. In some countries (for example, the United States and the United Kingdom), copyrights expire at the end of the calendar year in question.

The length and requirements for copyright duration are subject to change by legislation, and since the early 20th century there have been a number of adjustments made in various countries, which can make determining the duration of a given copyright somewhat difficult. For example, the United States used to require copyrights to be renewed after 28 years to stay in force, and formerly required a copyright notice upon first publication to gain coverage.

In Italy and France, there were post-wartime extensions that could increase the term by approximately 6 years in Italy and up to about 14 in France. Many countries have extended the length of their copyright terms (sometimes retroactively). International treaties establish minimum terms for copyrights, but individual countries may enforce longer terms than those.

Exclusive Rights Granted by Copyright

Copyright is literally, the right to copy, though in legal terms"the right to control copying" is more accurate. Copyright are exclusive statutory rights to exercise control over copying and other exploitation of the works for a specific period of time. The copyright owner is given two sets of rights: an exclusive, positive right to copy and exploit the copyrighted work, or license others to do so, and a negative right to prevent anyone else from doing so without consent, with the possibility of legal remedies if they do.

Copyright initially only granted the exclusive right to copy a book, allowing anybody to use the book to, for example, make a translation, adaptation or public performance. At the time print on paper was the only format in which most text based copyrighted works were distributed. Therefore, while the language of book contracts was typically very broad, the only exclusive rights that had any significant economic value were rights to distribute the work in print.

The exclusive rights granted by copyright law to copyright owners have been gradually expanded over time and now uses of the work such as dramatization, translations, and derivative works such as adaptations and transformations, fall within the scope of copyright. With a few exceptions, the exclusive rights granted by copyright are strictly territorial in scope, as they are granted by copyright laws in different countries. Bilateral and multilateral treaties establish minimum exclusive rights in member states, meaning that there is some uniformity across Berne Convention member states.

The print format means that content is affixed onto the content can't be easily or conveniently manipulated by the user. Duplication of printed works is time-consuming and generally produces a copy that is of lower quality. Developments in technology have created new formats and new means of distribution. Particularly digital formats distributed over computer networks have separated the content from its means of delivery. Users of content are now able to exercise many of the exclusive rights granted to copyright owners, such as reproduction, distribution and adaptation.

Types of Work Subject to Copyright

The types of work which are subject to copyright has been expanded over time. Initially only covering books, copyright law was revised in the 19th century to include maps, charts, engravings, prints, musical compositions, dramatic works, photographs, paintings, drawings and sculptures. In the 20th century copyright was expanded to cover motion pictures, computer programmes, sound recordings, choreography and architectural works.

Idea-expression Divide

Copyright law is typically designed to protect the fixed expression or manifestation of an idea rather than the fundamental idea itself. Copyright does not protect ideas, only their expression and in the Anglo-American law tradition the idea-expression divide is a legal concept which explains the appropriate function of copyright laws.

Related Rights and Neighboring Rights

Related rights is used to describe database rights, public lending rights (rental rights), artist resale rights and performers' rights. Related rights may also refer to copyright in broadcasts and sound recordings.

Related rights award copyright protection to works which are not author works, but rather technical media works which allowed author works to be communicated to a new audience in a different form. The substance of protection is usually not as great as there is for author works. In continental European copyright law, a system of neighboring rights has thus developed and the approach was reinforced by the creation of the Rome Convention for the Protection of Performers, Producers of Phonograms and Broadcasting Organizations in 1961.

First-sale Doctrine and Exhaustion of Rights

Copyright law does not restrict the owner of a copy from reselling legitimately obtained copies of copyrighted works, provided that those copies were originally produced by or with the permission of the copyright holder. It is therefore legal, for example, to resell a copyrighted book or CD.

In the United States, this is known as the first-sale doctrine, and was established by the courts to clarify the legality of reselling books in second-hand bookstores. Some countries may have parallel importation restrictions that allow the copyright holder to control the resale market. This may mean for example that a copy of a book that does not infringe copyright in the country where it was printed does infringe copyright in a country into which it is imported for retailing. The first-sale doctrine is known as exhaustion of rights in other countries and is a principle that also applies, though somewhat differently, to patent and trademark rights. It is important to note that the first-sale doctrine permits the transfer of the particular legitimate copy involved. It does not permit making or distributing additional copies.

Limitations and Exceptions

The expression"limitations and exceptions" refers to situations in which the exclusive rights granted to authors, or their assignees under copyright law do not apply or are limited for public interest reasons. They generally limit use of copyrighted material to certain cases that do not require permission from the rights holders, such as for commentary, criticism, news reporting, research, teaching or scholarship, archiving, access by the visually impaired etc.

They essentially create a limitation, or an exception to the monopoly exclusive rights that are granted to the creator of a copyright work by law.

Copyright theory teaches that the balance between monopoly granted to the creator, and the exceptions to this monopoly are at the heart of creativity. *i.e.* Exclusive rights stimulate investment and the production of creative works and simultaneously, exceptions to those rights create a balance that allows for the use of creative works to support innovation, creation, competition and the public interest.

Limitations and exceptions have a number of important public policy goals such as market failure, freedom of speech, education and equality of access (such as by the visually impaired.)

Some view"limitations and exceptions" as"user rights" - seeing user rights provide an essential balance to the rights of copyright owners. There is no consensus amongst copyright experts as to whether they are"rights" or not. The concept of user rights has also been recognised by courts, including the Canadian Supreme Court in CCH Canadian Ltd v. Law Society of Upper Canada (2004 SCC 13), which classed"fair dealing" as such a user right. These kinds of disagreements in philosophy are quite common in the philosophy of copyright, where debates about jurisprudential reasoning tend to act as proxies for more substantial disagreements about good policy.

Changing Technology and Limitations and Exceptions

The scope of copyright limitations and exceptions became a subject of significant controversy within various nations in the late 1990s and early 2000s, largely due to the impact of digital technology, the changes in national copyright legislations for compliance with TRIPS, and the enactment of anti-circumvention rules in response to the WIPO Copyright Treaty. Academics and defenders of copyright exceptions fear that technology, contract law undermining copyright law and copyright law not being amended, is reducing the scope of important exceptions and therefore harming creativity. This has resulted in a number of declarations on the importance of access to knowledge being important for creativity, such as the Adelphi Charter in 2005 and at a European level in May 2010 a declaration entitled Copyright for Creativity - A Declaration for Europe.

The declaration was supported by industry, artist, education and consumer groups. The declaration states that"While exclusive rights have been adapted and harmonised to meet the challenges of the knowledge economy, copyright's exceptions are radically out of line with the needs of the modern information society.

The lack of harmonisation of exceptions hinders the circulation of knowledge based goods and services across Europe. The lack of flexibility within the current European exceptions regime also prevents us from adapting to a constantly changing technological environment."

Competition Law/ Anti-Trust Law and Limitations and Exceptions

Copyright is typically thought of as a limited, legally sanctioned monopoly. Because of this, copyright licensing may sometimes interfere too much in free and competitive markets. These concerns are governed by legal doctrines such as competition law in the European Union, United States antitrust law, and anti-monopoly law in Russia and Japan.

Competition issues may arise when the licensing party unfairly leverages market power, engages in price discrimination through its licensing terms, or otherwise uses a licensing agreement in a discriminatory or unfair manner. Attempts to extend the copyright term granted by law - for example, by collecting royalties for use of the work after its copyright term has expired and it has passed into the public domain - raise such competition concerns. In April 1995, the US published"Antitrust Guidelines for the licensing of Intellectual Property" which apply to patents, copyright, and trade secrets. In January 1996, the European Union published Commission Regulation No.240/96 which applies to patents, copyright, and other intellectual property rights, especially regarding licenses.

The guidelines apply mutatis mutandis to the extent possible. The interplay of copyright law and competition law is increasingly important in the digital world, as most countries laws allow private contracts to override copyright law. Given that copyright law creates a legally sanctioned monopoly, balanced by"limitations and exceptions" that allow access without the permission of the copyright holder the overriding of copyright law by private contracts can create monopoly activity.

Well known limitations and exceptions include fair dealing in the UK and Canada, as well as the fair use doctrine in the US. The undermining of copyright law, and in particular limitations and exceptions to copyright by contract law is an issue frequently raised by libraries, and library groups such as International Federation of Library Associations and Institutions. As a result of this, this issue is increasingly being looked at and discussed at a national governmental level *e.g.* UK as well as international level such as WIPO - as part of the Development Agenda.

International Legal Instruments and Limitations and Exceptions

Limitations and exceptions are also the subject of significant regulation by global treaties. These treaties have harmonized the exclusive rights which must be provided by copyright laws, and the Berne three-step test operates to constrain the kinds of copyright exceptions and limitations which individual nations can enact. On the other hand, international copyright treaties place almost no requirements on national governments to provide exemptions from exclusive rights; a notable exception to this is Article 10(1) of the Berne Convention, which guarantees a limited right tō make quotations from copyrighted works.

Because of the lack of balance in international treaties in October 2004, WIPO agreed to adopt a significant proposal offered by Argentina and Brazil, the "Proposal for the Establishment of a Development Agenda for WIPO" also known simply as the "Development Agenda" - from the Geneva Declaration on the Future of the World Intellectual Property Organization. This proposal was well supported by developing countries. A number of civil society bodies have been working on a draft Access to Knowledge, or A2K.

Fair Use and Fair Dealing

Copyright does not prohibit all copying or replication. In the United States, the fair use doctrine, codified by the Copyright Act of 1976 as 17 U.S.C. § 107, permits some copying and distribution without permission of the copyright holder or payment to same. The statute does not clearly define fair use, but instead gives four non-exclusive factors to consider in a fair use analysis.

Those factors are:

1. The purpose and character of the use;
2. The nature of the copyrighted work;
3. The amount and substantialness of the portion used in relation to the copyrighted work as a whole; and
4. The effect of the use upon the potential market for or value of the copyrighted work.

In the United Kingdom and many other Commonwealth countries, a similar notion of fair dealing was established by the courts or through legislation. The concept is sometimes not well defined; however in Canada, private copying for personal use has been expressly permitted by statute since

1999. In Australia, the fair dealing exceptions under the Copyright Act 1968 (Cth) are a limited set of circumstances under which copyrighted material can be legally copied or adapted without the copyright holder's consent. Fair dealing uses are research and study; review and critique; parody and satire; news reportage and the giving of professional advice (*i.e.* legal advice). Under current Australian law it is still a breach of copyright to copy, reproduce or adapt copyright material for personal or private use without permission from the copyright owner.

Other technical exemptions from infringement may also apply, such as the temporary reproduction of a work in machine readable form for a computer. In the United States the AHRA prohibits action against consumers making noncommercial recordings of music, in return for royalties on both media and devices plus mandatory copy-control mechanisms on recorders. Section 1008.

Prohibition on certain infringement actions. No action ever may be brought under this title alleging infringement of copyright based on the manufacture, importation, or distribution of a digital audio recording device, a digital audio recording medium, an analog recording device, or an analog recording medium, or based on the noncommercial use by a consumer of such a device or medium for making digital musical recordings or analog musical recordings.

Later acts amended US Copyright law so that for certain purposes making 10 copies or more is construed to be commercial, but there is no general rule permitting such copying. Indeed making one complete copy of a work, or in many cases using a portion of it, for commercial purposes will not be considered fair use.

The Digital Millennium Copyright Act prohibits the manufacture, importation, or distribution of devices whose intended use, or only significant commercial use, is to bypass an access or copy control put in place by a copyright owner. An appellate court has held that fair use is not a defence to engaging in such distribution.

Educational use is regarded as "fair use" in most jurisdictions, but the restrictions vary wildly from nation to nation. Recent Israeli District Court decision dated Sep. 2, 2009 accepted the defence of fair use for a site linking to P2P live feeds of soccer matches. The main reasoning was based on the public importance of certain sporting events, *i.e.* - the public's rights as counter weight to the copyright holders rights.

Licensing, Transfer, and Assignment

Copyright may be bought and sold much like other properties. In the individual licensing model the copyright owner authorizes the use of the work against remuneration and under the conditions specified by the license. The conditions of the license may be complex since the exclusive rights granted by copyright to the copyright owner can be split territorially or with respect to language, the sequence of uses may be fixed, the number of copies to be made and their subsequent use may also be specified. Furthermore sublicenses and representation agreements may also be made. A contractual transfer of all or some of the rights in a copyrighted work is a known as a copyright license.

A copyright assignment is an immediate and irrevocable transfer of the copyright owner's entire interest in all or some of the rights in the copyrighted work. Copyright licensing and assignment cover only the specified geographical region.

There are significant differences in national copyright laws with regards to copyright licensing and assignment. Copyright licenses, as a minimum, define the copyrighted works and rights subject to the license, the territories or geographic region in which the license applies, the term or length of the license, and the consideration (such as a one of payment or royalties) for the license. The exclusive rights granted by copyright law can all be licensed, but they vary depending on local law.

Depending on how the work may be used different licenses need to be acquired. For example, the activity of distributing videocassettes of a motion picture will require the license for the right to reproduce the motion picture on a videocassette and the right to distribute the copies to the public.

Because the ratio of a television screen is different from that of a wide-screen cinema, requiring the cutting of the wide-screen"ends", it may also be necessary to obtain a license for the right to modify the motion picture. If the motion picture is to be edited or modified the copyright owner may include control over or approval of the editing process, or of the final result. Existing contractual agreements between the copyright owner and the director, may also require approval from the director to any changes made to the copyrighted work.

Different types of exclusive licenses exist, such as licenses that excludes the licensor from use of the licenced copyrighted work in the relevant region and for the stated time period. Or exclusive licenses may prevent the licensor from licensing other parties in the geographic region and during the license term.

There are also various types of non-exclusive licenses, including the right of first refusal should the licensor elect to offer future licenses to third parties. If a licensing agreement does not specify that the license is exclusive it may nonetheless be deemed exclusive depending on the language of the contract. Depending on local laws the owner of an exclusive license may be deemed the"copyright owner" of that work and bring charges for copyright infringement.

The term or length of the copyright license is not allowed to exceed the copyright term specified by local law. Licenses may establish various pay arrangements, such as royalties as a percentage of sales or as a stepped up or down percentage of sales, *e.g.* 5 per cent of sales up to 50,000 units, 2.5 per cent of sales in excess thereof.

The trigger for royalty payments may be sales. Minimum royalty payments are arrangements whereby a minimum up-front payment is made and then recouped against the percentage of sales. The up-front payment may be non-refundable if sales royalties do not reach the amount of the payment. Minimum royalty payment arrangements may be accompanied by marketing duties for the licensee, *e.g.* best effort and reasonable effort to market and promote the copyrighted work.

Collective Rights Management

Collective rights management is the licensing of copyright and related rights by organizations acting on behalf of rights owners. Collective management organisations, such as collecting societies, typically represent groups of copyright and related rights owners, such as authors, composers, publishers, writers, photographers, musicians and performers.

The following exclusive rights granted under copyright law are commonly collectively managed by collecting societies: the right to public performance, the right to broadcasting, the mechanical reproduction rights in recorded music, the performing rights in dramatical works, the rights of reprographic reproduction of literary and musical works, and related rights, for example the rights of performers and producers in recorded music when used in broadcasts.

The collective management of copyright and related rights is undertaken by various types of collective management organisations, most commonly collecting societies. Collecting societies act on behalf of their members, which may be authors or performers, and issue copyright licenses to users authorising the use of the works of their members.

Other forms of collective management organisations include rights clearance centres and one-stop shops. One-stop shops are a coalition of collecting societies and rights clearance centres offering a centralised source for users to obtain licences. They have become popular in response to multi-media productions requiring users to obtain multiple licences for relevant copyright and related rights.

Extended Collective Licensing

The first extended collective licensing (ECL) laws were established in Denmark, Finland, Iceland, Norway and Sweden in the 1960s. ECL is a form of collective rights management whereby ECL laws allow for freely negotiated copyright licensing contracts for the exclusive rights granted by copyright. ECL laws are designed specifically for mass use, where negotiating alone will rarely allow a single right owner to fully financially benefit from their exclusive rights. Under ECL laws, collecting societies negotiate ECL agreements with users, such as a TV broadcaster, covering the types of copyrighted works for uses specified in the ECL licence.

Subject to certain conditions collecting societies can under ECL law apply to represent all rights owners on a non-exclusive basis in a specific category of copyrighted works. The collecting society can then negotiate an ECL agreement with a user for certain uses.

This agreement applies to members of that collecting society, as well as non-members. ECL laws require that collecting societies treat rights owners who are non-members in the same way they treat their members. Non-members are also given the right to individual remuneration, *i.e.* royalty payment, by the collecting society, and the right to exclude their work from an ECL agreement.

Compulsory Licensing

In some countries copyright law provides for compulsory licenses of copyrighted works for specific uses. In many cases the remuneration or royalties received for a copyrighted work under compulsory license are specified by local law, but may also be subject to negotiation. Compulsory licensing may be established through negotiates licenses that provide terms within the parameters of the compulsory license.

Article 11bis(2) and Article 13(1) of the Berne Convention for the Protection of Literary and Artistic Works provide the legal basis for compulsory licenses. They state that member states are free to determine the conditions under which certain exclusive rights may be exercised in their national laws. They also provide for the minimum requirements to be set when compulsory licenses are applied, namely that they must not prejudice the author to fair compensation.

Future Rights under Pre-existing Agreements

It is commonplace in copyright licensing to license not only new uses which may be developed but also works which are not yet created. However, local law may not always recognise that the wording in licensing agreements does cover new uses permitted by subsequently developed technology. Whether a license covers future, as yet unknown, technological developments is subject to frequent disputes. Litigation over the use of a licensed copyrighted work in a medium unknown when the license was agreed is common.

Enforcement

Copyrights are generally enforced by the holder in a civil law court, but there are also criminal infringement statutes in some jurisdictions. While central registries are kept in some countries, which aid in proving claims of ownership, registering does not necessarily prove ownership, nor does the fact of copying (even without permission) necessarily prove that copyright was infringed. Criminal sanctions are generally aimed at serious counterfeiting activity, but are now becoming more commonplace as copyright collectives such as the RIAA are increasingly targeting the file sharing domestic Internet user.

Infringement

Copyright infringement, or copyright violation, is the unauthorized use of works covered by copyright law, in a way that violates one of the copyright owner's exclusive rights, such as the right to reproduce or perform the copyrighted work, or to make derivative works. For electronic and audio-visual media under copyright, unauthorized reproduction and distribution is also commonly referred to as piracy.

An early reference to piracy in the context of copyright infringement was made by Daniel Defoe in 1703 when he said of his novel The True-Born Englishman"Had I wrote it for the gain of the press, I should have been concerned at its being printed again and again by PIRATES, as they call them, and PARAGRAPHMEN: but if they do justice, and print it true, just as to the copy, they are welcome to sell it for a penny, if they please: the pence, indeed, is the end of their works.".

The practice of labeling the act of infringement as"piracy" predates statutory copyright law. Prior to the Statute of Anne 1709, the Stationers' Company of London in 1557 received a Royal Charter giving the company a monopoly on publication and tasking it with enforcing the charter. Those who violated the charter were labeled pirates as early as 1603.

Orphan Works

An orphan work is a work under copyright protection whose copyright owner is difficult or impossible to contact. The creator may be unknown, or where the creator is known it is unknown who represents them.

Public Domain

Works are in the public domain if their kind is not covered by intellectual property rights or if the intellectual property rights have expired, have been forfeited, or have never been claimed. Examples include the English language, the formulae of Newtonian physics, as well as the works of Shakespeare and the patents over powered flight.

Copyright as Property Right

Copyright as a property law was initially conceived of as a"chose in action", that is an intangible property, as opposed to tangible property. In the case of tangible property the property rights are bundled with the ownership of the property, and property rights are transferred once the property is sold.

In contrast copyright law detaches the exclusive rights granted under property law to the copyright owner from ownership of the good which is regarded as a reproduction. Hence the purchase of a book buys ownership of the book as a good, but not the underlying copyright in the book's content. If a derivative work based on the content of the book is made, permission needs to be sought from the copyright owner, not all owners of a copy of the book.

The Statute of Anne specifically referred to copyright in terms of literary property that is limited in time. Many contemporaries did not believe that the statute was concerned with property"in the strict sense of the word" and the question of whether copyright is property right dates back to the Battle of the Booksellers.

In 1773 Lord Gardenston commented in Hinton v. Donaldson that"the ordinary subjects of property are well known, and easily conceived... But property, when applied to ideas, or literary and intellectual compositions, is perfectly new and surprising..." It was in the 19th century that the term intellectual property began to be used as an umbrella term for patents, copyright and other laws.

The expansion of copyright and copyright term are mirrored in the rhetoric that has been employed in referring to copyright. Courts, when strengthening copyright, have characterised it as a type of property. Companies have strongly emphasised copyright as property, with leaders in the music and movie industries seeking to"protect private property from being pillaged" and making forceful assertions that copyright is absolute property right.

With reference to the expanding scope of copyright, one commentator noted that"We have gone from a regime where a tiny part of creative content was controlled to a regime where most of the most useful and valuable creative content is controlled for every significant use."

Graham Dutfield and Uma Suthersanen copyright is now a"class of intangible business assets", mostly owned by companies who function as"investor, employer, distributor and marketer". While copyright was conceived as personal property awarded to creators, creators now rarely own the rights in their works.

Copyright and Authors

Copyright law emerged in 18th Century Europe in relation to printed books and a new notion of authorship. In the European Renaissance and Neoclassical period the writer was regarded as an instrument, not as an independent creator.

The writer was seen as using external sources to create a work of inspiration. In the 18th Century a changing concept of genius located the source of inspiration within the writer, whose special talents and giftedness was the basis for creating works of inspiration and uniqueness. The concept of the author as original creator and owner of their work emerged partly from the new concept of property rights and John Locke's theory that individuals were"owners of themselves". Locke individuals invested their labour into natural goods, and so creating property.

Authors were argued to be the owners of their work because they had invested their labour in creating it. Patterson and Livingston there remains confusion about the nature of copyright ever since Donaldson v Beckett, a case heard in 1774 by the British House of Lords about whether copyright is the natural law right of the author or the statutory grant of a limited monopoly. One theory holds that copyright's origin occurs at the creation of a work, the other that its origin exists only through the copyright statute.

Copyright and Competition Law

Copyright is typically thought of as a limited, legally sanctioned monopoly. Because of this, copyright licensing may sometimes interfere too much in free and competitive markets.

These concerns are governed by legal doctrines such as competition law in the European Union, anti-trust law in the United States, and anti-monopoly law in Russia and Japan. Competition issues may arise when the licensing party unfairly leverages market power, engages in price discrimination through its licensing terms, or otherwise uses a licensing agreement in a discriminatory or unfair manner.

Attempts to extend the copyright term granted by law - for example, by collecting royalties for use of the work after its copyright term has expired and it has passed into the public domain - raise such competition concerns. In April 1995, the US published"Antitrust Guidelines for the licensing of Intellectual Property" which apply to patents, copyright, and trade secrets. In January 1996, the European Union published Commission Regulation No.240/96 which applies to patents, copyright, and other intellectual property rights, especially regarding licenses.

The guidelines apply mutatis mutandis to the extent possible. The interplay of copyright law and competition law is increasingly important in the digital world, as most countries laws allow private contracts to over-ride copyright law.

Given that copyright law creates a legally sanctioned monopoly, balanced by"limitations and exceptions" that allow access without the permission of the copyright holder the over-riding of copyright law by private contracts can create monopoly activity.

Well known limitations and exceptions include fair dealing in the UK and Canada, as well as the fair use doctrine in the US. The undermining of copyright law, and in particular limitations and exceptions to copyright by contract law is an issue frequently raised by libraries, and library groups such as International Federation of Library Associations and Institutions.

As a result of this, this issue is increasingly being looked at and discussed at a national governmental level *e.g.* UK as well as international level such as WIPO - as part of the Development Agenda.

Copyright and Economic Development

The historian Eckhard Höffner the 1710 introduction of copyright law in England and later in France acted as a barrier to economic progress for over a century, while Germany prospered in the same time frame due to the lack of copyright laws. Höffner argues that copyright laws allowed British publishers to print books in limited quantities for high prices.

ENTREPRENEURIAL MARKETING

What differentiates businesses that deliver sustained market leadership from those that don't? Michael Treacy and Fred Wiersema, as outlined in their book "The Discipline of Market Leaders," studied more than 80 companies, some acknowledged market leaders, some with less impressive results, to discover what accounted for the success of one group and the poor results of the other. To provide a framework for their findings, Treacy and Wiersema developed a concept they call "value disciplines," which identifies three fundamental ways that businesses drive their organizations to achieve leadership in their marketplaces: operational excellence, product leadership and customer intimacy.

The market leaders that Treacy and Wiersema studied exhibited high standards of performance and intense focus on one of these three disciplines, and used it to define their business. This does not mean that the other value disciplines were ignored; market leaders are competitive in all of the three values but have "honed at least one component of value to a level of excellence that puts all competitors to shame." We believe this model can be used by businesses of all sizes to develop a winning strategy and lay a foundation for competitive advantage.

MANAGING PRODUCT MOVEMENT

In addition to enlisting the assistance of retailers and wholesalers to make products available to customers, marketers also face additional concerns when trying to meet their distribution objectives. We examine the tasks that must be carried out in order to physically move products to customers. In some cases the marketer will take on the responsibility of carrying out some functions, while other tasks may be assigned to distribution service providers. Whether handled by the marketer or contracted to others, these functions are crucial to having a cost-effective and efficient distribution system.

We explore the movement of product by first examining how physical distribution decisions often involve analysing the trade-off between the service level the marketer offers to customers versus the costs associated with providing these services.

Next we provide an in-depth examination of three major tasks that the marketer or distribution service providers may need to carryout in order to ship products to customers.

These tasks include:

- Ordering and Inventory Management
- Product Storage
- Transportation

It is worth noting that while most physical distribution is concerned with moving tangible products, some of the issues covered here are also applicable to intangible products, such as services and to digital products.

TRADE-OFF ANALYSIS: SERVICE-LEVEL VS. COST

The distribution activities we discuss in this part of the Principles of Marketing tutorial are important elements in the marketer's overall customer service package. Marketers strive to deliver an optimal level of service to their customers. However, "optimal" does not always translate into providing the "best" service options to customers. The service-level marketers' offer for their distribution activities, like the service-level offered by other company-related activities that impact customers (e.g., customer help desk), is determined using trade-off analysis.

With service-level trade-off analysis, the marketer compares the number and quality of distribution features (e.g., speed of delivery, ease of placing orders, order tracking, etc.) they would like to offer versus the cost of providing the features.

For instance, when it comes to transportation options (e.g., truck, railroad, air, etc.), trade-off analysis may show that choosing the fastest method for delivery may not make economic sense since options for fast delivery often are very expensive compared to slower methods. While the customer may appreciate having their order arrive quickly, the marketer may find fast delivery to be an expensive proposition that significantly reduces their profit margin.

Since most distribution activities are non-revenue producing (i.e., are used to support the selling of a product but do not actually create a sale) and, thus, represent a cost to the marketer, it should be understood that the marketer's distribution system choice may not be the overall best available in terms of getting the product into customer's hand as fast as possible.

Rather, the marketer's choice for what is optimal will be determined by analysing distribution features and costs and evaluating how these fit within the marketer's overall objectives (e.g., financial objectives, product positioning, etc.).

ORDERING AND INVENTORY MANAGEMENT

Having products available when customers want to make purchases may seem like a relatively straightforward process. All a seller needs to do is make sure there is product (i.e., inventory) in their possession and ready for the customer to purchase. Unfortunately, being prepared for customer purchasing is not always easy.

Having the right product available when the customer is ready to buy requires a highly coordinated effort involving order entry and processing systems, forecasting techniques, customer knowledge, strong channel relationships and efficiency at physically handling products.

Order Entry and Processing System

The marketer must have a system allowing customers to easily place orders. This system can be as simple as a consumer walking to the counter of small food stand to purchase a few vegetables or as complicated as automated computer systems where an electronic order is triggered from a retailer to a manufacturer each time a consumer purchases a product at the retailer's store.

In either case, the order processing system must be able to meet the purchasing needs of the customer. In some cases, an efficient ordering system can be turned into a competitive advantage. Firms such as Amazon.com, turned their order handing system into a product feature with the patented "1-click" ordering option that streamlines online ordering by reducing the number of clicks needed to make purchases.

Forecasting

Inventory management is often an exercise in predicting how customers will respond in the future. By predicting purchase behaviour the marketer can respond by making sure the right amount of product is available. For most large-scale resellers effective inventory forecasting requires the use of sophisticated statistical tools that look at many variables, such as past purchase history, amount of promotional effort that triggers an increase in customer ordering, and other market criteria to determine how much of the product will be needed to meet customer demand.

Customer Knowledge

Inventory management can be fine-tuned to respond to customer's needs. As a marketer learns more about a customer they begin to observe trends in how and when purchases are made. Combining customer knowledge with forecasting techniques allows the marketer to better estimate product demand and inventory requirements. The key to understanding customers is to have in place a customer relationship management (CRM) system that tracks all customer activity and allows for data mining activities that analyse customer information in order to identify patterns in customer activity.

Channel Relationships

While the marketer who uses channel members to sell consumer products has access to information for their immediate customers (e.g., resellers) they often do not have access to sales and customer behaviour information controlled by the party selling to the final consumer (e.g., retailer). Knowing the demand patterns at the final consumer level can give marketers good insight into how the reseller may order.

Developing strong relationships with the holder of consumer information can result in the reseller sharing this information with the marketer. In fact, some retailers allow marketers direct access to real-time, store-level inventory information so the marketer can monitor how products are selling in stores and be in a position to respond quickly if inventory needs change.

Physical Product Handling

An often overlooked area of inventory management involves the actions and skills needed to prepare a product to move from one point to another. Some products require special attention be given to ensure the product is not damaged during shipment. Such efforts must be carefully balanced against increased costs that arise (e.g., stronger packaging) in order to provide greater protection to products. Because of this, many marketers will accept the fact that some small level of damage to occur during the distribution process.

PRODUCT STORAGE

The second important element in physical distribution concerns storing products for future delivery. Marketers of tangible products, and even digital products, may have storage concerns.

Storage facilities, such as warehouses, play an important role in the distribution process for a number of reasons including:

- *Hold Wide Assortment:* Many resellers allow their customers to purchase small quantities of many different products. Yet to obtain the best prices from suppliers, resellers must purchase in large quantities. The need, thus, exists for storage facilities that not only hold a large volume of product, but also can hold a wide-variety of resellers' inventory. Additionally, these facilities must be organized in a way that permits resellers to easily fill orders for their customers.
- *Meet Unanticipated Demand:* Holding products in storage offers a safeguard in cases of unexpected increases in demand for products.
- *Needed for Large Shipping Quantities:* As we noted in our discussion of transportation, manufacturers generally prefer to ship in large product quantities in order to more effectively spread transportation costs. This often means manufacturers must create

storage areas in which the manufactured goods can build up in the quantities needed for such shipments to occur.

- *Offer Faster Response:* Additional storage facilities, strategically located in different geographical areas, allows a marketing organization to respond quickly to customers' needs. The ability to respond with quick delivery can be a major value-added feature since it reduces the buyer's need to maintain large inventory at their own locations.
- *Security and Backup:* For digital products, additional storage facilities are not only needed to offer customers faster access to products (e.g., online content and software) but are also needed to protect against technical glitches and security threats.

Types of Warehouses

The warehouse is the most common type of storage though other forms do exist (e.g., storage tanks, computer server farms).

Some warehouses are massive structures that simultaneously support the unloading of numerous in-bound trucks and railroad cars containing suppliers' products while at the same time loading multiple trucks for shipment to customers.

Below we discuss five types of warehouses:

- *Private Warehouse:* This type of warehouse is owned and operated by channel suppliers and resellers and used in their own distribution activity. For instance, a major retail chain may have several regional warehouses supplying their stores or a wholesaler will operate a warehouse at which it receives and distributes products.
- *Public Warehouse:* The public warehouse is essentially space that can be leased to solve short-term distribution needs. Retailers that operate their own private warehouses may occasionally seek additional storage space if their facilities have reached capacity or if they are making a special, large purchase of products. For example, retailers may order extra merchandise to prepare for in-store sales or order a large volume of a product that is offered at a low promotional price by a supplier.
- *Automated Warehouse:* With advances in computer and robotics technology many warehouses now have automated capabilities. The level of automation ranges from a small conveyor belt transporting products in a small area all the way up to a fully automated facility where only a few people are needed to handle storage activity for thousands of pounds/kilograms of product. In fact, many warehouses use machines to handle nearly all physical distribution activities such as moving product-filled pallets (i.e., platforms that hold large

amounts of product) around buildings that may be several stories tall and the length of two or more football fields.

- *Climate-Controlled Warehouse:* Warehouses handle storage of many types of products including those that need special handling conditions such as freezers for storing frozen products, humidity-controlled environments for delicate products, such as produce or flowers, and dirt-free facilities for handling highly sensitive computer products.
- *Distribution Centre:* There are some warehouses where product storage is considered a very temporary activity. These warehouses serve as points in the distribution system at which products are received from many suppliers and quickly shipped out to many customers. In some cases, such as with distribution centers handling perishable food (e.g., produce), most of the product enters in the early morning and is distributed by the end of the day.

MODERN MARKETING MANAGEMENT

From earliest history, man has been dependent upon agriculture and upon some forms, however crude, of handicraft or manufacturing activity. Only in very recent times have people, especially in the United States, lived in an economy dominated by marketing-oriented organizations. The rather youthful character of our marketing system as it exists today may be better understood by giving very brief attention to historical changes from primitive times, through the emergence of a middleman system, down to current marketing conceptions.

EARLY DEVELOPMENTS

The origin of marketing is lost in antiquity. Certainly there is ample evidence of the existence of trade among the ancient Egyptians. Numerous references to trade are to be found in the Old Testament, and the Phoenicians in their heyday were regarded as a nation of wholesalers. Both wholesale and retail trade were well developed during the era of Greek supremacy and in the period of Roman domination.

To be sure, articles traded in the early days of civilization were few. They were restricted largely to luxuries purchased by the rich, due to the costliness and dangers of transportation and the low standards of living.

Differentiation of production in the various parts of a country and deficiencies in essentials such as common salt and spices in certain countries also stimulated trade, but in relatively few items. Even as late as the year 1000, villages were characterized by their agrarian, independent nature and by economic self-sufficiency. In every village attempts were made, by methods now considered crude and wasteful, to raise the necessary food supply and to produce other necessaries of existence. With the fall of the Roman Empire, trade seems to have suffered an eclipse for some centuries.

Beginning with the latter part of the Middle Ages the advance from the manorial or village system to the town was rapid. The town became a place of craftsmen and traders. In this handicraft stage, skilled workers set themselves up in their homes as craftsmen, making goods to order. Enterprising craftsmen began to use apprentices and often produced a surplus which was sold at local markets or fairs.

This resulted in the organization of markets and in the holding of fairs at periodic intervals. Craftsmen soon organized into guilds, which controlled both manufacturing and marketing by minute regulations, much to the detriment of progress in both. The domestic system, whereby the products of the craftsmen were sold by businessmen, superseded the handicraft stage. With increased protection by stronger and more stable governments, towns grew rapidly and markets gradually expanded. Toward the close of the fifteenth century a period of discoveries began.

It resulted in marked improvements in maritime transportation, thereby supplying an added impetus to commerce. With the development of national governments, guilds finally outlived their usefulness, and during the early part of the sixteenth century mercantilism became the guiding principle of state policy.

In brief, mercantilists argued that a country could become opulent if it sold more merchandise and services to foreigners than it bought from them. Only in this way could it increase its stock of precious metals that was received in payment required by a "favorable balance of trade" and which, at that time, was considered the ultimate desideratum. Naturally, this movement stimulated commerce to no small degree.

The Industrial Revolution

In the latter part of the eighteenth century the Industrial Revolution began to usher in marked improvements in form utility production. These were continued throughout the early part of the nineteenth century, but were greatly accelerated in the United States in the period following the Civil War. The domestic stage of manufacture was supplanted almost entirely by factories in which large numbers of specialized workers were employed. Elaborate steam- or motor-driven machinery replaced handicraft methods. Industry became localized, largescale output became the goal of manufacturers, and a minute division of labour began to be considered an essential prerequisite to efficient operation.

Specialization reached such a point that whole communi-ties or areas sometimes devoted a major part of their energy to the making of a single commodity.

Thus, Pittsburgh and Gary became known for iron and steel products; Detroit for automobiles; Wisconsin for cheese and other dairy products; California, Florida, and the Rio Grande valley for citrus fruits; and so on. xhe geographical chasm separating farm or factory and consumer widened considerably.

The agricultural producer, the processor, or the manufacturer cannot ordinarily seek out the final consumer or user of his wares. He finds it more economical to devote his major effort to physical production, where he is presumably of maximum service, and for the most part allows a marketing system to dispose of his finished goods and even to assemble his raw materials for him.

Similarly, the consumer or business user finds that any attempt on his part to purchase the numerous commodities necessary to satisfy his increasing and varied wants, directly from their makers, is the height of absurdity. He is, therefore, only too glad in the vast majority of cases to be relieved of the necessity of buying direct and to let the marketing system do it for him.

Effect of Industrial Revolution

It thus becomes obvious that the present middleman system is the outgrowth of changed conditions, the outcome of a growing civilization and industrial progress. As long as towns were economically self-sufficient, producer-consumer contact was feasible except for trade between countries. As localized, large-scale physical production developed, and cities grew in importance, maladjustments made their appearance, marketing risks increased, and an elaborate middleman system was called into existence to bridge over the ever-widening gap that separated the consumer or business user from the manufacturer.

To these factors may be added the constant pressure to increase both the scale of industrial output and production for sale instead of own use, both of which are direct results of our factory system.

Need for Middlemen

From this brief historical sketch it is apparent that few, if any, middlemen existed in primitive society—a condition that still obtains in underdeveloped parts of the globe.

There is hardly any surplus to exchange in primitive or highly underdeveloped communities. Each family is making practically all that is used in the home. Whenever any surplus of products of the soil, chase, or craftsman's art becomes available, the members of the tribe or village effect exchanges directly among themselves. Even during the early part of the handicraft stage in Europe, consumers either visited the shops of craftsmen or the latter abandoned their loom or bench at frequent intervals in order to find buyers for their wares.

On the other hand, whenever a country advanced in civilization, trade flourished as it did in ancient Sumeria, Babylonia, Phoenicia, and Egypt. In later years the Persians, Greeks, and Romans engaged in trade to a considerable extent, which decreased in importance as these nations declined in power. In modern times the ascendancy of trade resulted largely from the Industrial Revolution. This presented in its early days what appeared to be insuperable marketing problems. Marketing functions were therefore shifted more and more to middlemen who specialized in their performance, so that in the latter part of the nineteenth century the basis for the present system of marketing was fairly well established.

Even today in the transfer of title to goods, direct contact may be established. Manufacturers sometimes buy raw materials directly from original producers, and they often purchase semimanufactured goods, parts, equipment, and supplies direct.

Similarly, the consuming public buys a limited amount of merchandise direct from farmer or manufacturer. The bulk of farm products and manufactured goods, however, is bought and sold indirectly through one or more middlemen.

Middlemen are, then, individuals, firms, or corporations that stand between prime producers and ultimate consumers, assume title or assist directly in its transfer, and receive a profit for the risks they assume in addition to being paid for the cost of their services or take whatever losses are incident to the assumption of an entrepreneur's functions. Salesmen are excluded from this group, for they are not in business for themselves and, consequently, assume none of the risks of entrepreneurs and receive no profit, nor do they sustain losses from their sales efforts as such.

Classification of Middlemen

Undoubtedly the most useful classification of middlemen is that based on ownership of the goods. From both legal and practical aspects the relationship to the transfer of title is a most significant factor in defining the position of any group of middlemen. On this basis, *all middlemen can be divided into merchant and functional middlemen. Merchant middlemen buy the goods outright and necessarily take title to them.*

Wholesalers and retailers are common examples. *Functional,* or nonmerchant, middlemen ordinarily assist directly in effecting a change in ownership, but they *do not themselves take title to the goods in which they deal. They specialized in the performance of a single marketing function or of a limited number of such functions,* one of which is usually related to the transfer of title. Functional middlemen are best represented by auction companies, brokers, commission houses, manufacturers' agents, and selling agents.

Growing out of the major distinction between merchant and functional middlemen is a difference in degree of risk. All middlemen bear entrepreneurial risks, since they are in business for themselves and they may or may not be successful in securing the necessary volume for profitable operation. Merchant middlemen must, however, bear the additional risk resulting from the uncertain ability to dispose of the goods they own at remunerative prices.

Functional middlemen, on the other hand, act for others in the purchase or sale of goods; hence the risks of a changing price level and of uncertain demand or supply conditions are borne by the principals in whom title to the goods vests. There are, of course, other organizations, institutions, or agencies which facilitate the performance of marketing functions by acting in some specialized capacity.

They are not, however, generally regarded as middlemen or as strictly marketing institutions, chiefly because they render no direct assistance in the transfer of title to goods—a characteristic peculiar to all bona fide middlemen and marketing organizations. Among these are railroads, commercial banks, insurance companies, ordinary warehouses, cold storage plants, marketing research agencies, inspectors, and graders.

To the extent that they perform distributive and selling functions in certain lines of merchandise, warehouses may be classed among the functional middlemen, and to that extent they constitute an integral part of the marketing system.

Evolution of the Marketing Concept in Industry

Even though marketing functions have long been performed and a middleman system of marketing was well established in the last century, great changes have taken place in the significance attached to marketing by all kinds of companies.

In general, this has been a transition from emphasis on selling what a company had to the producing of goods and services that are wanted by the customers that made up the demand side of the market. In the marketing literature of the late 1950's and early 1960's, the newer emphasis has been described as *the marketing concept, marketing orientation, or marketing management philosophy.*

Example of Transition

The evolution may be illustrated by the experience of a well-known manufacturer, The Pillsbury Company, which, like many other organizations, moved through four eras of emphasis. First, there was the era of *manufacturing dominance.* The company was founded in 1869 by Charles A. Pillsbury on the basis of availability of high-quality wheat and proximity of water power.

Major concern was with manufacturing—not marketing. According to a company executive, company philosophy in the era of manufacturing dominance might be stated as follows: "We are professional flour millers. Blessed with a supply of the finest North American wheat, plenty of water power, and excellent milling machinery, we produce flour of the highest quality. Our *basic function is to mill high-quality flour,* and of course (and almost incidentally).

The second era was one of *sales orientation.* By the 1930's, competition had become more significant and the problems of reaching the market had grown much more complex. Company officials became somewhat aware of consumer wants and needs, and formed a commercial research department to develop facts about markets.

More attention was given to strengthening the distributing organization, consisting of wholesale and retail grocers. Company philosophy in this era is described as follows: "We are a flour milling company, manufacturing a number of products for the consumer market. We must have a first-rate sales organization which *can dispose of all the products we can make* at a favorable price. We must back up this sales force with consumer advertising and market intelligence. We want our salesmen and our dealers to have all the tools they need for *moving the output of our plants to the consumer."*

A third era of *marketing orientation* did not begin until the early 1950's. The company had experienced substantial post-World War II sales growth in new products, principally cake mixes. It realized that it could produce hundreds of new products, and faced the necessity of selecting the best ones. It was considered essential to build into the company organization *a new function* which would coordinate the heretofore separate company responsibilities of selling, advertising, marketing research, and product planning, and provide guidance for other areas.

This function was called "marketing," and marketing developed the criteria for determining which products to market. Emphasis shifted from manufacturing and mere sales considerations to a determination of which products would best fit the needs of the company's customers. Company policy for the 1950's was stated as follows: "We make and sell products *for consumers."*

At the beginning of the 1960's the company was moving into a fourth era of *marketing control,* described by a company official as follows: "Marketing today sets company operating policy short-term. It will come to influence long-range policy more and more.... At Pillsbury, as our fourth era progresses, marketing will become the basic motivating force for the entire corporation. Soon it will be true that every activity of the corporation—from finance to sales to production—is aimed at satisfying the needs and desires of the consumer."

OPERATIONAL EXCELLENCE

The operationally excellent organization is driven by logistical excellence, consistency, speed and quality. It typically provides lower-cost solutions than the competition. This organization is process obsessed and strives to measure and set new standards for efficiency, consistency and quality. Think of the process excellence of McDonald's in manufacturing a hamburger of consistent quality and low cost around the world, or of Dell Computer delivering a made-to-order computer from instructions received from the customer over the Internet. Wal-Mart is a pioneer in the field of retail operational excellence, using efficiency to drive its low-price promise.

Product Leadership

The product leadership organization focuses on product innovation, providing a superior product and continuously pursuing new products or enhancements.

The company's products are leading edge and exhibit design or technological advancement. Intel is a prime example of a product-focused market leader that continually pushes the technology envelope; 3M also leads its markets through new product development, and Sony led the consumer electronics market through its innovative product focus for several decades.

Customer Intimacy

The customer-intimate organization provides superior customer service by providing unique or customized products or services that stem from a deep understanding of each customer's, or market segment's, needs. It consistently meets and exceeds customer expectations, providing the best total solution to the requirements of a group of customers who are prepared to pay for it, or who will reward the value proposition by entering into a long-term relationship.

Four Seasons Hotels and Resorts states that its growth stemmed from a singular concept: what the global business traveller wanted most was round-theclock, personalised service. Home Depot revolutionized the retail building products industry and connected with an emerging consumer segment by hiring professional contractors to provide free, expert advice to the do-ityourself home renovator.

Applying the Model

Treacy and Wiersema found that the market leaders that they observed were focused on excelling in one of these three drivers, rather than all three. The authors put forward the notion that a business cannot become a market leader by trying to be all things to all people. After choosing a value discipline that defines what the company does best, market leaders work diligently to align all elements of their business in support of this value. When we discuss this model with business leaders, many have difficulty with the notion of losing focus on any of these key disciplines.

Using the value discipline model to develop a business strategy does not mean choosing one of the three drivers and ignoring the others. In the extreme, customer intimacy without some level of operational excellence would allow you to become close to a customer, but unable to deliver any kind of product or service to them. It is essential to deliver satisfactory results in all three areas while striving to deliver extraordinary results in one. To apply this model to your organization, start by determining your current positioning. Where is your organization now? Are you a product leader? Are you trying to be both customer intimate and operationally excellent?

Once you determine where you are now, think about where you would like to be in the future and how your organization would look should you choose one discipline as the foundation for your business strategy.

In the safety of an internal planning session, you and your management team might think about how each of these drivers would change your business over the next three to five years if it were your focus. Which of these three best matches with your market opportunities and strengths? Defining competitive positioning and strategy is all about setting key priorities for the organization and choosing where to place your bets.

Business Strategies

Good entrepreneurs understand the role of business strategy in growing a business. Here, we discuss numerous business strategies that might work for you. It's a competitive world out there. Make sure your strategies are up to the job of outperforming the competition and helping you to achieve your business goals.

A strategic alliance is a cooperative agreement with another company to combine resources in a way that is beneficial to both parties. Unlike a merger, both companies maintain their individual identities, goals, mission, etc. The purpose of the alliance is simply to create opportunities for the two companies to work together to achieve a specified goal - promotion, purchasing, product manufacturing, or something else entirely.

Understandably, many small business owners are hesitant to partner with other businesses, particularly businesses that operate in the same industry. After all, what good could possibly come from helping the competition? But suppose you own a pizza parlor and a competitor approached you about joining forces to place a combined order that would reduce the cost of your tomato sauce by 35%.

Sure, your competitor would reduce his expenses, but so would you. More importantly, it would give both of your companies a competitive advantage over all the other pizza parlors in the area. That's the power of a strategic alliance. Both companies benefit and realise a marketplace advantage they would not have been able to achieve independently.

Setting-Up Strategic Alliance

The important thing is to make sure that both partners are aware of what they are expected to do and what they can expect to receive as a result of the alliance. Regardless of how you decide to structure the alliance, it's important for both partners to share the risks and the benefits. If your company is left to carry all the risk for half the benefit, then you're probably being taken advantage of and need to look elsewhere for a new alliance partner. Yet many business owners fall into the rut of offering products that are nearly identical to the competition.

To stand out from the crowd, all you need is a healthy dose of creativity to take you back to your entrepreneurial roots. Here's how to get started.

Making Good or Better Product

You have a good product. But the competition has a good product, too. In fact, the market is filled with good products and the last thing your customers need is another product of average quality cluttering the buying process. More than anything else, customers are looking for a great product that leaves all the other ones in the dust.

Gather your team together and begin brainstorming about ways to improve your existing product and position yourself above the competition. Emphasize improvements that create additional features or add value - anything that will stand out from the other "been there, done that" products the industry already offers.

New Applications

Sometimes the problem isn't the product itself, but rather the product's field of use. In some industries, product use is limited to a narrow range of applications defined by the way the product has been used in the past.

However, there is a good chance that your product has applications beyond its current usage. With a little diligence and a few minor modifications, you may be able to find new applications for your product and increase demand by widening the market.

New Products

Right now, someone is wishing they had a product that doesn't exist. Yet. Innovative entrepreneurs succeed by creating new products to fill gaps in the marketplace. The way they discern those gaps is through patience and hard work. Begin by asking your existing customers for suggestions about new products that would make their life a little easier. Then use their ideas as fodder for new product concepts, consistently returning to the customers for input throughout the development process. Before the product even hits the market it will be in demand by the customers whose input you used to produce it.

Cross-Pollinate for Ideas

Another source of ideas for new products is to cross-pollinate with other industries. For example, if your business is accounting, regularly expand your horizons by touching base with other non-related industries like healthcare, advertising, or graphic design.

Along the way, you might run across tidbits of information that spark an idea for improving your services or creating new ones altogether. You might also be able to leverage new insights and new contacts to expand your market into other industries.

Take Risks

Know why many business owners find themselves stuck in a crowd? Because they are afraid of how their business might be perceived if they stood out from the crowd. Innovation is risky business.

Successful entrepreneurs embrace a certain level of calculated risk in order to differentiate themselves from the competition. Don't let risk hold you back from acting on innovative ideas. Identify the risks ahead of time, take the necessary steps to minimize them, and step out of the crowd with confidence.

MARKET STRATEGY

Sometimes it does, but sometimes waiting for someone else to break new ground is a surer way to achieve long-term success. The key to finding the right time for the release of your product is knowing upfront the potential advantages and disadvantages associated with being the first to market.

Advantages of Being First to Market

- *Consumer Impact*: First movers enjoy the ability to make a significant impact in the minds of consumers, setting a standard for others to follow. Product characteristics, service delivery methods, price points, and other factors combine to create a level of expectation that you can progressively be refined to strengthen your brand.
- *Name Recognition*: If you are the first to bring a product to market, you will experience exclusive name recognition during the initial stages of the product's life. As long as you are able to maintain a strong market presence, your name will continue to be identified with the product even after others have entered the market.
- *Lack of Competition*: This may seem obvious, but being a first mover grants you exclusive market rights - at least for a while. By leveraging your temporary position as the sole provider, you can make significant gains in the short term and plot a strategy to remain competitive when the market gets crowded.

Disadvantages

- *Market Ignorance* - When you create a new product, you are (in effect) creating a new market. As a first mover, the new market will look to your company to shoulder the burden of introducing the product to consumers and educating them about its use. This translates into time, effort, and resources that later competitors don't have to worry about.

- *Product Development* - First movers also bear the cost of developing a product to the point of marketability. For some products, research and development costs aren't a major factor. But for more complex products, it's definitely something you need to factor into your decision. Ultimately, you might be better off letting someone else work out the kinks so you can focus on creating a lasting market presence.

Cheap Knockoffs: If your product is a success, someone is inevitably going to try to steal market share by offering a cheaper alternative. Unless you can clearly articulate the value of your product compared to a cheap knockoff, you may find yourself priced out by someone who hasn't invested anything in the product's design or development.

If your product doesn't stand out from the crowd, the marketplace will view it as a commodity and you'll be forced to compete on price - bad news for a business eager to boost its bottom line. The problem is that standing out is easier said than done.

Commoditization is becoming an increasingly familiar problem in some industries, leaving small business owners scrambling to price their products at a competitive level. Rather than trying to compete on price, you can beat the system and avoid the commodity trap by altering the market's perception of your product. Here are five ways to differentiate your product and avoid being lumped in with the rest of the pack.

Unique Characteristics

The first step out of the commodity trap is to examine what makes your product or service different from everyone else's. Do you have better customer support? Is your product designed better than the competition? Is your service tailored to a specific segment of the market? There's a good chance there is something that sets you apart from others who provide the same product. Finding your unique characteristics is crucial because it provides a starting point for the entire differentiation process.

Value-Added Services

Once you have identified your unique characteristics, you can begin to explore new ways to add value to your product. Use your imagination to consider how you can offer additional value while at the same time highlighting your product's strengths.

Many add-ons can be done without a substantial cost increase. In fact, some of the best ones cost very little, yet draw a significant amount of attention from the marketplace.

Target Marketing

Another effective way to differentiate your product or service is to customise it for specific industries or market niches.

Interview potential customers within a given industry to determine which features are currently missing in the marketplace and then tailor your product to meet their needs. If you play your cards right, it's possible to customise your product to the extent that it becomes a standard within the industry, safely distancing it from being perceived as a commodity.

Create a Network

An isolationist attitude in a glutted market will only make the situation worse. The businesses who rise above the competition are the ones who have created strategic relationships with vendors, consultants, and others who offer complementary products and services. The larger your network, the more likely it is that your product will find its way to the top of the heap.

Value vs. Cost

The surest way to avoid competing on price is to stop pushing price as a selling point. Instead, educate your sales staff to focus on the value of your product compared to the competition. Buyers are almost always willing to spend a little more as long as they understand the additional benefits they will receive from the more expensive product. Developing strategy can be very exciting for a business owner.

Break It Down

When you communicate a business strategy to your staff, you need to help them see how they fit into the big picture. They want to have a general idea what the big picture looks like, but more importantly they want to understand how it will impact them.

Will your new strategy affect their role in the company? Is their job still secure? What new expectations will be placed on them? These questions and many more will need to be answered before your employees can wholeheartedly commit to the strategy.

Speak their Language

It's not uncommon for business owners to immerse themselves in the language and culture of a new strategy. The problem is that employees haven't immersed themselves in the same language and culture, and may need some time to catch up. Until they do, it's important to communicate in their language, using terms and phrases they already understand.

Establish Benchmarks

Benchmarks help employees contextualize the strategy and understand the timeframe for its implementation. Each person's role in executing the strategy becomes easier to swallow when the strategy is presented in a staged format with manageable "bite-sized" goals along the way. It also becomes easier to assess progress and red flag problem areas when they arise.

Provide Updates

Once you've established strategy benchmarks, you'll need to revisit them every once in a while and communicate your progress to your employees. If you are on-schedule, your employees will want to share in your satisfaction. If you are behind schedule, your employees may be able to help you nail down the reason why and make suggestions about how to get back on track.

Avoid E-mail

One last thing about communicating strategy to your employees: If at all possible, avoid using e-mail as a communication device. E-mail is fine for everyday business correspondence. But when it comes to something as important as strategy, employees appreciate the courtesy of a face to face meeting.

Meetings also have the added benefit of bringing the entire team together to brainstorm ideas and coordinate between departments. If your business is in fast-growth mode, you need to stay alert for trouble signs before it's too late. Here are five of the most common fast-growth snafus worth watching.

Growing Beyond Your Infrastructure

Infrastructure is the backbone of your business. It consists of the capital resources, systems, and processes that you use everyday to run your business effectively. If growth outpaces infrastructure, resources run thin and systems get stretched to their limits. In other words, your business becomes less effective. Planned growth buys the time you need to upgrade your infrastructure to maintain the same level of quality that made your business a success in the first place..

Losing Quality Staff

An overheated growth cycle is stressful on a business. However, quick growth is especially difficult on key employees who are typically leaned on in a pinch. Lean on them too much and you will likely lose them to competitors whose work environment reflects a more normal pace of life. Instead of losing them, engage key employees in a dialogue about how your growth is affecting the company and share your plans to remedy the situation as soon as possible.

Stretching Human Resources

Key employees aren't the only ones who are affected by rapid growth. All of your employees will be forced to deal with the reality of trying to squeeze more work into their work week.

When business is booming, it's tempting to put off hiring additional staff as a way to beef up the bottom line. But the extra profits you reap will pale in comparison to the extra headaches that come with a disgruntled workforce. A more reasonable approach is to map out a schedule of new hires that is gauged to benchmarks of growth. Solicit input from department heads to determine how many additional workers you'll need and when you will need them.

Create New Products

One way to reinvent an industry is to create entirely new products that meet needs and position your business at the top of the heap. While the competition is struggling to catch up, you'll enjoy the advantages that go along with being first to market.

You'll also enjoy the ability to define future expectations regarding your new product, meaning that instead of being controlled by the market, you will be in the driver's seat. Although under certain circumstances being the first to market can be a disadvantage, it's definitely an option worth considering.

Redesign Product Delivery

You don't necessarily have to create a new product to be innovative. Sometimes all it takes is a radical redesign of the manner in which your product is delivered to customers. For example, Starbucks didn't invent the coffee shop concept. However, they revolutionized the industry by transforming a simple cup of coffee into a gourmet coffee experience. With a little creativity, you can transform your industry by changing the way customers experience products you already sell.

Customise

Niche marketing has traditionally been a tool used by businesses to differentiate themselves from the competition. But you can also employ niche marketing techniques to customise your products for various segments of the market. While everyone else is offering a generic, one-size-fits-all product, you can offer an array of products designed to accommodate your customers' specific needs and applications.

Creating Strategic Partnerships

If you can't beat the competition, maybe you can join them. Strategic partnerships leverage the strengths of individual businesses to form an alliance that is beneficial to both parties. When partner companies possess complementary strengths, the result is a powerhouse that leaves other competitors scratching their heads.

Change Your Emphasis

Yet another way to turn the industry on its head is to refocus the prevailing emphasis. If the industry is focused on cost, you can focus on service. If the industry is focused on service, you can focus on cost. If it succeeds, you will soon find yourself on the cutting edge of an industry trend that you have shaped and molded to your company's strengths. Conventional wisdom says that a sure way to increase demand for a product is to slash its price.

But is that really true? Is being the lowest cost provider the best strategy for increasing sales and bumping the bottom line? On the first day of Econ 101, your professor explained a fundamental economic concept: Lower the price and demand will increase.

In a perfect world, that would always be true. The problem is that we don't live in a perfect world. Price is only one factor in determining demand for products and services. Other factors (e.g. marketing strategy) also play a significant role in attracting customers. In fact, sometimes being the lowest priced product on the market can even have a negative effect on demand.

Low Product Perception

A low-priced product is often perceived to be inferior to its higher priced counterparts, regardless of its actual quality. Think about it: If given the choice between a $10 hamburger and a $1 hamburger, chances are you will assume the $10 burger is larger, tastes better, and contains better ingredients based on nothing other than price. By choosing to compete on price, you run the risk of inviting a similar perception from your customer base. In some industries the risk may be minimal, but in others it may be a formidable obstacle to overcome.

Brand Inferiority

Another common perception that can be caused by low pricing is that your company and your brand occupy a mediocre standing within the industry. Consumers are typically willing to pay more for a brand name product. New consumers will inevitably assume lower priced products are offered by a brand that is less established or less capable of delivering quality merchandise.

Poor Service

In the mind of a typical consumer, the cost of a product doesn't just include the cost of the merchandise inside the box. It also includes the cost of back-end products such as customer service and product warranties. If your product is priced lower than everyone else's, consumers will naturally assume that it doesn't come with the same assurance of support as products that are priced higher. This perception might not be far from reality since a lower priced product may necessitate cost-cutting measures that affect the level of follow-up service you are able to provide.

It's important to remember that the price you establish for your product communicates a wide range of intangibles to potential customers. Rather than trying to offer the least expensive product, you might want to consider strategic pricing to properly position yourself within the market.

Begin to view price as a tool to communicate the quality and value of your product in relation to your competitors. Done right, this can be a powerful way to establish market presence and eliminate the need to compete on price alone. It is important to have goals for the direction of your business outside of purely monetary gain.

By setting goals, you are defining a guideline for the future of your business, and if you set goals effectively, you lay the framework for making those aspirations a reality. Measuring actual performance against your goals can provide an effective barometer for the performance of your business against desired performance. Not only does goal setting provide an introspective into overall performance, but is also an effective management tool used in businesses of all sizes in all industries.

The feasibility of goals is another issue that you will encounter as a small business owner. By setting goals that are too easily attainable, you may not be pushing your business to its maximum potential, allowing for wasted potential.

This is certainly not a scenario you would want to encounter. Conversely, by setting very lofty goals, you may be fostering some unrealistic notions and setting yourself up for disappointment.

While it is important to be ambitions, striking a healthy balance between ambition and feasibility is important to the effectiveness of goals that you set for your business.

By knowing the fundamentals of effective goal setting, you can be sure that the goals you set are effective in spurring the performance of your business and inspiring confidence in your employees in their drive for continuous progress. But growing a company takes a lot more than good intentions. You need a plan. With dozens of strategies to choose from, here are four that could put your company on the fast track to growth. Not every growth strategy is appropriate for every small business. The key to finding the right growth strategy is properly matching it to your company and its specific marketplace. Since the wrong strategy can devastate your business, it's important to determine whether you are selling new or emerging products in a new or existing market.

Diversification

Diversification is a high-risk growth strategy, largely because both the products and the market are unproven territory for the entrepreneur. Though trailblazing emerging products and markets can be exhilarating, it can also be terrifying given the fact that neither you nor anyone else can rely on prior experience for reassurance.

Market Development

A more common scenario is one in which a small business owner attempts to develop a new market for their existing products and services. The new market can be geographical (e.g. foreign export) or an untapped segment of a domestic market. It's even possible to develop a new market for existing products by adjusting the product's packaging or expanding the product's distribution channels.

In any event, a market development growth strategy requires a working knowledge of existing markets and the ability to gaps in the marketplace that can be exploited to your advantage.

Product Development

A growth strategy based on product development is the mirror image of a market development strategy. Instead of pioneering a new market with existing products, you attempt to roll out a new product(s) in a market with which you are already familiar.

Many small business owners are more comfortable working in this kind of scenario because they already possess an awareness of prevailing market conditions. However, a product development strategy can be just as challenging as a market development strategy because it often requires the business to develop new abilities and continuously adapt the products until they achieve marketplace success.

Market Penetration

Businesses that find themselves in a situation that involves neither new markets nor new products are forced to grow through a market penetration strategy, a strategy that is designed to give the business a greater percentage of market share. This type of strategy usually seeks to gain a competitive edge through pricing, marketing, or other initiatives. Additionally, market penetration can be achieved by increasing customer usage through loyalty programs and incentives targeting your existing customer base.

Day-to-day toil shouldn't distract you from certain practices that will not only keep your business afloat, but are essential in making it thrive.

SUCCESSFUL BUS}INESS

Improve Capital Funding

Everywhere you turn there are gurus, middlemen and business development specialist who have their own "To-Do" lists readily offered up to anybody seeking capital for the start-up or expansion of a business venture.

In most every case, a business plan is as important as a loan application in the process of seeking that money. What follows is a list of 12 topics you want to address when preparing your presentation for solicitation of funding:

Be Prepared: Write a Business Plan

By going through the process of writing your business plan you will have thought through all of the issues that an investor considers when judging the viability of your business. Even if they don't look at your entire business plan on the first pass you'll be prepared to respond to important issues and concerns of the potential investor or lender.

The Executive Summary should contain the following:

- The primary objectives of your company.
- Your key personnel.
- The market you address, its needs, how those needs are currently met, and how you address its short-comings.
- Detailed description of your product or service, including how it addresses customer needs and desires.
- Financial projections for five years, profit point, break-even point, and ROI for investors.

Be Flexible to Change in Your Business Model

As you begin to implement the business plan the real world may not embrace your business model. Determine what works and doesn't work. Be willing to alter your plans accordingly. You may even find greater market potential that requires re-thinking the entire business plan.

Consider Alternatives to Product Distribution

Failing to understand how your product should be distributed is a sure way to turn away investors. Do your homework on the various distribution channels. Know their expectations and working models.

Find the channel that works with your pricing model and facilitates your growth requirements. If possible, develop partners with brand names that can provide credibility and growth potential.

Be Flexible with Investors on Issues of Control

Don't focus on retaining control of your company. Focus on what makes the company profitable. Investors need to see that you are willing to assume some level of risk and are not intent on hoarding stock.

Great businesses have been built by entrepreneurs that understood their limitations and hired executives who knew more than they did. Focusing on profits creates capital opportunities. Focusing on control creates potential barriers to investors.

Develop a Strong Management Team

A business plan is only as good as the people responsible for making the business succeed. Identify who will run the business, their achievements and ability to make the business a success. Get commitments from qualified personnel for operations, financial management, development, marketing and sales. If not yet identified, make note of those key positions for which you must identify and recruit the appropriate individual who retains the necessary education and experience. Don't hide your weaknesses or shortcomings. Identify them and how you intend to overcome.

Give Customers a Reason to Buy from You

There must be a need and desire for your product. No longer will a clever idea, by itself, bring in the money. You need customers willing to test your product. Paying customers validate your pricing strategy.

Be Reasonable and Conservative on Near-term Revenues and Profit Projections

The biggest red flag to an investor is revenue projections that increase by the same per cent each year. You should anticipate various increase levels as your business progresses through different stages of growth. Your engineering, sales and marketing expenses will also change with these growth stages. Conduct the research of your industry to determine expected ratios for expenses and revenue per employee. Investors will take you seriously when they see that you have a clear understanding of the financial implications.

Give Investors Alternative Exit Strategies

Understand what motivates an investor, their expectations, exit strategy, and their minimally acceptable return on investment (ROI). The investor has many alternative investment opportunities. If the investor is going to take a risk on your concept he or she has to "BELIEVE". Demonstrate your potential for profitability with thorough descriptions of the market, your personnel and your product concept.

Don't Ignore the Competition

Customers always have a choice. They can either choose to do things the way they have always done them, find alternative solutions, or purchase your product. Identify your competitors, their strengths, and weaknesses and emerging technologies. Without this knowledge you will not be able to plan on how to respond to their retaliation.

Accurately and Honestly Define Your Market

Do your market research. Investors can easily discern between substantive and superficial data. Define and locate your market niche then determine its TAM (Total Available Market) and SAM (Served Available Market). Through the use of surveys (primary data) and secondary data you can calculate the approximate percentage of the SAM your company can penetrate, and how much to increase the SAM. Stating that you will capture the entire TAM is a clear indicator you don't understand the market and your potential in that market.

Don't Ignore Requirements of Incorporation, Patents, Trademarks and Copyrights

In some industries (i.e. pharmaceuticals) it is critical that competition be dissuaded through the use of patents, which protect your research and development investments and provide a window of opportunity to realise a share of revenues before competitive offerings arrive in the marketplace. Trademarks, copyrights, non-disclosure agreements, employee agreements, etc. are a necessary part of the protection of a company's intellectual assets and branding. Incorporation will help to protect the investors and company assets in the event of legal proceedings against your company.

Identify the Methods and Costs of Getting Your Message to the Marketplace

Investors want to know what methods will be employed to gain customer attention, customer acquisition costs, average and target per-customer revenues, customer breakeven milestones and product life cycles. They also want to see your future plans for retaining existing customers. In most every business sector the returning customer represents the most reliable source of near and long-term revenues and profits.

STEPS TO A GREAT BUSINESS PLAN

A business plan serves two purposes:

- It provides a road map for your business.
- It helps you obtain outside financing.

If you're going into business for yourself, you must have a business plan - period. Numerous studies have shown that one of the major reasons new businesses fail is poor planning.

- Are you an entrepreneur?
- Start your own small business

The good news is that developing a business plan is not as hard as it seems. In order to develop a solid business plan, you need to have a thorough understanding of the business you're entering. Next, you need to determine how you'll use the plan and who your target audience is. Finally, you should create a complete a business plan that is comprehensive and concisely written. We'll explore each of these steps in detail.

Step 1: Know Your Business

In order to prepare a business plan, you must know the business you are entering inside and out. This means lots of research. Research comes in two forms: reading everything you can about the industry and talking to those who are already in it. Learn everything you can about your business and industry.

Step 2: Determine your Purposes for the Plan

A business plan serves to crystallize your business vision and guide you in fulfilling that vision; it is also frequently used to entice potential investors.

- 6 steps to a better business budget
- Can you handle a home-based business?

If you are self-financing your business, you design the plan mostly for your benefit, but if you're seeking outside investors, you'll need to target them. As such, before you create your plan, determine whether you will solicit outside investors.

Step 3: Determine your Audience

If you plan to recruit investors, you need to build a plan to suit them. Outside investors, who range from friends and family members to banks and venture capitalists, will invest through either loaning you the money, buying shares in your company or some combination of the two.

Determine their level of sophistication and what they are looking for in a potential business investment. Remember that regardless of their level of sophistication, they are all looking for four things:

Financial Confidence

Clearly articulate the risks of investing in your business. Also, show investors how they can recoup their money - whether your venture succeeds or fails.

A good return on investment - Over the period of 1928-2007, the geometric (exponential) return for stocks was 9.8 per cent, while for 10-year Treasury bonds, it was 5 per cent.

Historical private-equity returns are more difficult to measure, but, in general, investors will expect a premium of anywhere from 2-5 per cent over public-equity market returns. The return on equity for your new business must be in the private-equity range. Typically, investors will look to beat a certain internal rate of return. Your job is to make sure your projected returns are in line with those of similar industries.

Step 4: Create your Business Plan

First, develop an outline of your business plan. Consider every aspect of your business and how it will affect your business plan. Remember, this business plan is a road map. It must guide you. It must also communicate to investors what you're doing and why they should invest with you.

The order in which your plan is presented should be something like the following:

- Mission Statement
- Executive Summary
- Product or Service Offerings

- Target Market
- Marketing Plan
- Industry and Competitive Analysis
- Pro-Forma Financials
- Resumes of the Company Principals
- Your Offering (what type of financing you're seeking)

Mission Statement

The mission statement is a concise, one- to three-paragraph description of your business objectives, or your business's guiding principles.

In this section, you should state your unique selling point, or what separates your company from all the others in the industry that are otherwise just like it.

This is a one- to two-page summary of your business. Potential investors will read this to decide whether they want to look at the rest of your plan.

Product or Service Offering

Create a section describing your product or service offerings in detail, as well as how much you'll charge for what you're selling.

Target Market

Present your primary and secondary target markets, along with any research that demonstrates how your target market will benefit from and consequently purchase what you're offering.

Marketing Plan

Present your marketing plan, which should show in detail how you'll reach your target market. This part of the plan will include advertising and promotional strategies.

Industry and Competitive Analysis

Include a complete and thorough industry and competitive analysis that includes all stakeholders in your business. Don't forget to include governmental and regulatory agencies.

Financial Statements

These must be complete, accurate and thorough. Each number on your spreadsheets must mean something. Don't estimate payroll, for instance; determine what it will actually be. Your income statement must reconcile to your cash flow statement, which reconciles to your balance sheet. Your balance sheet must balance at the end of every period. You must have supporting schedules (e.g. depreciation and amortisation schedules) to back up your projections.

If you are having trouble building your pro-forma financial models, which should project out for at least five years, seek outside help from a qualified professional. Use realistic projections. In estimating the growth of your business, you will make certain assumptions, which should be based on thorough industry research combined with a strategy for how you'll compete.

Also, analyse how quickly you'll achieve positive cash flow. Investors vary in their standards, but most like to see positive cash flow within the first year of operation, particularly if this if your first venture. In order for your projections to be accurate, you must know your business. If you've built an accurate and realistic model, but still project negative cash flow for more than 12 months, rethink your business model.

Resumes of Company Principals

Include the bios and professional backgrounds of all significant employees of your business. You will want to emphasize how their backgrounds have prepared them to take on the challenge of running your new startup. Also, if an employee's business background is in a significantly different industry, you might want to emphasize how this can be an advantage instead of a detriment.

Your Offering

Present what level of investment you're seeking and for what purposes you will use the funds. If you're selling business units, state the individual price per unit. Once you've put together all of this key information, make sure to present your plan professionally.

It should be typed, margin aligned and neatly bound. Use colour graphics and pictures where possible. Do not handwrite changes or corrections. The inside of your business plan should be near book or magazine quality.

After you've finished your plan, have a professional you trust, such as a Certified Public Accountant or attorney, look it over. This person may catch details, errors or omissions you've made. They also will be able to give you a more objective opinion of the viability of your business.

MARKET EXPANSION STRATEGIES

The Quarterly global survey of business executives reports that 84 per cent of executives consider growing number of consumers in emerging markets as an important trend but a lesser number of executives (63 per cent) view these consumers as a future source of profits and a still lesser number (41 per cent) of executives say that their companies have pursued this opportunity.

Real challenge lies in converting non-customers of an industry into customers. However, traditionally, strategy researchers and practitioners have focused their attention on the problem of dealing with competition and how to get and keep market share.

Kim and Mauborgne conceptualize a "blue ocean" strategy framework for creation of demand in an untapped market. They visualize it as an alternative strategy to market share growth.

However, not every one agrees that market expansion and market share growth are mutually exclusive strategies. Some of the strategies suggested in this framework do not lead to market expansion in the same sense as we define it in this chapter. A "blue ocean" strategy framework provides tools and techniques for dealing with competition at different levels.

But it does not pay enough attention to the exogenous factors affecting market demand such as the purchasing and consumption abilities of potential customers.

Prahalad with other scholars like Hammond and Lieberthal has developed a "bottom of the pyramid (BOP) marketing framework" as a means of expanding low income markets. In the context of developing countries, a BOP framework is more relevant than a "blue ocean strategy" framework.

Although a "BOP" framework is useful for development of a general framework for market expansion, conceptually expansions of markets do not necessarily mean expansion of "bottom of the pyramid" markets.

A "BOP" framework puts strong emphasis on the creation of consumption capacity among the poor. However, like a "blue ocean strategy" framework, it does not adequately address a very important consumer behaviour related issue of how to bring an unwilling customer into the market. "BOP" framework also ignores the competitive dimension in the formulation of strategy.

Much before the writings on "blue ocean strategy" and "bottom of the pyramid marketing," Kotler wrote about demand creation activities. He had identified specific situations in which a company needs to undertake demand creation efforts.

Although he wrote about marketing tasks in each such situation, these tasks do not constitute a holistic framework, especially in the context of developing countries. Moreover he did not write specifically about demand for a product as against demand for a brand.

The objective of this chapter is to conceptualize a market expansion strategy in such a way that a generic framework can be developed which should be useful for the expansion of markets of any type, including the bottom of the pyramid markets in developing countries.

METHODOLOGY

We develop a framework without making any assumption as to whether market expansion is a strategic alternative to market share or not. We look into the fundamental issues such as: what is a market and what is market expansion. We synthesize some significant contributions to the market expansion-related strategy literature with relevant concepts and theories from literature in other areas. On the basis of the survey of the literature, we first clarify the domain of the market expansion construct and market expansion strategy. Then we identify the antecedent conditions that drive market expansion.

We also identify the moderating conditions under which the effect of antecedents is enhanced or ameliorated. On the basis of the identified antecedents and moderators, we develop a process-based framework for implementation and measurement of market expansion strategy. We also present a series of research propositions in the spirit of propositional inventories such as those developed by scholars like Kohli and Jaworski.

In the marketing literature the term "market" is referred to a set of actual and potential buyers of a product. Size of the market is measured in terms of demand. Demand for a product category as a whole is termed as primary demand while demand for a particular brand of a product is called selective demand.

The upper limit of market demand is called market potential. In the marketing and strategy literature, primary demand creation and selective demand creation have been identified as distinct strategic options. Companies selling in mature markets often take primary demand as given. They concentrate their marketing resources on building selective demand. However in countries which are characterized by huge but largely untapped market potential, some companies attempt to build primary demand as well as preference for their brands.

Demand for a product category can be expressed in terms of volume (i.e. quantity or number of units) or value (i.e. monetary units). Whether the growth in the sales volume or value of a product category can be considered as market expansion or not depends on the source of the demand's growth.

We can visualize three sources of the growth in the demand for a product category:

- Demand from the first time buyers i.e. existing non-customers of the industry,
- Increase in the usage rate of existing customers of the industry,
- Value growth because of some customers upgrading to higher priced products.

Besides this, most products have replacement demand. We define a market expansion strategy as a strategy of increasing primary demand for a product category by converting non-customers into customers of an industry and/or by increasing the usage rate of industry's existing customers.

Focus on increasing the usage rate is especially relevant in case of products with high penetration levels but low per capita consumption.

For example, expansion of market of consumer non durables (i.e. toilet soaps and detergent cakes/powders) in India, can take place through increase in its usage rate.

"Expansion" and other similar terms used in the business and corporate strategy literature do not always mean market expansion.

For instance, Glueck and Jauch suggest concen-tration, integration, diversification, cooperation, and interna-tionalization as different routes to expansion. But these strategies do not necessarily lead to expansion of market for a particular product category.

Similarly, Ansoff in his product-market growth matrix talks about "market extension strategy" and "market penetration strategy." But extension of a market by reaching out to new market segments in present geographic markets is not the same as regional, national, or international geographic expansion of the company's sales.

The former option leads to an increase in primary demand for the product category. But in the latter case, a company might grow its sales by gaining market share from existing competitors in new geographic markets. Similarly, if market penetration is sought by converting non-customers into the customers of the industry's products, it leads to increase in the primary demand.

But if market penetration is brought about by attracting competitor's customers, it leads to increases in the selective demand. This chapter is concerned with market expansion for a particular product category and not corporate level expansion of overall sales revenue.

In order to measure market potential, it is necessary to define boundaries of a market. For defining market boundaries, Brooks conceptualizes "market" as a set of customers served by a set of suppliers, where both sets are defined in terms of products and services and in terms of geographic locations.

This means for each of its products in a chosen geographical area, a company can have different estimates of market potential depending on the definition of respective product's market boundaries in terms of competition.There exist two approaches to the definition of competition.

Demand-oriented approaches define competitors with respect to customer needs and wants, while supply-oriented approaches focus on physical product and manufacturing processes.

Levitt highlights the importance of demand side perspective in his article on 'Marketing Myopia' wherein he asks companies to focus on customer needs rather than the products that they sell. Marketing strategists generally define competitors from a consumer behaviour perspective.

By using four levels of competition as a framework, we can conceptualize different levels of market expansion. We can measure market potential for a product form (i.e. low cost airlines/motorbikes/herbal shampoo) or for a product category (i.e. airlines/two wheelers/shampoos) or for a generic need (i.e. travel/personal transport/hair care).

At one extreme end, a firm may try to increase sales of its specific brand without attempting to increase the market potential of the product form to which the brand belongs. Resultant increase in the sales of that brand can not be termed as market expansion. A company can make efforts to increase the sales of a product form within a product category. For example, Air Deccan popularized the low cost air travel format in Indian domestic air travel market.

3

Business Planning: Myths and Realities

EFFECTIVE BUSINESS MODEL

Business planning is the process of setting goals, explaining the objectives and then mapping out a document to achieve these goals and objectives.

A well-written Business Plan lays out the best growth path and strategy, as well as the rationale for the selection of the strategy over other alternatives. In essence, a Business Plan is the articulation and explanation of why the chosen game plan for building the company makes sense, what resources it will need to implement the vision, who the team will be that will have the skills and leadership to execute the vision, and what path they will follow to get there. Nobody has a crystal ball to predict what will work and what won't, not even a savvy investor or veteran entrepreneur.

The better the analysis, the better the chances that most of the goals set forth in the Business Plan will be achieved. A well-written Business Plan doesn't oversell the good, undersell the bad or ignore the ugly!

It is essentially an articulation of the entrepreneurial company's plan for managing the risks and challenges involved in building or expanding the business. As such, it should acknowledge that growth and success are moving targets by anticipating as many future events or circumstances that will affect the company's objectives. Business Plan, Business Model.

MYTHS AND REALITIES

In developing a Business Plan and a Business Model, entrepreneurs need to be aware that there are myths and misconceptions about the process.

Among the most common are the following:

- *Myth*: Business plans are only for start-up companies.
  - *Reality*: Companies at all stages of development need to prepare Business Plans either for the planning and financing of a specific project, general expansion financing, mergers or acquisitions, and the overall improvement of the company's financial and managerial performance. A company operating for 15 years or

more will need to draft a Business Plan in order to raise the necessary capital to reach the next stage in its development.

- *Myth*: Business plans should be as detailed and slick as possible. The longer the plan, the better chance that the company will be financed.
  - *Reality*: Sophisticated investors will not have the time to review hundreds of pages of text. The plan must be concise, well-written and should focus on the lender's or investor's principal areas of concern, and not be cluttered with lots of exhibits or irrelevant market studies. Companies should typically prepare an Executive Summary, a 10-page version and a 30- to 40-page version. Avoid overly technical descriptions of the company's processes or operations. Investors will commit funds based on the quality and clarity of the document, not its thickness. Although a Business Plan ought to be presented professionally, a very expensive binder or overly lavish presentation will often demonstrate inefficient resource management.
- *Myth*: Business plans should emphasize ideas and concepts, not people.
  - *Reality*: Many entrepreneurs fear that if the success of a company depends too heavily on any specific person, an investor will shy away. Although this is partially true, individual financiers and venture capitalists alike actually would prefer to invest in a company that has great people and only a good concept, rather than one with a great concept and a weak management team. Ultimately, lenders and investors will commit funds based on the strength of the management team.
- *Myth*: only the founding entrepreneur should prepare business plans.
  - *Reality*: Most entrepreneurs are highly skilled in a particular profession or area of management. As a result, they may not necessarily possess the ability to prepare a Business Plan in a form which prospective lenders or investors are accustomed. Ideally, the Business Plan should be developed by a team of managers within the company and then reviewed by qualified experts, such as accountants, attorneys and the board of directors. Conversely, it should never be prepared solely by outside advisors without the input of internal management. A veteran investor will be quick to recognize a "cooked" plan or one that reflects the views and efforts of professional advisors rather than the company's management team who are responsible for running the company on a day-to-day basis. The entrepreneur or founders must be in a position to defend the

assumptions that support the Business Plan in meetings with prospective investors or strategic partners.

- *Myth*: Business plans should be distributed as widely as possible.
  - *Reality*: The Business Plan will inevitably contain information that is proprietary and confidential to the company. Therefore, distribution should be controlled and careful records kept about who has received a copy of the plan. The cover sheet should contain a conspicuously positioned management disclaimer reminding the reader that these are only the plans of the company, the success of which cannot be assured, as well as a notice of proprietary information. All applicable federal and state securities laws must be carefully considered if the Business Plan is intended as a financing proposal; however, the Business Plan should not be used in lieu of a formal private-placement memorandum. Finally, certain institutional investors will consider investments only in certain kinds of companies or industries. Research these criteria before sending a Business Plan in order to save both the time and resources of all concerned parties.
- *Myth*: A business plan should follow a specified format, regardless of the industry in, which the company operates.
  - *Reality*: While it may be true that all companies face certain common challenges in the areas of marketing, management, administration and finance, companies at different stages of growth (and thus facing different problems) and those operating in different industries will require that different sets of topics be included in the Business Plan. For example, plans for a start-up manu-facturing company may be far more concerned with financing of the plant, equipment, patents, inventory, and production schedules than an already established service-oriented company, which may be more focused on personnel, marketing costs and the protection of trade secrets and goodwill.
- *Myth*: In preparing the business plan, optimism should prevail over realism.
  - *Reality*: The Business Plan should demonstrate the enthusiasm of the founders of the company as well as generate excitement in the reader; however, it should be credible and accurate. Investors will want to know all of the company's strengths and its weaknesses. In fact, a realistic discussion of the company's problems, along with a reasonable plan for dealing and mitigating these various risks and challenges, will have a much more positive impact on the prospective investor. As a general

rule, investors will feel more comfortable investing in someone who has learned from previous business failures rather than a person who has never managed a company. Finally, any budgets, sales projections, company valuations, or related forecasts should be well substantiated with accompanying footnotes, for both legal and business reasons. Unrealistic or unsubstantiated financial projections and budgets will reveal inexperience or lack of attention to detail, or even lead to litigation by disgruntled investors if there are wide disparities between what was represented and reality.

- *Myth*: A well-written business plan should contain an executive summary, which should be written before the full text of the document is prepared.
  - *Reality*: Institutional investors are exposed to hundreds of Business Plans in any given month, and as a result will initially only devote a few minutes to the review of each Business Plan. The Executive Summary (generally one to three pages in length) will be the first and possibly the last impression that the company makes on the investor. Thus, if the reader's attention is not captured in these first few minutes, he or she is not likely to complete the review of the document. The Executive Summary should contain all of the information that will be critical in the investment decision, such as the nature of the company and its founders, the amount of money sought, the allocation of the proceeds, a summary of key financial projections, and an overview of marketing considerations. The mistake often made by entrepreneurs in preparing the plan is writing the Executive Summary first (before the main components have been drafted). It is much more effective to prepare the main body of the plan, then draft the Executive Summary last in order to ensure consistency. The Executive Summary is then truly a preview of the details of the plan.
- *Myth*: Business plans are only written when a company needs to raise capital.
  - *Reality*: Although most Business Plans are written in connection with the search for capital, a well-written Business Plan will serve a variety of beneficial purposes to the company and its management team, among them a management tool to use as a road map for growth, a realistic self-appraisal of progress to date as well as against projected goals and objectives, and a foundation for the development of a more detailed strategic and

growth management plan (especially after a proposed financing has been successfully completed).

SENSITIVITY ANALYSIS

The company's ability to identify the specific tasks and translate them into a specific schedule will be affected by ever-changing capital markets, customer-demand patterns, the entry of new competitors, and general market conditions.

The Business Plan must deal with these "what ifs?" and be reflective of changing business models.

For example, if the success of the Business Plan relies upon the company's products being faster, cheaper, more reliable and capable of solving more complicated problems than those offered by their competitors, then how does the strategy change when a competitor introduces a product better, faster and cheaper than theirs?

Or what if the customer is slow to adopt or even recognize the benefits of the new product or service? Sensitivity analysis is a tool for looking at a wide range of variables and assumptions in the Business Plan to determine the impact on the company and the viability of the plan if and when these planning assumptions change - which they invariably and inevitably will.

Sensitivity analysis raises questions such as the following:

- Will our Business Plan still be viable if 20% of the target customers that we assume will adopt this new product do not? 30%? 40%?
- What will be the impact on our Business Plan if two of the key potential competitors we have identified become actual competitors?
- What will be the impact on our Business Plan if we can't attract new employees or strategic partners that we have identified as critical to implementation?
- What if we can't raise the equity capital we need to implement the Business Model? What if we have to give up more ownership and control than we had anticipated to raise the capital? What if we need to raise more debt capital?
- If we planned to borrow money to implement the Business Model, what impact would higher interest rates have on the economics of the model? If our customers will need to borrow to buy our products and services, what impact will higher rates have on these buying decisions?
- What if the market rejects the pricing structure that underlies the introduction of the new product or service? What if deeper discounts need to be offered to encourage customers to make the switch? What impact will this have on our margins?

The bottom line is that overly optimistic or weakly researched assumptions in a Business Plan can and will come back to haunt the entrepreneur.

Assuming conservative assumptions and adequate research, there are still many variables that can and will change that will have an impact on the Business Plan and the company.

Sensitivity analysis seeks to anticipate the changes in these variables so that owners are not caught by surprise.

Variables Affecting Implementation

- No matter how carefully the Business Plan is prepared, things can and will change. Hundreds of variables will go into the development of the Business Plan, which means that thousands of things could go wrong (or right) that will affect the company's actual-to-plan performance. The actual growth results may vary depending on a wide variety of factors, including:
- Demand for the company's products and services
- Actions taken by the company's innovation team, including new product introductions and enhancements
- Ability to scale the company's network and operations to support large numbers of customers, suppliers and transactions
- Ability to develop, introduce and market new products and enhancements to existing products on a timely basis
- Changes in the company's pricing policies and business model or those of its competitors
- Integration of the company's recent acquisitions and any future acquisitions
- Ability to expand the company's sales and marketing operations, including hiring additional sales personnel
- Size and timing of sales of the company's products and services, including the recognition of a significant portion of its sales at the end of the quarter
- Success in maintaining and enhancing existing relationships and developing new relationships with strategic partners, including systems integrators and other implementation partners
- Compensation policies that compensate sales personnel based on achieving annual quotas
- Ability to control costs
- Technological changes in the company's markets
- Deferrals of customer orders in anticipation of product enhancements or new products

- Customer budget cycles and changes in these budget cycles
- General economic factors, including an economic slowdown or recession.

Final Thoughts

- Effective business planning is not an easy process. Entrepreneurs and executives are likely to make classic mistakes. Having worked with hundreds of companies of all sizes and in many different industries over the years in reviewing Business Plans and developing growth strategies, I have pulled together below some tips, thoughts and observations that should govern the planning process, as well as the review and support of that process.
- Have the right mix of talent to develop and maintain the Business Plan. The wrong planning team will yield the wrong planning decisions, leading the company down a path of disaster.
- Think long-term but act short-term. Be ready to modify the plan based on changes in market conditions but without taking your eye off the long-term goals.
- Effective business planning is a continuing process, not a stand-alone task.
- Don't buy into the mantra that planning is a thing of the past. There are some who believe that market conditions are too dynamic and uncertain to make long-term business growth-oriented strategic planning possible - SIMPLY NOT TRUE! In fact, fast-moving business conditions make the need for strategic planning that much more critical, provided that the plan does not sit on a shelf but rather are monitored and modified as conditions may warrant.
- Invest in systems that will gather competitive intelligence. Information rules! If the company does not have reliable data on the trends affecting its competitors and customers, then they are dead in the water. The data gathered becomes a key component of the Business Plan and becomes the trigger point for changes to the plan or strategy selected.
- Protect key assets. An entrepreneur can develop Business Plans until blue in the face, but if the success of the company's business model depends on the ability to keep and leverage key intangible assets - then owners must take the time to protect intellectual property and to reward and motivate employees.
- Be sure to connect the dots. A well-drafted Business Plan understands and anticipates how all of the market forces and players fit together, taking into account social, environmental, political and

economic influences and figuring at how these factors come together to afford your growth plans. One common mistake is when the strategic assumptions underlying financial projections do not fit squarely with the written text of the plan. The ability to view things at 40,000 feet, 20,000 feet as well as at ground level, and the ability to see the dynamics of your markets at all of these levels is key to effective growth planning. And because these market conditions are never static and the relationships that connect the dots constantly change, you need to keep climbing the mountain to look down on the valley.

- Build an organization that has a deeply rooted commitment to growth. The commitment must begin with the leader or founder of the company, whose mission and passion become contagious, and everyone in the company focuses their efforts on meeting business growth objectives. To achieve this, the company's leadership must clearly communicate and reinforce the growth plans, objectives and strategies, reward those who contribute to the achievement of these goals and monitor the company's progress, changing its course and direction as may be necessary. If the course does need to change, these shifts in direction must be regularly shared with the company's employees, together with an explanation for the need for the change. Employees at all levels will resent a change in direction without knowing it or understanding it and if they are not told how or why their positions and tasks must change to meet these new challenges.
- Don't be afraid to measure and monitor performance. It is critical to develop an objective set of metrics for each key area of the Business Plan that can be continuously monitored and periodically measured against key goals. The metrics may include sales, profitability, the number of new customer relationships added, the growth market partners, the number of new employees, customer satisfaction, the level of employee turnover, inventory cycles, the number of new offices opened, warranty returns or even the number of new rounds of capital raised at favourable valuation rates. Regardless of the specific metrics selected, the growing company must build systems to track and measure these performance indicators and have the expertise in place to understand, analyse and properly react to this data once it has been reported.
- Develop high quality products and services. As veteran entrepreneurs and professional advisors will always say, a Business Plan will be completely ineffective if the "dogs will not eat the dog food." At the end of the day, all Business Plans must revolve around a set of high-quality products and services that customers genuinely want and need.

STARTING A BUSINESS

A business enterprise is an economic institution engaged in the production and/or distribution of goods and services in order to earn profits and acquire wealth. The scope of a business is very wide. It includes a large number of activities which may be classified into two broad categories i.e. Industry and Commerce.

Production of goods is the domain of 'Industry' and distribution comes under 'Commerce'. Every entrepreneur aims at starting a business and building it into a successful enterprise. The term 'entrepreneur' means to undertake and pursue opportunities and to fulfill needs and wants of people through innovation.

He/she innovates and combines resources in the form of men, materials and money and brings them together to make the business venture profitable. He/she is prepared to take risk and face challenges. Thus, innovation and risks are the two basic elements of a good entrepreneurship.

The whole process of starting a business begins with writing a business plan. A good business plan is the key to setting up a successful business. Once a plan is prepared, the entrepreneur faces various challenges while implementing the plan. The Commissionerates or Directorates of Industries are the nodal agencies in different States which assist and guide new entrepreneurs in starting up an industrial unit in the concerned State.

They provide an interface between industry and other agencies for industry inputs and enable the entrepreneur to get different industrial approvals and clearances from various departments at a single point-Single Window. They sanction incentives to eligible industrial undertakings and create a transparent and automatic system of allotment of scarce raw materials to industrial units. Hence, a new entrepreneur must approach the concerned commissionerate while setting up a business firm.

CREATING BUSINESS PLAN

Every new venture should have a business plan. A business plan is the formal written expression of the entrepreneurial vision, describing the strategy and operations of the proposed venture. The business plan also goes by other names, depending on its intended audience. Presented to a banker, it may be called a "loan proposal." A venture capital group might call it the "venture plan" or "investment prospectus." The advantages of writing a business plan far outweigh the costs. The purpose of the plan is to enable the top executives of the firm to think about their business in a comprehensive way, to communicate their objectives to individuals who may have a stake in the firm's future, to have a basis for making decisions, and to facilitate the planning process.

Entrepreneurs should undertake the task of preparing the business plan personally. Although outsiders - consultants, accountants, and lawyers -

should be tapped for their advice and expertise, the promoter or the initial top management team should be responsible for the writing. Personally drafting the plan will enable the entrepreneurs to think through all aspects of the proposed business and ensure that they are familiar with all the details, for they will have to make decisions about the new venture and be responsible for those decisions. Moreover, investors expect the founders to be involved in and knowledgeable about the proposed enterprise.

BENEFITS OF BUSINESS PLANNING

The business plan can personally benefit the entrepreneurial team. Founding a new business can be enormously fulfilling and exhilarating, but it is also an anxiety-ridden and tense experience. Usually a great deal of money is at stake, and the consequences of poor decisions can affect many people for a long time.

In developing and writing a business plan, the entrepreneurial team reduces these anxieties and tensions by confronting them in advance. By projecting the risks of the new venture into the future, the team comes to grips with potential negative outcomes and the possibility of failure. The knowledge that comes from this experience can reduce the fear of being taken by surprise by problems that could have been foreseen and provided for at the very outset. Every Business Plan must have: cover page, table of contents, executive summary, development and production, resource requirement, format and presentation, writing and editing, summary.

MAKING A PRODUCT CHOICE

After choosing the form of the business organisation the next start up problem is the choice of the particular product or service to be manufactured by the firm. It is an important decision because rest of the challenges of setting up a business is based on the type of the product the firm wants to produce. This decision can be taken through a comparative analysis of the several products or services that the firm can provide.

The analysis involves assessing the size and structure of the market for the products; determining the future demand pattern for each of them; comparing their competitive positions in the market; graphing the life cycle of each product; finding the shelf life of each product. The ease of availability of raw materials, technology for production as well as the manpower are other important determinants.

Government policies and regulations can also help the entrepreneur in taking the decision. Central Government and the State Governments provide incentives for manufacture of certain products by small scale units. The most important promotional measure being the reservation of several products for exclusive manufacture by small scale industries. Large/Medium units can, however, manufacture such reserved items provided they undertake to export 50% or more of their production. Also, there are some agencies and organisations which provide entrepreneurs with the necessary information required in making a product choice. The Commissionerates or Directorates of industries of different States provide guidance to the entrepreneurs with respect to the particular State. An entrepreneur can also study the industry clusters of India to get an idea about the type of products best suited for production in particular areas.

SETTING INFRASTRUCTURE

A new business enterprise after deciding upon the location of the industry needs to set up the basic infrastructural facilities for commencing its operations. It includes, purchasing the land for the construction of the industry. The site must be well connected to the nearest transport network i.e. rail, road or port. Besides, the availability of the basic amenities like, water, power supply is equally essential. Also, setting up of a good telecom facility for the industry is necessary for the growth and expansion of the business.

The State Government offers incentives like land and building tax concessions, providing land at cheaper rates through the State Government Agencies to new and existing entrepreneurs. It also offers concessions in water tariff, power subsidy, subsidy on generating sets, transport subsidy, incentive for pollution control and quality equipment depending on the location, size of investment and category of the industry.After all these requirements are met the commercial production of the product can commence.

NAMING AND REGISTERING A BUSINESS

In India, incorporation of a company is governed by the Companies Act 1956. It is the most important piece of legislation that empowers the Central Government to regulate the formation, financing, functioning and winding up of companies. It applies to whole of India and to all types of companies, whether registered under this Act or an earlier Act. But it does not apply to universities, co-operative societies, unincorporated trading, scientific and other societies.

The Act is administered by the Central Government through the Ministry of Corporate Affairs and the Offices of Registrar of Companies, Official Liquidators, Public Trustee, Company Law Board, Director of Inspection, etc. The Registrar of Companies (ROC) controls the task of incorporation of new companies and the administration of running companies.

The Official Liquidators who are attached to the various High Courts functioning in the country are also under the overall administrative control of the Ministry.

The set-up at the Headquarters includes the Company Law Board, a quasi-judicial body, having the principal Bench at New Delhi, an additional principal bench for Southern Region at Chennai and four Regional Benches located at New Delhi, Mumbai, Kolkata and Chennai.

The organisation at the Headquarters also includes two Directors of Inspection and Investigation with a complement of staff, an Economic Adviser for Research and Statistics and other Officials providing expertise on legal, accounting, economic and statistical matters.

The four Regional Directors, who are in charge of the respective regions, comprising a number of States and Union Territories, interalia, supervise the working of the Offices of Registrars of Companies and the Official Liquidators working in their regions.

They also maintain liaison with the respective State Governments and the Central Government in matters relating to the administration of the Companies Act, 1956. Registrar of Companies (ROCs) appointed under Section 609 of the Companies Act, covering various States and Union Territories, are vested with the primary duty of registering companies floated in the respective States and the Union Territories and ensuring that such companies comply with the statutory requirements under the Act.

Their offices function as registry of records relating to the companies registered with them.

For registration and incorporation of a company, an application has to be filed with Registrar of companies. Application for registration of a company accompanied by the selected names, Memorandum of Association and Articles of Association and other necessary documents is to be filed with the Registrar of companies of the State in which the company is proposed to be incorporated. Under the Companies Act, an entrepreneur can form two types of companies, namely a private company or a public company.

A Private Company is one, the articles whereof contains the following restrictions:

- Restricts the minimum paid up share capital to such an amount as may be prescribed but which shall not be less than rupees one lakh;
- Restricts the rights of members to transfer its shares, if any;
- Limits the number of its members to fifty excluding the past or present employees of the company who are members of the company;
- Prohibits any invitation to the public to subscribe for any shares or debentures of the company;
- Does not invite or accept any deposits from persons other than its members, directors or their relatives

Also, the minimum number of members in a private company is two and such a company must have the words 'Pvt Ltd' as the last part of its name.

A Public Company, as defined in the Companies Act, has the following features:

- Its shares are freely transferable;
- There is no ceiling on its membership;

- It can invite general public to subscribe to its shares;
- It has a minimum paid up capital of Rs.5 lakhs or such higher paid up capital as may be prescribed;
- It is a private company which is a subsidiary of a public company.

Also, the minimum number of members in a public company is seven and such a company must have the word 'Ltd' as last part of its name.

Choosing a Form of Business Organisation

A business enterprise can be owned and organized in several forms. Each form of organization has its own merits and demerits. The ultimate choice of the form of business depends upon the balancing of the advantages and disadvantages of the various forms of business.

The right choice of the form of the business is very crucial because it determines the power, control, risk and responsibility of the entrepreneur as well as the division of profits and losses. Being a long term commitment, the choice of the form of business should be made after considerable thought and deliberation.

The choice of the form of business is governed by several interrelated and interdependent factors:

- The nature of business is the most important factor. Businesses providing direct services like tailors, restaurants and professional services like doctors, lawyers are generally organised as proprietary concerns. While, businesses requiring pooling of skills and funds like accounting firms are better organised as partnerships. Manufacturing organisations of large size are more commonly set up as private and public companies.
- Scale of operations i.e. volume of business (large, medium, small) and size of the market area (local, national, international) served are the key factors. Large scale enterprises catering to national and international markets can be organised more successfully as private or public companies. Small and medium scale firms are generally set up as partnerships and proprietorship. Similarly, where the area of operations is wide spread (national or international), company ownership is appropriate. But if the area of operations is confined to a particular locality, partnership or proprietorship will be a more suitable choice.
- The degree of control desired by the owner(s). A person who desires direct control of business, prefers proprietorship, because a company involves separation of ownership and management.
- Amount of capital required for the establishment and operation of a business. A partnership may be converted into a company when it grows beyond the capacity and resources of a few persons.

- The volume of risks and liabilities as well as the willingness of the owners to bear it, is also an important consideration.
- Comparative tax liability.

CHOOSING THE LOCATION OF THE INDUSTRY

Every entrepreneur is faced with the problem of deciding the location for his/her factory or plant. Location of the business is the most important factor influencing its success or failure. It is a long-term decision which should take into consideration not only the present requirements of the organisation but also its future expansion plans. Errors in location may be very difficult and expensive to rectify.

Location of a plant has a bearing on the layout of machinery and equipment as well as on the process of production. The objective of a locational plan is to find out the optimum or best location for the particular plant. Such a location not only results in lowest cost per unit but also facilitates orderly growth of the firm. Hence, the most advantageous location is that at which the cost of gathering material and fabricating it plus the cost of distributing the finished product to the customers will be at a minimum.

It is not necessarily the most favourable location but rather the site at which all the considerations are optimised. There is no ideal location for all firms or even for one firm at all times. The choice of location depends on several important factors.

It is influenced by the kind of products being manufactured, costs of production and distribution. The location of the plant should also be able to meet the environmental guidelines and other regulations set by the Government specific to a particular industry. The choice of an optimum location requires judicious balancing of all these factors.

Pricing your Product

Fixing the right price for a product is the most difficult task as it affects the volume of sales of the product of the firm as well as the profits of the firm. Although non-price factors have become more important in recent decades, price remains one of the important elements in determining the market share and profitability.

Prices are set by a firm by taking into consideration factors like costs, profit targets, competition and perceived value of products. Taking into account the various factors, the steps generally followed in setting the price of a product are:

- *Setting the Pricing Objective of the Firm*: It is the most important step as it varies from firm to firm. Setting a lower price may attract more customers and thus fetch a larger market share for the firm's product. But charging a higher price might reflect a high quality and prestige product.

- *Determining the Demand for the Product*: Demand for the product sets a ceiling price. Penetration pricing is used when the product has a highly elastic demand and there is strong competition in the market. Under this policy, prices are fixed below the competitive level in order to obtain a larger share of the market. Once your product is in demand or is accepted in the market, the price of your product is increased. But when the demand for the product with respect to price is more inelastic, higher prices are charged for the product. This policy is generally followed during the initial stages of introduction of the new product.
- *Estimating the Costs and Profits*: Costs set a floor price. Amount spent and return expected is the key factor in deciding the price. The various costs involved in producing the product must be covered in pricing the product. On a long term basis also the price must take into consideration the costs of doing business. This also includes sales forecast and profit margin.
- *Determining the Competition for the Product*: Competitors prices and the price of substitutes provide an orientation point. The number of competitors for the product in the market as well as the policy followed by them is also an important factor. Competitive pricing is used if the market is highly competitive and the product is not differentiated from that of the competitor's.
- *Considering the Governmental Regulations*: Government policies and incentives are also taken into account. Prices are also affected by various tax liabilities which a company and the product is subjected to. It includes, excise duty, sales tax and local taxes like octroi. Sales tax is levied on the sale of moveable goods in India at the rates which vary depending upon the type and nature of goods and the State in which sale has taken place. The Central and State Government are both empowered to impose sales tax. The Central Sales tax deals with transactions in the nature of inter-state sales. While the State sales tax deals with intra-state sales. Octroi is a tax levied on the entry of goods into a municipality or any other specified jurisdiction for use, consumption or sale. Goods in transit are exempted from it.
- *Selecting a Suitable Pricing Method/Policy*: Right price for the product can be determined through pricing research and by adopting test-marketing techniques. The various pricing methods are:
- *Perceived value pricing*: In which a firm sets its price in relation to the value delivered and perceived by the customer. Perceived value is made up of several elements like buyer's image of the product performance, warranty, trustworthiness, esteem, etc. Each customer

gives different weightage to these elements. Some may be price buyers, others may be value buyers and still others may be loyal buyers. If either the price is higher than the value perceived or the price is lower than the value perceived, the company will not be able to make potential profits.

- *Value pricing*: In which companies develop brand loyalty for their product by charging a fairly low price for a high quality offering.
- *Going rate pricing*: is followed if it is difficult to ascertain the exact costs involved and the competitive response. Hence, firms base their price on competitor's price by charging the same, more or less than the major competitor.
- *Introducing a product at a premium price*: When a product is innovative and competition is low or non-existent, this policy can be applied. Thus profits are optimised. But when competition arises prices are lowered.
- *Ethical pricing*: - Price is fixed keeping the welfare of the society in mind. For many life saving drugs, this particular policy is used. The product is sold at the lowest possible price with either a very reasonable margin or no profit at all. Profit may be earned from other products.
- *Full Line pricing*: If you are selling a range of particular product for example pickles, then you price the product in a particular range, this way you may earn more profit in one flavour and less on the other. But, you cannot sell only the one that gives you maximum profit, or else a customer may switch over to another brand where he would be able to exercise an option for other flavours.

The Central and State Governments have passed certain legislations in order to control production, supply, and distribution as well as price of a number of commodities. The Essential Commodities Act,1955 is one such important legislation.

Under the Act, the State Governments/UT Administrations have issued various control orders to regulate various aspects of trading in essential commodities such as foodgrains, edible oils, pulses kerosene, sugar etc.

The Central Government regularly monitors the action taken by State Governments/UT Administrations to implement the provisions of the Act.

The Government is empowered to enlist any class of commodity as essential commodity as well as regulate or prohibit the production, supply, distribution, price and trade in any of these commodities for the following purposes: Maintaining or increasing their supplies.

- Equitable distribution and availability at fair prices of the commodities concerned.

- Securing any essential commodity for the defence of India or the efficient conduct of military operations.

The list of commodities declared as "essential" under the Essential Commodities Act, 1955 is reviewed from time to time in the light of changes in the economic situation and particularly with regard to their production and supply.

For example, keeping in view production and demand of some of the commodities, it was felt that these could be removed from the list of essential commodities.

The list of commodities declared essential under the Essential Commodities Act, 1955:

A. Declared under Clause (a) of Section 2 of the Act:

- Cattle fodder, including oilcakes and other concentrates.
- Coal, including coke and other derivatives.
- Component parts and accessories of automobiles.
- Cotton and woollen textiles.
- Drugs.
- Foodstuffs, including edible oilseeds and oils.
- Iron and Steel, including manufactured products of Iron & Steel.
- Paper, including newsprint, paperboard and strawboard.
- Petroleum and Petroleum products.
- Raw Cotton, either ginned or unginned and cotton seed.
- Raw Jute.
- Declared as essential through notifications under sub-clause (xi) of clause (a) of Section 2 of the Act
- Jute textiles.
- Fertilizer, whether inorganic, organic or mixed.
- Yarn made wholly from cotton.
  - Seeds of food crops and seeds of fruits and vegetables,
  - Seeds of cattle fodder
  - Jute seeds

The Act has been amended from time to time. The Essential Commodities (Special Provisions) Act, 1981, makes certain special provisions by way of amendments to the Essential Commodities Act,1955, for a temporary period for dealing more effectively with persons indulging in hoarding and black marketing of, and profiteering in, essential commodities and with the evil of vicious inflationary prices and for matters connected therewith or incidental thereto.

Information on retail prices is received on daily basis from 18 centres of the country. Similarly, information on wholesale prices is received from 37 centres of the country on weekly basis. Accordingly, the price monitoring cell issues the following reports on daily and weekly basis:

- *Retail Prices*: Daily
- *Wholesale Prices*: Weekly

The objective of such price and distribution controls is: promotion of equity or distributive justice; ensuring the quality of goods and services; prevention of monopolistic, restrictive and unfair trade practices that are hindering public interest; augmentation of the supply; ensuring availability of essential goods at reasonable prices to the vulnerable sections in all areas; control of inflation and deflation; etc.

REGULATORY REQUIREMENTS

Once an entrepreneur has taken all the important decisions relating to starting a business, he/she has to take into account the basic regulatory requirements which are to be followed for setting up the organisation. The most important regulation is the Companies Act, 1956, which regulates all the affairs of a company.

It contains provisions relating to the formation of a company, powers and responsibilities of the directors and managers, raising of capital, holding company meetings, maintenance and audit of company accounts, powers of inspection and investigation of company affairs, reconstruction and amalgamation of a company and even winding up of a company.

The Ministry of Corporate Affairs, earlier known as Department of Corporate Affairs under Ministry of Finance, is primarily concerned with administration of this Act as well as other allied Acts and rules & regulations framed there-under.

The next important regulation relates to environment. The environmental regulatory requirements envisage a wide legislative framework covering every aspect of environment protection like air, water, noise, forest conservation, wildlife protection, etc.

Also, separate set of laws and rules for emission of hazardous wastes have been enacted. The Ministry of Environment and Forests (MoEF), is the nodal agency for regulating all such environmental aspects.

It undertakes conservation & survey of flora, fauna, forests and wildlife; prevention & control of pollution; afforestation & regeneration of degraded areas. Every industry has to abide by all such guidelines and parameters for environmental protection because only this will ensure its sustainable progress and growth.

FINANCING A START UP BUSINESS

One needs money to make money. Finance is the lifeline of business. A business firm requires finance to commence its operations, to continue its operations and for its expansion and growth.

There must be continuous flow of funds in and out of business. Sound plans, efficient production and marketing are all dependent on smooth flow of finance.

Hence, a financial plan needs to be prepared, which indicates the requirements of finance, sources for raising the finance and the application of funds.

Financial planning for starting a business begins with estimating the total amount of capital required by the firm for the various need of the business.

The financial plans of an enterprise should be formulated by taking into consideration the following factors:

- The financial objectives of the company
- Nature and size of the business
- The image and credit-worthiness of the enterprise
- Growth and expansion plans
- Capital market trends
- Government regulations

Managing your Finance

Managing the finances of the firm in an efficient manner is the most important aspect of managing a business. It means controlling and managing the firm's financial resources. The process of managing finances involves cash flow management which is concerned with the inflow and outflow of money in and out of a business.

For this a cash flow statement is prepared which records a company's income and expenses in a systematic form. Cash flow statement is a financial tool used by the companies to measure its cash receipts and disbursements over a period of time. It lists cash to and cash from operating, investing and financing activities along with the net increase or decrease in cash for the period. For proper management of a company's finances, the knowledge of accountancy, particularly the principles of double entry book keeping is an essential requirement.

Accountancy tells us how to prepare and maintain the various accounts of a company and how to communicate such accounting information to the concerned parties. A 'general ledger account' is the most important account prepared by a company.

It records all the financial transactions of the company by means of two entries called debit and credit. Besides, every company is statutorily required under the Companies Act, 1956 to keep and maintain books of accounts. Such books are necessary because they give a true and fair view of the state of affairs of the company.

For auditing these books of accounts, it is mandatory for the companies (under the Act) to provide for compulsory appointment of an independent person as the 'auditor' of the company. It is the duty of the auditor to check the arithmetical accuracy of books of accounts and submit its report on the accounting standards and goodwill of the company.

This whole process of financial management gives the true financial position of the company. A good financial standing of a company so indicated reinforces its credit worthiness and competitive position in the market. It is thus essential for smooth and successful functioning of the enterprise in a profitable manner on a long term basis.

Sourcing Process

Once the firm has decided on the foremost issues of which product it wants to produce and the location of the industry, the next important step is to select appropriate technology and equipment to produce the same. In addition to this, the source of raw material has to be decided upon.

The requirements of all these can either be met through domestic sources or can be imported subject to the regulatory requirements of the Government.

The regulatory requirements pertaining to the import procedures vary depending on the item of import. In case of raw materials, the Export Import Policy of the Government regulates imports. However, in the case of technology, the Foreign Direct Investment (FDI) Policy and the Foreign Technology Transfer Agreements govern the imports.

The firm should do a careful cost and benefit analysis before going ahead with the process of placing the orders to minimize the production costs and hence increasing the profit margins. Various sources of Capital should be explored and the cost of capital should be analysed cautiously.

Process Selection

Once the choice of the product is made, selection of the right process technology becomes important.

The process technology required may be:

- *Indigenously developed*: In India, technologies are being developed at CSIR and Defence Research Labs. There are some intermediaries like APCTT (Asian and Pacific Centre for Transfer of Technology), TBSE (Technology Bureau for Small Enterprises) which can help you to locate the relevant technologies. Besides there are some In-house R & D centres of companies which develop technologies and sell them to interested parties. Indigenously developed process know-how has intrinsic benefits like appropriateness, relative inexpensiveness and possibility to work with technology developer.
- *Imported*: For some complex products, process know-how has to be imported. In such cases agreements for technology transfer should

be made with due care in order to safeguard nation's interest. Government of India facilitates foreign technology induction both ' either through the automatic route under the powers delegated to the Reserve Bank of India or otherwise by the Government.

While choosing the process technology, the following considerations are essential:

- The level of skilled workers or complex machines required by the process.
- The quantity of water and/or power required.
- If any process or product patent is needed in order to utilize the selected process technology.
- Any special Pollution or Environmental regulation is to be followed.
- The appropriateness of the technology to the Indian environment and conditions.

Raw Materials

Raw Material procurement and planning are critical to success, of a start-up unit.

The raw materials required may be:

- *Domestically available* (within the country): As we know that our country is a resource rich country with abundance of specific raw materials in different States. (For details, please refer to 'Investment opportunities and incentives' section). Accordingly appropriate suppliers of raw materials have to be selected.
- *Imported from abroad*: For importing the raw materials the Government rules and regulations have to be followed. The imports are regulated by the Foreign Trade (Development and Regulation) Act, 1992. The Act provides for the appointment by the Central Government, of a Director General of Foreign Trade for the purpose of the Act. The DGFT shall advise Central Government in formulating export and import policy and implementing the policy. (For details, please refer to 'Legal Aspects' section).

Whatever be the source of raw materials it must be bought from reputed dealers and agencies only. Before ordering, compare the prices and get quotation from at least 3-4 places and also check whether price is inclusive or exclusive of transportation costs.

While receiving the delivery, check the quality and quantity of the materials. Proper planning is essential because non-availability of the required raw material may result in production hold-ups, idle machinery and manpower. On the other hand if too much is ordered too soon considerable amount of working capital gets locked up. All this will lead to increased production costs. But proper inventory management can lead to manageable cash flow situations. For imported raw material whose lead time are large, proper planning is all the more essential.

Machinery and Equipments

The next important step is choosing and ordering of right machinery and equipments. The machinery and equipments required may be either domestically available or imported from abroad.

For importing machinery and equipments, the Government rules and regulations have to be followed. The imports are regulated by the Foreign Trade (Development and Regulation) Act, 1992.

The Act provides for the appointment by the Central Government, of a Director General of Foreign Trade for the purpose of the Act. The DGFT shall advise Central Government in formulating export and import policy and implementing the policy. Generally, technology or process provides with the necessary specifications relating to machinery and equipment required.

Otherwise, an extensive techno-economic survey of the available machinery and equipment may be carried out. International trade fairs and engineering fairs are good places to look at available options.

The entrepreneur may also consult experts, dealers/suppliers as well as users, prior to making a selection of equipment and machinery. Many entrepreneurs buy second hand machines and equipments.

But this leads to the problem of prevalence of outdated production and management methods hindering the efficient operation of business units. The advice of SISI and NSIC can also be sought.

There are 30 SISIs (Small Industries Services Institutes) set up in State capitals and other industrial cities all over the country. The main objective of National Small Industries Corporation (NSIC) is to provide machinery and equipment to small industrial units offering them long repayment period with moderate rate of interest.

It has been found that small industrialists are unable to install modern machinery and equipment due to lack of investable funds. Hence many schemes and incentives are available to assist them. Now, small scale firms can acquire industrial machinery, office equipment, vehicles, etc, without making full payment through hire purchase. With the help of assets acquired through hire purchase, they can produce and sell. From the earning of production, they can make payments in installment. Ultimately the ownership of assets can be acquired.

National Small Industries Corporation (NSIC) provides machinery and equipment to small scale units on hire purchase basis and on lease basis.

NSIC follows the following Hire Purchase procedure and Hire Purchase Scheme for financing plant and machinery to small scale units:

- The hire purchase application is to be made on the prescribed form.
- The Director of Industries of the State under whose jurisdiction the

applicant falls, forwards the application to the head office of the NSIC at Delhi with his recommendation and comments.

- All applications for indigenous or imported machines are considered by acceptance committees comprising of the representatives of the Chief Controller of Imports, Development Commissioner, Small Scale Industries and other concerned departments.
- Decisions of these committees are conveyed to the parties concerned with copies to the regional offices of the NSIC and the concerned Directorate of Industries.
- It is open to an applicant whose case has been rejected to get his application reviewed by a high powered committee.
- Once the hirer completes all these formalities, instructions are sent to the suppliers to dispatch the consignment (duly insured for transit risk) to the hirer and to send the R/R or C/R as the case may be, to the regional office.
- The NSIC after ensuring that the hirer has paid all dues, releases the R/R or C/R to him for taking delivery of the machines.
- In case of imported machines, the procedure is slightly different in as much as the shipping documents are sent to the clearing agents for clearing the consignment from the Customs and dispatching it to the hirer.

HIRING HUMAN RESOURCE

Human Resource is also an important determinant of business location and functioning. Factors such as the availability of labour of different skill levels, productivity and cost of labour, flexibility of labour, attitude and behaviour patterns of labour, nature of trade unionism etc. are important to a business.

The whole process begins with the task of hiring manpower for starting a business for filling the present and prospective vacancies in the company. The objective of hiring manpower is to procure the right number of employees, with the required qualifications to do the right type of jobs. The hiring process involves four main steps i.e. manpower planning, recruitment, selection and placement. Each of these steps and sub-steps help the employer obtain more and more information about the candidates and thus help in obtaining the best possible manpower for the firm.

This function must be performed carefully because any error committed at the time of hiring manpower may prove to be very costly for the firm both in the short as well as long term. These costs will be in the form of waste of time, money and energy in repeated hiring process. The training costs incurred on them will go waste. The efficiency of the organisation will go down due to hiring of unsuitable candidates. At the same time the rate of absenteeism and labour turnover will be higher.

Hence, an effective hiring procedure includes the answers to the following questions:

- What are the requirements of the jobs to be filled?
- What kinds of persons are needed?
- How many persons are needed?
- What sources of recruitment may be utilised?
- What steps should be taken to select the right type of candidates for employment?

ENTREPRENEURIAL FINANCE

Financial planning is very important for the *entrepreneur* to manage the finance of the business wisely. The most important function of the modern business is to allocate capital efficiently in productive channels. The funds of the firm must be utilized to purchase long-term or fixed term assets effectively. These decisions are known as capital budgeting decisions or capital expenditure and they affect firms growth, profitability, risk and value of the business.

In simple words, companys decision to invest funds to acquire long-term or fixed asset is known as capital investment. Fixed assets do not directly generate income to the business but the process of production is carried smoothly only if fixed assets are employed into the business. The firms investment decisions include expansion, modernization, modification and replacement of fixed assets and it includes any activity that brings profitability to the business. The investment decisions are risky and have long-term consequences.

Such decisions are very important for the *entrepreneur* because they affect firms competitive position in the market and its profitability. The investment decisions once made cannot be revised. They affect the cost structure of the business. If a firm decides to purchase a new plant then they must incur additional expenses for labour, rent and insurance etc. after investing huge amount for the plant they are not yielding expected profit then they must spend a fixed cost for labour, rent till the loss incurred is written off completely. The first stage of investment decision is to identify the investment opportunities.

This job may be complex because numerous investment opportunities are available to a promoter but it is difficult to recognize the most promising investment activity. Therefore he must have knowledge regarding the governmental regulatory framework and policies as they have bearing on different investments. He must study the suitability of the investments proposal with regards to the firms strength and weakness. The demand and supply conditions prevailing in the different industries should be studied. The industrys present level of capacity utilization, profitability factor and the new project planning should be studied by conducting a survey through market researchers. There are some projects that are successfully capitalized.

When the Food specialties launched Maggie noodles in the market, the degree of consumer acceptance was very high and it was understood that fast food is the highly cherished by the general public and therefore can rapidly attract demand. Later the Food specialities Ltd was surrounded by a number of competitors then. Spark plug in India was a product only manufactured by the MICO group, but when Modi recognized that MICO alone cannot fulfill the demand throughout the nation it promoted a new brand and thus successfully launched its product. The government is keen on promoting export-oriented units and import substitution units and grants *finance* to startup the business.

The promoter can analyse the trends of exports and imports after five to six years to be able to identify investment opportunities. India earlier imported cold-rolled coils worth ₹ 1500 crore every year but when Ispat profiles India ltd identified the drawback in India it recognized this opportunity and their product is largely accepted by the consumers.

An entrepreneur, quick in grasping the social trends and human behaviour can find opportunities easily. Today even the middle-class people are turning less reluctant buying goods on credit basis and so noticing this many finance companies are introducing many *finance* schemes. The consumption pattern depends upon many factors like age, geographical area, climatic conditions or traditions and culture of a particular nation. Reviving a sick unit is also an opportunity for a proprietor.

If it takes over a loss-making unit it can increase the profitability by manufacturing a by-product. When the company plans to increase the existing operation capacity or widen the distribution network knowledge of capital investment is necessary. Such decisions are risky and complex. They are taken by the top management after analyzing the report. Diversification involves planning to manufacture a new product or change the location of the business. It also includes merging with the other business firm to expand the unit. It is purely a managerial decision.

In order to improve the quality of the product and increase the production efficiency it is essential to replace the old assets and install new assets that are more efficient. New assets reduce the total production costs to be incurred. Due to the advancement in technology the old assets become obsolete and it becomes necessary to change the asset. This decision is known as cost-reduction investment decision.

Apart from the following investments that are meant to increase the profitably of the business concern sometimes investment decisions are taken to comply the statutory requirements.

Examples of mandatory decisions are purchasing fire-equipments, pollution control equipments, medical and recreational facilities to the staff etc. these decisions are taken to comply the statutory requirements and the managerial decides how to fulfill the requirements by investing minimum. Capital budgeting involves the element of risk and uncertainty. But risk and profitability are directly proportional to each other. If the risks are greater, the profits are also higher. Risk analysis the most complex aspect of capital budgeting. Investment begins with identification of investment opportunities, and then followed by preliminary screening, feasibility study, implementation and performance review.

Preliminary screening includes analysis of the list of most promising investments identified from various sources. The opportunities identified must meet the government regulatory framework and must be compatible to the promoter. The raw materials should be adequately available and the process of transportation must be quicker. It should minimize the cost of production. The inherent risk in the project also should be studied. Once the project is accepted after screening feasibility study should be conducted to study the marketing, technical, financial and economic aspects of the project. Estimation is made regarding the project cost and profitability and sales figure is forecasted.

The structure of raising capital and production cost are also studied the aim of the feasibility study is to ensure whether to choose the particular project or not. Implementation of the project means actually translating the proposal into a project. The implementation stage includes construction of building and other civil works and preparation of blueprints. Negotiations are made with the financial institutions, entering into contracts and supply of machinery and marketing of the companys products etc. Finally, the equipments are installed and the workers, technicians and engineers are trained.

4

Financing Constraints and Entrepreneurship

ENTREPRENEURIAL FINANCE

Venture Associates is a firm with a long, successful history of its knowledge of entrepreneurial financing. It has consulted to and worked with hundreds of companies in practically all industry segments.

These projects have ranged from initial conversations with prospective entrepreneurs in assisting them in their analysis of the viability of their project, all the way through the process of taking their companies public as well as advising on sellouts and mergers. If you're exploring or have questions regarding the financing of your project, you're welcome to contact the firm via the following methods:

STAGES OF ENTREPRENEURIAL FINANCING

Obtaining money for an entrepreneurial company is really pretty simple—it's just another sale. Your customer has something you want their money. You have something they want, equity or a piece of the action of the potential growth of your enterprise.

The key, as in all sales, is to determine the right price and close the sale. To do that, you have to develop a financial marketing mindset. Just as you would prepare a marketing programme to sell your product or service, you need to prepare a financial marketing programme.

That means you prepare a business plan, a Private Placement Memorandum and then develop and practice a verbal pitch, develop a marketing scheme, present the package, and close the sale. It takes intimate knowledge, unbounded enthusiasm, and a scuff resistant ego.

By consulting with your peers, legal counsel, accountants and company consultant, you will have determined the most proper legal structure for your company as well as the proposed valuations. From this, you can then develop your financial marketing programme which in turn will help you narrow in on the type of investor you will be seeking.

For seed and concept companies, this invariably means the entrepreneur starts with "family and friends" money, and then proceeds on to obtaining informal private investor financing prior to attracting the interest of the more formal investors such as venture capital firms. It will be helpful if you understand the accepted "stages of growth" used by all financing sources.

UNDERSTANDING THE STAGES

Prior to delving into the details of entrepreneurial financing, it's helpful to establish an understanding of the traditional stages of development for entrepreneurial companies. These are: Seed or Concept, Startup, First, Second, Third, and Harvest. They are briefly described with Status,
Tasks, and Financing as follows:

Seed or Concept

Status

This is the wild-eyed, perhaps incurable, inventor stage. There is an idea, a concept, no management team, no prototype, and patentability has not been determined. No business plan, timetable, or market research has been assembled. Founder(s) may be technicians.

Tasks

To begin development of a prototype, assemble some key management, develop a business plan, assess market potential, structure the company, and assess patentability or proprietary standing.

Financing

Traditional venture capital firms have little interest in funding a company at this stage. The risk level is just too high, and the time for achieving a payout or harvest is not determinable.

Personal savings or friend and family money funds this stage. It ends with the completion of a seed stage business plan and the formation of the company.

Start-up

Status

At least one principal person of the company is pursuing the project on a full-time basis.

The prototype is being developed or the service is being discussed with potential users, the business plan is being refined, a management team is being identified, market analysis is being undertaking, and beta tests are being set up or initial customers are identified. More formal funding is being accomplished.

Tasks

Complete and test the prototype or beta test the service to obtain evidence of commercial interest. Assemble and identify an initial management team, finish the business and marketing plans, establish manufacturing and initiate sales.

Financing

Traditional venture capital firms may show an interest at this stage, assuming that a top-rated management team is assembled, patentability or proprietorship is proven, and marketability is demonstrated. Fund raising is a major effort at this stage and it may take from several months to a year or more.

First Stage

Status

The company is now a going concern. The product has proven manufacturable and is selling. If it's a service company, some customers have tried the service.

The initial management team is in place, the company has experienced some setbacks, customers can confirm product or service usage, marketing is being refined, adjustments are being made in the business plan and the money raising efforts continue.

Tasks

To achieve market penetration and initial sales goals, reach close to break even, increase productivity, reduce unit costs, build the sales organization and distribution system.

Financing

At this stage, traditional venture capital firms are interested in investment in fact, it's their most preferable stage. Financing is needed to get the production bugs worked out and to support initial marketing efforts.

Second Stage

Status

Significant sales are developing as are assets and liabilities. The company is sporadically achieving break even, and cash flow management becomes critical.

Second-level management is being identified and hired. Export marketing is being explored and more sophisticated management systems are being put into place.

Tasks

To obtain consistent profitability, add significant sales and back orders, expand sales from regional to national, identify international marketing plans, and obtain working capital to expand marketing, accounts receivable, and inventory.

Financing

More sophisticated and second-round venture capital financing comes into play at this stage. The founders and investors are forming plans for the harvest.

Third Stag (also Mezzanine Stage)

Status

All systems are really go and the potential for a major success is beginning to be apparent. Snags are being worked out in all areas from design and development of second-generation products; to marketing and distribution; to management and all its applied systems.

Tasks

To increase market reliability, begin export marketing, put second-level management in place, begin to "dress up" the company for harvest.

Financing

At this stage, the company may need to obtain "bridge" or "mezzanine" financing to carry increased accounts receivable and inventory prior to harvest. There is a great amount of pressure to prove second- and third-generation products, increase profitability records, improve the balance sheet, and firmly establish market share and penetration.

Stage Four: Or is the Harvest Near?

The end may be near for entrepreneurial companies. The company is sifting and sorting out its options including going public, being acquired, selling out, or merging. What started out as a dream has become an entrepreneurial reality. The next challenge is to start all over again, but this time with a pocketful of dollars.

TYPES OF ENTREPRENEURIAL FINANCING

Entrepreneurial managed companies are constantly on the search for new capital and it is seldom easy to come by. Top entrepreneurs understand that raising money is a way of life. Experienced entrepreneurs realise that the financing of companies is done in stages and that they have to be flexible in identifying the latest trends in financing. Many first-timers erroneously believe that they can successfully generate sufficient cash flow on a near-term basis, then bootstrap their way to financial success. This does not work in today's fast-moving business climate, especially in many medium and high-tech areas. This section discusses this fact and other potential problems. The next section offers many solutions for the sourcing of financing.

DEBT AND EQUITY

Contrary to the dreams of many startup entrepreneurs, initial financing can be the hardest part of launching their new business. There are many popular misconceptions that an idea, a startup team, and a preliminary business plan will get them in the venture capitalist door.

They expect to exit, happily, with the check in hand. They don't realise that traditional venture capital-venture capital funds that are supported by institutional investors-only finance a fraction of a per cent of the new companies started each year.

They are not cognizant of the fact that 90 per cent plus of startup money comes from private sources and its up to the individual entrepreneur to identify and sell their project to these financing sources. It's tough, tough work!

The first thing to do is to put together a business plan to use as a fundraising too.Second is the actual raising of the financing, or financial marketing. Each alternative to raising money requires a different approach to the business plan. Financing never happens quickly; it is never simple.

In fact, it is usually quite painful and exasperating. Entrepreneurs can find themselves chasing down blind alleys if they don't prepare properly.

There are a number of sources of financing and a variety of forms of capital. Some are used to finance seed or startup companies while others are used for expansion. Start-ups are usually limited to the type of financing they can get, like personal savings used as equity or personally secured subordinated debt. On the other hand, companies with a proven track record have a much larger choice of financing alternatives—such as banks, venture capital firms, private or public offerings.

What all entrepreneurs soon discover is that there are several factors that they must constantly reckon with, in pursuit of the elusive dollar.

These are:

- The dilution of equity ownership,
- Potential restrictions on daily operating flexibility, and
- Debt-imposed constraints on future growth.

CHOICES FOR FINANCING

For all intents and purposes, the entrepreneur has two basic choices when considering financing: debt or equity, pledging a part of one's soul or giving away a piece of it. Commonly, one does both. In simple terms, debt is borrowed money secured in some fashion with some type of asset for collateral. Equity, on the other hand, is contributed capital, usually hard dollars. Debt may be secured by a personal signature only, and equity can also be in the form of a contributed asset. But most often new businesses require long-term debt or permanent equity capital to support major expansion and anticipated rapid growth.

The advantage of borrowing is that it is a relatively simple process to arrange. It does not take a great deal of time and does not dilute equity ownership. The disadvantages are that it is a high-risk strategy as far as company growth is concerned, in that incurring debt subjects the company to a firm obligation, usually including the principals as cosigners. A downturn in business or an increase in interest rates could result in the inability to service debt payments with the consequences being that the co-signers have to personally pay the company's debt.

SUCCESSFUL ENTREPRENEURS COMBINATIONS

Unlike oil and water, debt, equity, self-funding, and external funding do mix well. In fact, it's an entrepreneurial secret. The best managed companies mix their financing sources and choices. Which to use, and when, becomes a matter of individual option, although there are some pretty well established precedents. Founders' personal investments, including both personal assets and family and friends' equity and loans, are usually what finances concept or seed stage companies.

Development or Start-Up stage companies commonly seek funding from Private Placement's (Regulation D), early-stage venture capital firms, and various grants from both foundations and government sources. Early/First-stage or production companies may receive financing from bank loans, leasing companies, and research and development partnerships (for incremental product development). Strategic partnerships are often entered into at this stage with potential customers, suppliers, and manufacturers.

Companies at the next stage of ramping up (Second Stage), which is full-scale production and expanded marketing, often receive additional dollar injections. These come from second and larger rounds of traditional venture capital, larger companies that are looking for product distribution opportunities, institutional investors, more venture leasing companies (for manufacturing equipment), and additional strategic partners (often seeking secondary manufacturing and distribution rights both domestically and for foreign countries).

After this stage, the entrepreneuring company has some heavy choices to consider. Here is where the harvest point (Third and Forth Stage) is a natural if the plan has been to build a company and then sell out. They still need more money (what's new), but their choices are a lot broader: more venture capital, bridge or mezzanine financing while going public, being acquired (perhaps by one of the earlier-stage strategic partners), or selling out to a cash-rich company.

Debt or Equity

If we're saying that entrepreneurs use combinations, how do we distinguish which and when? The use of debt almost always requires that some equity has come in first. A rough rule of thumb is that a dollar of early stage equity can support a dollar of debt, if there is some additional security to further back the debt. Lenders feel that a start-up has little ability to generate sales or profits. Consequently, the lender wants to have their debt secured, and even then, they feel that the asset value will be decreasing with time and there's always the possibility that management may not be up to the company-building challenge at hand.

This debt will most likely be short-term debt (one year or less) to be paid back from sales. Short-term debt is traditionally used for working capital and small equipment purchases.

Long-term borrowing (one year or maybe up to five) can be used for some working capital needs, but usually is assigned to finance property or equipment that serves as collateral for the debt. While commercial banks are the most common source of short-term debt, there are more choices for long-term financing. Equipment manufacturers provide some, as does the Small Business Administration (SBA), various state agencies, and leasing companies. More examples are given in the following section.

It's true, entrepreneurs can finance start-ups with more debt than equity, but there are some distinct disadvantages. As an example; if they negotiate extended credit terms with several suppliers, this restricts their flexibility to negotiate prices. Heavily leveraged (i.e. debt-financed) companies are constantly undercapitalized and will experience continuing cashflow problems as they grow. Paying close attention to strained cashflow requires a that lot of management time be diverted from company operations. It also affects the balance sheet, making it difficult to obtain additional equity or debt.

On the other hand, there is one big positive in using debt. Debt does not decrease or dilute the entrepreneur's equity position and it provides nice returns on invested capital. However, if credit costs go up, or sales don't meet projections, cashflows really get pinched and bankruptcy can become reality. Top entrepreneurial companies use varying combinations of debt and equity. They determine which is the most advantageous for the particular stage of growth they're financing. Their aim is to create increasingly higher valuations or profit structures.

Enterprise formation is in the business of procreation. The founder entrepreneurs are entrusted with that task. In turn, market economies have entrusted the founder entrepreneur with the procreation of their future. The statistics is not good in this regard. Fifty per cent of the new born enterprises die within two years, and 90 per cent of them die within ten years. Obviously these founder entrepreneurs need help. The venture capitalists are the first to come to help. But the numbers that these venture capitalists could assist are extremely limited, when measured against the total number of firms given birth to every year. Obviously there is a need for more perva-sive help, and this is where the academic world could play a part...

What is it that the academic world could do that even venture capitalist could not do? How can the academic world make itself relevant and useful to the founder entrepreneurs? The answer is: theory. "There is nothing more useful than a good theory", as Kurt Lewin used to say. Most of the founder entrepreneurs act without good theory.

Most of them are running blind, without sound interpretative schemes and intervention theories. By theory here we concur with what Weisbord says: "A theory is not a method. It is a way of interpreting reality that helps you act with more certainty". This chapter firstly reports on the failure of an entrepreneurial venture, launched in part under the ae-gis of the Nature of Entrepreneurial Work Research Programme at the University of Hong Kong.

While attempting to save this venture, a search for relevant and useful knowledge in existence to guide the effort has ended in vein. The poverty such knowledge for the entrepreneurs locked in the founding process had come to be acutely felt. The most critical missing piece is the lack of perspectives and paradigms on the transactional space and how entrepreneurs could act with them and within it to ensure venture survival and prosperity. This triggered off a new field research initiative on the side, through participant observation. The finding of this initiative has resulted in a new way of conceiving the nature of the entrepreneurial firm, of the roles of founder entrepreneurs, and of the types of entrepre-neurial competencies needed to facilitate the earning of the birth right for a new born enterprise. This new set of hypotheses is then used to guide the founding of another entrepreneurial venture.

This second new venture has not only earned its birth right, but is now well on the way to move to newer height. The paper will share this experience and these new conceptualizations. It ends with a calling for more research into the transactional realm, an area critical to the life and death of enterprises. The experimental phase of the Nature of Entrepreneurial Work Research Programme A fascination with what the entrepreneurs really do in order that they could achieve phenomenal suc-cess has led to a life-long research programme. This programme has led to a typological understanding of entrepreneurial work. When the theoretical yield of participant observation was found to be approaching a limit, a decision was made to change the research strategy.

The researcher had re-signed from the University of Hong Kong, to be fully engaged in entrepreneurial work, from there to see if new insight into the entrepreneurial processes could be realized in the course venture experimentations. One of the gaps of knowledge which the researcher had not been able to gain access to is a consequence of the research method adopted in phase one.

Very little could be learnt through participant observation about the early enterprise formation period. This is because the researcher had invariably arrived at sites at a stage when the company's existence is already assured and assumed. We learnt that each of the successful enterprises has evolved its unique formula of success, and we could understand that these formulae fall into types and obey hidden evolutionary and systemic order. But as a rule the process of searching for the formula has been based on self reported data, without the researcher's involvement or presence.

Such lack of solid knowledge will prove to be fatal when the researcher en-tered into the phase of experimentation. Conducting venture creation experiments will thus enable the researcher to go through the initial stages of a firm's existence, before the realization of its formula of success. This would help us unearth and understand the preconditions, if any, for subsequent success.

On the one hand, conducting entrepreneurial experiment is an expensive endeavour, and could bring risks to whoever is committed to this exercise.

On the other hand, without direct involvement, research yield might only stay skin deep. To overcome the accessibility problem, the researcher decided to enter into ventures himself. Essentially this means that there is a social scientist willing take on the role of an entrepreneur, through such involvement to see what entrepreneurial work is really like, from the inside out, rather than from the outside in.

He is switching from being an observer to being a partic-ipant. Prior to this, the researcher has invested and co-founded an information technology business in Hong Kong. Over the years, it has evolved into a stable core business. It now comes to a stage when it could be restructured to become a holding company, in preparation for experimentation with new business formation around the core. That is the background to a series of venture experiments. Two of these experiments will be re-ported here.

ENTREPRENEURIAL EXPERIMENT ONE

The first experiment has involved a formation of a business related to the IT base. One of the projects which the mother company is engaged in has entailed an outsourcing arrangement with a Guangzhou data entry operation. The original data were scanned and shipped from Hong Kong via Internet to GZ for processing, the output was then returned to Hong Kong via the same electronic channel. It was then realized that if this could be done between Hong Kong and GZ, then theoretically this could be done between US and China. A business concept was thus born, to capitalize on the wage differential between the United States and China. The coming together of two groups of entrepreneurs, one from the US and the other from HK (the original founders of the holding company) resulted in a fifty-fifty joint venture.

There is to be a separation of duties between the two teams, one is to do with the securing of out-sourcing contracts from United States companies, and the other is responsible for the production and delivery part of the contracts in China.

The original production site has already been set up through outsourcing in GZ, providing service to Hong Kong. So what is required is a matter of gearing this facility up so that it could provide ser-vice in English and directing the service to the US market. Formerly it is providing service in Chinese. The operation was already quite sizable and has stable contracts from Hong Kong that will sustain a core of staff for the coming few years.

Problem and Solutions

While the China side is running in a stable path because of the Hong Kong contracts, the US side soon had their hope of securing contracts frustrated. There were a lot of set backs. One by one, those potential clients as listed in the original business plan projection had politely declined our offers. There were occasional interest shown, as indicated by the number of pilot and one-off projects, but most had not materialized into sizable contracts. There was a frenetic rush to find solutions.

Change of targeted industry was one. Change of targeted geographical territories was another. Growing into new business networks was the third. We began to eliminate more and more possibilities for lack of breakthrough through trail and error, until we come to realise that it might be our lack of marketing and sales competencies that could be the source of the problem. We began to engage marketing expert in the US to advice on go-to-market strategies. Then we began to experiment with employing professional salesmen in US one after another.

One pivotal turning point happened when the researcher went to see the top management of a leading company in Dallas, and along with my partners, explained the huge benefits of outsourcing to China. Within a week we heard from that company that they will be giving us a contract. If we were able to secure that contract, this will require us to scale up our operation in China ten times over within three years. The whole team was elated and the researcher returned to China to make preparation for the expanding volume of work. We eventually failed to secure that contract. We began to realise that for a complex sales situation, just employing one or two sales professional would not be enough to cover the vast decision making trees participating as a matter of routine. The whole entrepreneurial team would need to be engaged in the transactional act as well. We decided to battle on in spite of this huge set back. The discovery of a theoretically uncharted space.

While all the above were going on, just as everyone in the team did, the researcher on this end was desperately trying to make sense of this impasse. Being an academic by training, one of the actions taken was to see if the academic literature has anything to say about this phenomenon. It was at this juncture that the barren knowledge landscape on the relationship between entrepreneurship and transactional performance was first coming into view.

This poverty of academic interest in the transaction arena is surprisingly pervasive, and this is the case across the fields of strategy, management, organization, entrepreneurship and even within marketing.

This is strange, when one of their sister disciplines, economics, has completely constructed the core of the discipline around supply and demand (mainstream economics) and around transactional cost (institutional economics). "In virtually all discussions, the sale process is the missing piece of the puzzle.

Whether you're looking at Business Week or an inflight magazine or the latest report form the Harvard Business School, the world of sales and sellers is conspicuous by its absence. It is strange but true. Even though every business would stop dead in its tracks without the sale revenue, the sales process is never discussed in the same breath—or, for that matter, in the same room—as the "strategic" contributions of senior management" "In the business literature, on the corporate organization chart, and in the traditional mind-set of most senior managers, sales and management are viewed as separate entities, and there's little question about which is more important. " Serious" decisions are made by senior management. The sales force might pump the gas, but it can't drive the car".

This lack of managerial attention might have also affected our academic focus in subtle ways. As a result founder entrepreneurs are suffering from the poverty of understanding of what it is and how it is done, and what kind of innovation potentials exist within that space. There is a complete lack of documentation on the inner secrets of how to bring about transactional breakthroughs imaginatively.

Lack of Systematic Knowledge and Theories

The underestimation of the importance of transactional knowledge, competencies and imagination to entrepreneurial success is producing repercussions in the educational and training arena. This attitude has resulted in a complete lack of theory.

In a typical MBA programme, the topic of sales are usually re-legated to a minor section within marketing, and one would be lucky to find a few passing remarks about sales management. In executive seminars, the issue of buying and selling is usually covered by the sharing of experience with veteran sales professionals, and their experience rarely got distilled into theories by academics.

Academics tends to see sales activity as something that exist beneath the managerial level, something far removed from the strategy making role of directors, something that could be considered solved by the time the executive audience comes for professional upgrading. Why this lack is particularly serious for the entrepreneurial venture.

But transaction is something that makes or breaks a company. The continuing under development of knowledge, competencies and theories can be costly. For an entrepreneurial venture, nothing happens unless one can make a sale. And suffering from the liability of newness, having to make a deal without a brand, without track record, without client reference, without industry reputation could be a daunting challenge.

The future of market economies is based on new venture success, and we just throw these adventurers into the water to see if they could swim. Transactional success is the entry ticket to the market. It is the act of earning the birth-right for the venture. What kind of theory do founder entrepreneurs want? The theoretical payoffs for sustained effort in entrepreneurial research could be substantial.

We learnt from the findings of the Nature of Entrepreneurial Work programme that there are definite ways for entrepreneur to make impact to the world as well as to make impact to the firm. We understand that to obtain superior rewards it requires the actor to be in tune with the underlying logics in the system, a distinctive entrepreneurial universe. The opportunity to magnify the impact of one's talent through mechanisms does exist, because there are mechanisms for multiplication inherent within the market system, and are open to those who could decipher the rules. These vehicles for multiplication come in various forms.

An entrepreneur could exercise pervasive impact through innovations in prod-uct (as Steve Jobs), in process (as Henry Ford), in sourcing (as Mikimoto) and in distribution (as Ri-chard Sears), through leveraging market forces (as Warren Buffet), through exploiting state-market difference (as Soros), through political relations (as Schindler), through resource reconfiguration and re-deployment (as Iacocca). Each of these vehicles, when married to the right contextual shifts, produces quantum jump in performance. When these separate types are put together, a view emerges in which the actors, the multiplication mechanisms, the interpretative orientations, the profit logics, the contextual shifts, the causalities are all inter-linked functionally to form a coherent, self-organizing, and recurring universe.

With this background it would be possible for us to advance a view of participant reconstruction, a view which resonant with the calling for micro-foundations, actor dependent causalities and macrostructure. Commenting on the failure of the dominant literature to incorporate the role of the actor, and how the actor could impact on the larger entities, a few fellow academics have expressed grave concerns about the practical relevance of such form of theory building: "We are worried that the absence of micro-foundations in the capabilities view (the dominant view in strategic management) may contribute to the disappearing mandate for strategic management. In other words, the possibility of strategic action might become obscured by a firm emphasis on firm level constructs, such as routines and capabilities.

It would often seem critical to management scholars as well as strategic managers to understand and to be able to impute actions to individuals, rather than to collective variables.

And if indeed routines and capabilities are meaningful variables, both manage-ment scholars and strategic managers should take an interest in the micro-mechanisms through which they assert their influence on firm performance. Performance improvement might come about not by selecting new routines and capabilities, but also through changing and influencing the micro-mechanisms through which routine work their influence on performance".

The academic mandate in the eyes of the founder entrepreneurs could be regained. In this connection, we see the study of founder entrepreneurs as providing a natural fit for this advocated line of re-search pursuit.

The nature of founder entrepreneur's work demands theoretic insights that bridge the micro with the macro, insight that could inform actors on how to interpret and intervene to bring about venture survival and performance:

- Founder entrepreneurs, as micro-actors, are being asked to create macro-structures from ground zero. They need to be the originator of routines and capabilities, among other things.
- Founder entrepreneurs, as micro-actors, need to be armed with knowledge of actor-dependent cau-salities, so that the job of firm creation could begin with conscious understanding. Given the open-ended nature of firm creation, blind search could be very costly.
- For founder entrepreneurs, performance separates life from death. It is important that they be well informed on the underlying causalities which could bring about the right kind of performance.

With the current state of literature at hand, we do not know enough about the roles of the founder entrepreneurs. Within the entrepreneurial studies literature, there have been a lot of studies on the perso-nalities, rather than the work roles, of the entrepreneurs.

We do not know what special competencies, if any, are needed to fulfill the requirement of this daunting jobs of bringing a firm from concept to life, what sort of causalities one could leverage on to ensure the survival of the firms, and what kind of knowledge would be most useful to the task at hand. Yet this sort of understanding is mission critical. What should we be looking for? We learn from the first phase of our research programme that it is possible to systematically understand entrepreneurial roles, which could be typologically segregated. We also understand that these roles are stable, recurring and orderly because entrepreneurial performance is tied to market mechanisms.

There are only limited ways that the market mechanism could rewards the entrepreneurs. Once we know that entrepreneurial role systems are recurrent and stable, it would be meaningful for us to move on to the next stage of refined understanding.

We could start learning how as actors they could influence the development of the firm. A firm is a socially constructed entity and as leading actors founder entrepreneurs need to know what need to be constructed and how to influence that construction in order that a venture could earn its entry ticket..We understands that entrepreneurial interventions are triggered by how the realities are interpreted. And these interpretative schemes are typologically bounded. Different types of entrepreneur's functions within different types of realities. Within each type of reality, founders are responsible for the generation of the interpretative schemes, to ensure a unique approach to the reality for advantage.

A market forces player would need to devise an interpretative scheme so that one could following the movement of the market, make sense of it in ways so that one could exploit the situation to advantage. Thus the competence to construct a unique interpretive paradigm would be instrumental to the fulfill-ment of entrepreneurial role (for example, Warren Buffet and Templeton).

On the other hand, a product innovator would need to evolve its own ways of interpreting the changing modes and aspirations of customers, so that products that satisfy those could be designed in accordance with such reading (for example, Steve Jobs and Ralph Lauren). It would be great if the academic world could help them do so.

To regain the academic mandate, we also need to help founder entrepreneurs build theories that would enable them to perform in interactive contexts. In other words, we need to be in search of a type of knowledge which could explain and predict interactive causalities. Consider how we could help an entrepreneur tango with his or her competitors.

Consider how we could help an entrepreneur negotiate for contracts. Game theory, negotiation theory would be example that fit into this description. While we cannot predict in advance the specific ecology this kind of knowledge will be put to use, we could predict the form that will be. Entrepreneurs as actor need to become the causal mechanisms of firm's performance. In this regard, we are in agreement with the micro-foundation persuasion.

Research Design

While the sample base for the first phase of our research was extensive, encompassing ten industries over ten years, and hundreds of representative cases, the experimental phase will not have this luxury. What we are trying to do is to make this an exploratory, hypotheses generation exercise, in the spirit of Barry and Glazer, with regard to the discovery of grounded theory. The background is that all these experiments are stemming from the same holding company, which concentrates on large scale systems integration work. The business has been in existence for over sixteen years and has earned a strong reputation and track record with government, finance, banking, insurance, education and logistic clients.

Most of these clients are either institutions serving a global city, regional firms becoming global firm, or global firms entering China. All the experimental ventures are related in one way or the other to information technology and its diverse application areas. The information technology industry is in a very advantageous position be-cause it is penetrating into all aspects of institutions, industries, functions and levels. As such there is no shortage of new venture opportunities around the core. With this as background, all new ventures therefore are controlled experiments in a certain sense.

They are all stemming from the same industry, using the same base technology, invested with the same over-seeing management from the same holding company, working in the same region, into markets with the application of IT, and all with the participation of the researcher as one of the founders in both the holding and the new ventures. With these levels of control in place, it would enable the researcher to use the constant comparative method, for hypotheses generation purpose.

The in-depth involvement of researcher in this arrange-ment would allow him to find way to map micro-action, trace actor-dependent causalities and hypo-thesis on how action, interpretation and interaction could be linked to macro-structures and performance.

Entering an Uncharted Territory

With the above as the theory building ideal, and the matching research design in place, the researcher entrepreneur will try to undertake two tasks in parallel. Most of the decisions and communication exchange are stored in files and emails, leaving traces of evidence for subsequent analysis and comparative insight generation. He can, also switch into a phenomenological mode of operation, suspending his judgment as much as possible when he entered into the exploratory act. As the Zen master once said, you have to empty your cup before we could fill it up again with fresh insight. Learning to be humble in face of the transactional challenge.

Repeated failures at cracking the secret codes of transactional success, by a group of very intelligent founders (some of them have achieved international repute) had led all of us into a new kind of humbleness with regard to this particular profession. This experience had completely taken away whatever arrogance we might have with regard to the transactional vocation. Commenting on the management's lack of regards for the sales function, Sanchez et.al, specialists of the sales processes, have this to say: "The people who generate the revenue are often treated like Forrest Gumps. At best, their essential work is taken for granted.

At worst, senior managers view it as a necessary evil". They also quoted the work of Robert Atkins, a partner with Mercer Management Consulting, published in Business Week, as testimony: "I don't know a lot of CEO's who are paying any attention to their sales channels. They also tried to explain why this is so: "As dangerously counterproductive as this situation is, there are logical, or at least traditional, rea-sons why it exists.

One is the view of the sales rep as a slick-talking co artist—the kind of character who peddles refrigerators to Eskimos. Another is the image of the rep as a shuffling Willy Loman—somebody whose main ambition is to be "well-liked" and who is rightly seen as a loser. Underlying these stereotypes are a corporate peculiarity: the fact that, with a few notable exceptions (IBM's Thomas Watson comes to mind), CEOs and other senior managers have never done any selling them-selves.

Their careers started in operations and finance, and they have never been educated about what a salespeople do" Working with sales people, and venturing into taking up some sales functions by the founding teams themselves, had taught all of us, how hard it could be. The empathy was particularly strong with regard to how they need to handle rejections day in day out and still need to charge ahead with a smil-ing face. It is a tough act learning how to reinvigorate oneself defeats after defeats.

The Puzzle

But still the puzzle remained. After a few years banging our heads against the proverbial wall, we were still going no where. What does it take to close a complex deal? To us, and to the sales people that we have engaged to enter into the US market, there was an unfathomable mystery with regards to the other side of the exchange equation. There were no perspectives and paradigms which could be good enough to guide us to deal-making, to understand what potential clients really wanted and what was needed to close a deal. Meanwhile the resources for the venture were being drained away by the blind search. It was amid this crisis that a series of surprising discoveries begun to come to the fore.

Series of Surprising Discoveries

The turning point came, after a few years of struggle in securing contract from US without success, in the form of an accidental encounter with a sales master in Hong Kong. This encounter, along with the series of interviews and observations with other masters that follows, had completely reversed the researcher's understanding of the transactional universe. Eventually a new perspective for understanding the role of founder entrepreneurs in the transactional space emerged.

This new perspective will have multiple building blocks. The most fundamental part is: what does it take so that entrepreneur could make transaction possible? There in we find the unique recipe of conversion as a product of founder's search and deliberation. Then we find that on that basis of having achieved breakthroughs again and again, the entrepreneur will usually grow in confidence and gain a sense of masterly.

Over time some will move on and take up the challenge of re-structuring the context of transaction. This is a big step up because with this new framework thus coconstructed, large volume and continuous flow of contracts could be processed.

Therein we see the creation of conversion mechanisms. This framework by itself might not be sufficient enough for the entrepreneur to bring in the level of certainty that would be required to push the enterprise into a firm foundation. The next step up we see the founder entrepreneurs undertaking something more abstract in nature. This is to do with the uncovering of contextual shift, the mental tracing of the demand formation mechanisms, thereby finding ways to leverage the forces in the situation. Contextual shift will push the multitude of customers into the pipe-lines of the firm's conversion framework.

Levels of Transactional Performance

This series of discoveries would not be possible without first encountering a sales master. After having met with so many sales in US, and having formed a view of what sales is about, I have come to assume that complex sales must be met with a lot of hurdles, and that sales cycles must be long, and the reject rate must be around 80 to 90 per cent.

This sales master appeared against this background, and presented an immediate contrast. Observing how this sales master arrives at a deal is analogous to seeing how a chess master makes his moves. My first observation of him has lasted for hours, which included his explanation on how he would exhaustively prepare for the kill. After the deal has been struck, he would also explain how he did it, and why he did what during. This goes on for a few times until I got the sense of the pattern involved. The central thrust is simple. He does not sell.

He would thoroughly research the possible posi-tions of the counter part, and thought through the options of the counter-part well before the meeting. For each options he would find ways to structure a win-win structure so that the counterpart would find each irresistible. The ways he could always find a way to work out win-win structure is eye-opening, reflecting abundant resourcefulness. Should he not be able to find these structures, he would decline entering into a deal making situation. In other words, he would try to conceptually win the battle before he starts the war. During the interaction, his mind could always work out a few steps ahead of the counterpart, which give him ample time to cover contingencies and maintain control over the unfolding conversations. His performance is stellar. His success rate is the reverse of the norm, 80 to 90%.

His presence suggests that there is an alternative way of approaching the transactional situation, a complete reversal of the way of the low performing sales. He has evolved his own perspectives to make sense of his counterparts, who could come in different shapes and sizes. He has evolved schema of interactions which he could liberally deploy in different scenarios. He could thus anticipate the sales processes and work out scripts of standard response, saving energy for contingencies.

He would have many win-win solutions stored in his mind so that he could mix and match, modify to fit, or redesign spontaneously around basic blueprints. The existence of this alternative means that transactional situation is open to multiple interpretations, thus making it possible for actor to exercise influence over the course of development and per-haps control the outcome.

This encounter has ignited my curiosity and encouraged me to hunt for newer approaches to enhance sales performance. And there are. As more and more cases began to come in, they seem to fall into distinct categories. As far as the sample allows us to generalize, there are five levels of transactional performance we could discern.

Level One refers to those founders who do not have interest in sales, those who have been mindful about the sales situations they went through, and those have not developed the requisite sensitivity to the intrigue of sale. Sale is someone else's business. I belong to this type before I put myself through entrepreneurial experiments. Level Two refers to those founders who could not conclude deals no matter how hard they try. They might want to learn about sales but do not know how or from whom. They have not encountered sales masters, nor have they been inspired by the possibilities these master could open. They have not been able to appreciate the meaningfulness and challenge of sale.

Sale is a necessary evil. Sale is a duty, and is a hurdle to be overcome so that you could then move on to the real thing. Sale performance is a chancy affair. Level Three refers to those founders who could see the meaningfulness of transaction, challenged by it, and is excited by the kill. They have developed repertoire of scripts and standardized responses to map to multiple sale situations.

They could also improvise on the spot. They are passionate about the art of making deals and could read the counterpart like a book. They know how to bring deals to closure in spite of odds and perform well across a variety of customer types. They come to realise a unique approach to go beyond the hurdles and bring both parties to a deal. And the basic core of this conversion has a common form. It lies somewhere in the successful search, conception and construc-tion of a win-win structure.

Level Four refer to those founders who not only could excel in deal making. They could migrate to the entrepreneurial level and is capable of conceiving and constructing multiple and overlapping macro-structures. At the core it is an ability to dynamically construct symbiotic relationships across multiple participants in the external context and integrating them together to form durable structures, thereby forming value creation and value exchange flows.

Whereas level three is more concerned with concluding single transactional deals one by one, level four is concerned with the clustering of contextual units into grand structures so that large volume of deals could flow through. Because of this, the difference in the level of performance between level four and three could be quantum. We will la-bel this kind of work as context re-structuring, and illustration of how this works will follow.

Level Five refer to those who not only excel in deal making and those who could construct multiple symbiotic structures. It refers to those who had developed unique perspectives to decipher contextual shifts and could find ingenious ways to leverage those shifts to couple with the macro-structures to bring in permanence, stability and growth.

Again the performance difference between level five and level four is quantum, because of the rare competence to inter-relate the deal-processing mechanism to a massive demand pipeline. We will label this kind of work as contextual shifts leveraging, and illustration of how this work will follow. What separate transactional failure from transactional success: finding a unique recipe pertaining to the specific type of transactional interface.

The turn of fate for an entrepreneurial venture from failure to survival is finally becoming clear: the founder has to be in search of a unique win-win structure which could become the key to unlock the firm or industry specific transactional impasse. What separates the unsuccessful from successful sale lies in finding a unique way which might work the magic to overcome the specific kind of apathy, doubts, hesitations, anxieties, or whatever reasons which stop the potential exchange partner from crossing the line. The transactional impasse that we have encountered in our first entrepreneurial experiment is not unique. Consider the case of Larry Ellison, the founder of Oracle. When the relational database product was first present to the potential customers, it was considered a laughing stock and no body believed it could work. It was considered too much of a toy and could never become a work-horse in the enterprise computing universe. It had taken Oracle ten years of hard work and Larry's Ellison considerable ingenuity to overcome this anxiety and doubt.

The success in finding a win-win structure could be conceived as the pivotal, conversion trig-ger-event. How to ensure that the two parties could arrive at a win-win structure is something that is going to demand huge ingenuity and possibly conceptual jumps.

This is analogous to that of a task master who needs to work with the material for a long time so that he/she could discover a special way to converting the materials into product. Beyond that point, a piece of stone will no longer remain a piece of stone for long, when it reaches the hands of Michelangelo. A hamburger is more than a hamburger when it reaches the eyes of Ray Kroc. Artistic mastery and transactional mastery are analogous. Crossing that bar is what marks the novice from the master. The following case might reveal the same difference between what separated the McDonald brothers from Ray Kroc. The case is to do with one of the founders of a global courier company.

What does a courier company sells? The answer is that this is a glorified mail room outsourcing business. It involves helping companies to dispatch mails in a more efficient manner so that one could save on mail room cost. This way of conceiving the nature of this business would not be able to explain the phenomenal growth of the industry and would not be able to explain the differentiation of courier companies. For after all, how could you differentiate on the basis of having the messengers running between a company and the post office? This founder, who has a biology background, got a job in a factory in Hong Kong which required him to frequent the airport for the export of cargo.

There he began to be intrigued by the inner working of the cargo and logistic world. His biological background probably enabled him to construct his un-derstanding of the logistic world in terms of ecological cycles.

His entry into the courier world was by invitation of three original founders in the United States. These original founders were trying to expand their business to Hong Kong from the original base in California. He agreed to join them and started off with a modest base. He tried at first to build up his pool of contracts by providing courier service to those American banks with presence in Hong Kong, thereby ca-pitalizing on the geographic link between Hong Kong and United State for document flow management. Progress was relatively slow.

His real breakthrough had come from a new realization. He saw a new way of constructing a win-win structure at the cross-section between factory operations and banking service. He came to learn that specific to factories in Hong Kong, mostly export oriented, were in need of three sets of capital to operate. The first set was to be invested into fixed assets, including the factory premises, the machines and the like.

The second set was to be put into the employment, the raw materials, in the form of circulating capital. Then there is a third set. Because output were for export, the payment cycle could not be concluded without having to go through lengthy cycles. A typical cycle would incorporate time for shipment, custom clearance, ground distribution, warehouse acceptance, and shelving into stores.

The same applies to the documents that accompany the goods, having to pass the hands of forwarders, shippers, customs, ground handlers, clients, bankers. Only after all these cleared and verified will the exporters have their money back. Thus the third set could easily tie up more capital than the first two because most of the time the goods are either floating on the sea and in transit, and the document could be held up in the red tapes.

Here in lies the need for a solution: if the documentation could be speeded up, from months to days, then the amount of capital required for the third purpose could drastically shrink. This discovery fundamentally altered the fate of the courier enterprise in question.

So while the amateurs were selling cost saving for the mailroom, which was modest; he began selling the solution for using courier service to dramatically restructure the financial situation in factories. The gains are huge for both parties of the exchange. Less financial tied up, faster recycling of capital, huge saving in interest, more business with less money, opportunities enlargement for the factories.

For the courier company: exclusive access to the top echelon of factory management for a messenger service, locking factories into long term secured contracts, becoming an integral and critical part of the exporters business cycles, growing dependencies of the factories on the exporters' business as they grow, and the externalities benefit deriving from securing contracts from the entire value chain, once a player in the document flow process has granted entry.

Therein we see the power of the conceptual jump in changing the fate of an enterprise. The symbiotic opportunity so discovered, conceived, and converted into a win-win structure is, at its core, an entrepreneurial function. This is but one illustration of the kind of transactional imagination that needed to be in place in order that the transactional impasse so typical of new founded enterprises could be overcome. The contract is the product of entrepreneurial ingenuity. The process of arriving at the contract deserves serious entrepreneurial studies.

It is particularly critical for entrepreneurial scholar to grasp at the challenge of achieving sale at the founding stage. Because by the time a whole batch of sales pro-fessionals are being dispatch on the road to make the kill, they will be following the founder's innovated recipe. Studying transactional behaviour at this stage, as fait accompli, we will only get at something that has already been converted into routines and mostly been taken for granted.

The working of the micro-foundations and causalities could no longer be grasped at this stage. That is why most of the popular books on sale are for the sales professionals working within a taken-for-granted framework, and provide limited clues to the entrepreneurial challenge of how to construct the framework for the sales professional in the first place. Inventing the phone is very different from using the phone.

The transactional role of this courier service founder, Mr. Po Chung, who is now the retired chairman Asia of DHL at the time of the interview, is analogous to that of the founder of Estee Lauder. She was trying to sell perfume to the American ladies at a time of extreme social conservatism. Immediately after the war, the buying of perfume was a preserve of the boyfriends and husbands, or directly only by those who are engaging in night life. And these boyfriends and husbands were miles apart in guessing at the aromatic aspiration of the opposite sex to be making the right choice. But the social stigma would prevent these ladies to lay their hands on the perfume themselves.

At this transactional impasse, we saw the entry of Estee Lauder. She innovated in a completely new way. She will not be selling perfume. She will be selling Youth Dew, as bath solution instead. This stroke of genius has enabled the middle class perfume market to be made wide open. This transactional breakthrough is one of the foundation stones for one of the world's largest cosmetic companies. Just as Po Chung would not be selling messenger service, he will be selling capital re-structuring.

That opened a pathway to help the factories, right at the beginning stage of the industrial revolution in Hong Kong. Soon each and every industry—garment, fashion, toys, electronics, electrical, printing and packaging, watches, etc— that are coming into being would embrace this service, launching the DHL service to new height. Whereas at level three the founder entrepreneurs are entrusted with the role to search for a key to unlock the market, to invent a conversion methodology to make transaction possible, the kind of work on level four and five will represent entrepreneurial attempts to move the secret recipe onto a massive scale.

Sometime the realization of a recipe to solve the three upper levels challenges could happen at the same time, but this is rare. Here these three levels could be treated as analytically separate so that we could see the underlying logics in its entirety.

It is from the discoveries of these upper three levels of endeavour that we begun to see the link between micro-actor and macro-structures and then onto performance. In the following, we will describe in further details how these are done. But before we go into the details, we need to continue with asking the central question. How could such a critical role of founder entrepreneurship remain so invisible to the researchers? The first reason: by the time the field researchers arrived at site, by definition the transactional riddle must have been solved, or else there will be no firm to study. As we begin our discovery on the fourth level, we see the second reason.

This level of work has escaped the attention of the field researchers within the research sites because the bulk of transactional activities are usually conducted within client sites. This is especially true of the business to business kind of transactional activities, which both of our experiments are engaged in.

Because of the criticality of securing contracts to any company, researchers are rarely allowed to participate. And since complex sale easily takes a few months or even years to conclude, accessibility has always been a problem. Thus the transactional front had remained quite hidden to the academic world. Theoretical treatment on a subject without empirical reference is difficult to come by, as a result. "Even Michael Hammer and James Champy, who wrote Re-engineering the Corporation, reveal the same blind spot as other business gurus when they claim, "sales is not a process, but a depart-ment."

When () asked why he and Champy had included in their book so "few examples of re-engineered sales and marketing processes". Hammer's explanation? They "weren't available... They weren't ready to be discussed when we wrote the book". And it was only through privileged access as a result of participating in entrepreneurial experiments that the inner sanctum of the deal making world could come to be revealed. What is coming to view is startling, because there are large chunked of edifice constructed external to the organization, that are critical to the survival and prosperity of the venture, that has not been ac-counted for in the dominant literature.

The importance of the transactional phenomenon has been sanctified in the economics literature as the centre piece around which theories are constructed. In the strategy, management, organization and entrepreneurship literature, however, this phenomenon has been sidelined, diminished, underappreciated and relegated to an insignificant corner.

Our conception of the transactional challenge has been reduced to the act of sale. And sale is defined only in terms of the salesman job. While the popular literature is full of treatments on the art of salesmanship, the academic literature, however, has entirely missed the centrality and criticalness of the interactive relationship between entrepreneurship and the transactional sphere. There is no serious study on how the entrepreneur could or should relate to the transactional challenge.

Context Re-Structuring Work

Part of the reason why this kind of entrepreneurial work has remained invisible is that the results of the work, macro-structures, are usually scattered across multiple organizations. Those studying individual organization might find this of tangential interest, therefore insignificant and inconsequential. The following case will illustrate the point.

There are a few contextual elements scattered all over China. First are a few electronic factories in the coastal provinces. Second is a group of government officials in the interior provinces, thousands of miles away. Third, there is a huge group of young girls and boys working in farming communities under the provincial administration. Fourth is a batch of retired supervisors from electronic factories in the Southern provinces. They are totally unrelated to each other and each leads an existence separate from the other.

No transaction could possibly exist between them—without intervention. An entrepreneur comes into the picture. He discovered that the electronics factories are suffering from huge labour turnover, as the coastal provinces are increasing prosperous and full of alternative employment opportunities. For each worker recruited and trained to be ready for assembly work, the factories would have to spend RMB 5000 as cost.

He also discovered that those government officials are given a policy to find ways to relieve poverty in their remote provinces. Then he learnt that these young boys and girls working in the farms are dying to go to the cities and find work. A factory job could bring in multiple fold of what they could earn from a farm.

Armed with this knowledge, he struck a series of deals with the electronic factories, promising each that he could provide the needed labour for them. They will be recruited, trained and made ready for selection in accordance with their customized needs, for RMB 3000 each. The factories readily agreed. He then went to the government officials, to propose a poverty reduction solution: He would provide training free of charge for farm boys and girls, and if they are good they will be given jobs in the cities. To join this programme, the officials would need to select the best and the brightest from these farms that are available for this purpose. In addition, they need to provide training facilities, perhaps converting some underused government offices for that purpose.

These officials were delighted by this god-sent solution. They just ordered some of the government buildings to be allocated for this dedicated use. The boys and girls are overwhelmed by this arrangement. By nodding their head they earn training opportunities that are free of charge training and the prospect of securing a job in the cities. They will do this with the full support from government, and they will be migrating to a new place of work accompanied by friends. Those retired electronic workers find their way into becoming the teachers and trainers, a job which use their skills but paid higher. The entrepreneur has string together a multi-party symbiotic structure, creating value to each and every participating party. His cost of recruitment, training and dispatch is RMB 1000 per worker.

The training company, which the entrepreneur founded, has now successfully trained and dis-patched 10,000 youngsters. The target just within this industry is 100, 000. He plans to replicate this arrangement to other industries and other provinces. That is only one of the many examples that we have been exposed to.

There are numerous other ingenious designs of multiple and overlapping win-win-win structures which are being uncovered. The underlying FORM to these examples is: Mental switching is the prerequisite for an entrepre-neur to move one step up in the ladder, away from isolated deal making.

To make that transition from singular deal to structured flow of deals, there is yet to be a new kind of paradigm shift. This paradigm shift needs to result in an overall concept which could embrace and convert dispersed, unrelated contextual elements into resources. These resources are then stringed together to form a symbiotic struc-ture like piecing together Lego blocks.

This symbiotic structure is then made to function as a processing mechanism for converting raw contextual elements into ongoing value creation and value exchanges. It is meant to be able to process a flow of deals instead of just a one-off deal. The processes required to pull this off could very messy, involving multiple rounds of negotiation and bargaining, and multiple mixes and matches. We will gross over these messy steps in this chapter.

Conversion could take place on a massive scale Because our exclusive focus in this research has been on figuring out the nature of entrepreneurial work on the transactional sphere, which is on the interface between the firm and its context of exchange, we have so far put aside our focus on the operation core activities. This is where most of the exciting things are being reported to be happening: the locus of innovation and reinvention.

Here you have the likes of Menlo Park, a laboratory for experimentations on finding a transformation process to turn these raw materials into a light bulb, and those materials into a micro-chip. We might as well call this as the transformational space, in contrast to the transactional space this chapter is concentrating on.

But even here we are beginning to witness a striking parallel. If we consider the role of the operating core as a transformational mechanism, we could consider the role of these symbiotic structures as conversion mechanisms. It is about the conversion of contextual elements into resources so that they could create marketable value; it is also about the conversion of doubters into buyers so that transactional value could be realized. The massification of internal transformation requires the massification of external conversion as a precondition.

Through gaining access to these examples, the role of the founder entrepreneur in the transactional sphere has just come to view. When the singular deal structure is reconceived into a mechanism capable processing large scale deal flow, in other words into a mechanism of mass conversion, this is analogous to the reconceptualization of handicraft operation into an assembly line operation.

It is a Henry Ford kind of contribution, albeit that it is happening in the transactional sphere, not in the internal transformational sphere. Once we move onto the massification level, then the target of the transactional operation shift from individual to population, from singular preference to social aspiration. With this we now reach the point where we began to appreciate the need for contextual shift leveraging work. What has the more brilliant entrepreneurs been doing with regards to the other side of the transactional reality? To be able to make this mental shift is what has enabled Ralph Lauren, formerly a tie salesman, to become the grand master of dream fulfillment.

Contextual Shifts Leveraging Work

The first major breakthrough in our exploration has been the discovery of a bewildering variety of conversion mechanisms, conceived and constructed by founder entrepreneurs across industries. But even more surprising new discoveries are waiting for us around the corner. There is yet another level of transactional imaginativeness, which could push performance up another quantum level.

To fully appreciate this requires an ability to see the missing piece in the mass conversion mechanism construction. In our earlier work we have identified the importance of paying attention to the contextual shifts, but we have not seen how contextual shifts could be leveraged operationally.

A contextual shift refers to a convergence of discontinuities in the environment which collectively reconditions the existential circumstances of certain targeted population, thereby invalidating the usefulness and relevance of the current supply conventions. As a result of contextual shift, entire population will have their tested and truth existential based removed, and will be forced to move on in search of new solu-tions.

Because we had not been able to zoom into the transactional sphere in our first phase of research, the interpretive and interactive interplays with contextual shift in the concrete were not captured. This time we discover that there has to be a conversion process, but on the demand side of the exchange equation.

Again this is largely invisible to the non-discerning eyes. And this is usually kept as top business secret. Entrepreneurs would not want to publicize how they "see" their customer except for the part which could be released for public consumption.

The unique Customer Picture as a rule is not released to the public because of the need for the firm to differentiate. Need for contextual insight: the logic to bring this into the open for the purpose of this research, let us start by retracing the logic. Perhaps with the following illustration, we could have some idea about the kind of challenge these transactional innovators would have to face. The movement of China from a centrally planned economy to that of a market economy is a contextual shift. Prior to that there were the gathering of strong forces which collectively created this discontinuity, and given that these new set of forces will grow in intensity, this trend is predicted to last for a long time.

As a result the existential conditions of all Chinese in the Mainland are being fundamentally altered. But how do you convert your observations about the impact of this social reconditioning event, which is creeping out in every seams of the society in varying form, in different intensity, and in endless proliferation of ways into a coherent theme?

For without a coherent image of how these are being converted into concrete demand, your enterprise could not provide a focused, structured and stable supply of solutions through the transactional sphere. Without such understanding how could you visualize what the emerging transactional reality will likely be, and how would you position your company in advance for a leading position within this emerging reality? This is a test of interpretative excellence.

In other words, if social reconditioning will dislodge the existing consumers from their comfort zone, into what concrete pockets will they be forced into? Where is the new catchments area, and what should the entrepreneurs be building within that new catchments area so that the full benefits of the contextual forces pushing the potential consumers into new pockets could be leveraged and captured? The choice of this focal theme could determine whether an enterprise could become a great player or a passenger. There are a lot of passengers, those who had failed to leverage on contextual shifts.

Demand Formation Chain

The search of contextual insight should ideally end up with a mental product: the demand formation chain. Why do we need that kind of conception? The economics literature could start its theory construction effort with the concept of demand.

The entrepreneurship literature does not have the same luxury. Entrepreneur has to probe much deeper, to conduct an infinite regress into a series of pre-conditions which could giving rise to the demand, and in most case, to participate in the articulation of the vague feelings into concrete expression of demand. The infinite regress will hopefully guide us to the ground of certainty on which great enterprises could be built.

This focuses on the other fifty per cent of the transactional reality and requires another form of transactional imagination. Imagine an entrepreneur conducting business in a city facing the sea, on the brink of a continental block completely engulfed in Communist transformation. The city operates on a Capitalistic norm, a colony operating under British influence. This city's livelihood has always been based farming, fishing and on trade, which was interrupted by war in the Pacific.

After the war and the beginning of Com-munist transformation around the city there has been an influx of textile manufacturers, relocating from the Mainland, who brought in industrial production on a scale much larger than the recovering agricultural, fishery and trading sectors. Along with that came a natural extension of the textile foo-thold, the fashion and garment industry.

The industrial sector further gain ground as a plastic flower industry began to take off. You were one of the major plastic flower manufacturers, one of the few who could see the benefit of turning the refugee influx to be factory workers.

Business are working very well for you, your factory has been growing by leaps and bounds. If you were an entrepreneur living through the same set of circumstances, what future do you see? The entrepreneur in question saw a crisis that was coming and decide to completely withdraw from plastic flower industry. He sold it out at the peak of the industry, when everybody was still having a rosy dream. He also saw something else emerging on the horizon, and decided to switch into it, full force and full throttle. He saw something that most did not see, despite that fact that most contempora-ries are living through the same set of circumstance.

One of the hallmarks of an entrepreneur is that he/she could see what other people could not see. But there is no systematic study on what and how these entrepreneurs see, and why seeing what other people could not see are so important.

This "seeing" is the foundation of strategy-making and for the entrepreneur in question, strategy switching. To completely commit entrepreneurial resources to a direction for decades would call for the de-velopment of ingenious ways to ascertain the future. For without that sense of certainty how could en-trepreneurs develop macro-structures? Macro-structure needs to be sustainable, and within the context of exchange, large scale transactional processing must presume large scale demand flow.

There has to be a continuous reproduction of demand in order that these could be sustainable. And this reproduction mechanism needs to be discovered.

How could one construct a career structure for thousands of employees, and enable each of them to secure a long term future with the organization, without a sense of what the business will be coming from?

Creating a career structure for thousands of employee is different from seeking an employment in a company. It is a completely different task.

The entrepreneur in question saw the following:

- The influx of refugee was going to continue unabated. This would result in the swelling of the population. This influx was assured because of the ongoing transformational experiments in China. This would bring in an increasing number of workers and business talents from the rest of China. There would be additional inflow of capitalistic talents to this colony, beyond the first batch of textile manufacturers. When the trading heritage, competencies and global network were combined with industrial production competencies, there would be more and more export oriented industries being born to meet the need for worldwide increase in consumption. The cutting off of China would deprive China from competing with Hong Kong for this growing market. And the fact that Hong Kong had been able to carve out a niche from Japan in the textile and manufacturing field was an indication of the viability of an alternative industry formation model.

- These immigrants would need jobs and would need shelter. When the trading competencies and the industrial competencies coupled together with cheap and eager labour, the future expansion of industrial transformation could be assured.
- The land was fixed and not expandable. Demand for industrial and residential land would grow in leaps and bounds, dependent on the influx and the success in industrial expansion. Industrial land use pattern was fundamentally different from the trading land use pattern, therefore the existing way of thinking about the land use reality will increasing be invalidated. The transformation of land use pattern would give rise to new needs for which most existing players would find it difficult to comprehend. The trading operation requires limited space, and warehouse and shipping would need to be modernized. Hence there is a need for a new kind of land use providers.
- The existing pattern of residential land use would need to be different as well, thus invalidating the relevance of entrenched players who are content with low rise, small population logic.
- The unfolding scenario was predicted to be the acute shortage of land and the ever growing need for more space. Space would become the most critical shortfall, and as therefore the most valuable commodity.

He saw a land use revolution about to begin. He decided to abandon plastic flower work and switch to become a real estate player.

Logic distilled from empirical patterns. The above, in it's abstracted from, is not a unique case. In our phase one research, the cases covered ten industries and over 80 in depth samples. When combined with our new round of studies, we are now in a position to revisit our previous case, and fill in the details in between. The logical flow is now clearly discernable: —Contextual shift is a result of a convergence of discontinuities. It has two parts. On the one hand, one sees the weakening of the forces field which was responsible for the production, reproduction and maintenance of the existing transactional order. On the other hand, we see the gathering strength of the new set of forces.

This new set of converging forces—their continuing strength and gathering momen-tum would need to be carefully ascertained and constantly monitored—will collectively constitute a new force field, and bring about a new transactional reality. —This contextual shift will cause social reconditioning via the production of a new force field and the dissipation of the current force-field. What has been taken for granted as matter-of-fact will increa-singly be invalidated, events contradictory to the expected and normal will crop up to give signal to the discerning eyes. But the same impact of social re-conditioning might not elicit uniform response. This is because it is bound to be producing impact on a population with vastly different initial condi-tions, degree of entrenchment, response elasticity, and gain & loss calculus. Thus one could presume that there will be differential pockets of transactional readiness and affordability.

Only a minor set will have the right level of purchasing power to form a new demand structure. —To be able to ascertain the mechanisms responsible for the production and reproduction of the presenting phenomenon would be critical.

And there could be multiple mechanisms and cycles in op-eration. For example, the change from a farming background to an industrial background will signifi-cantly raise a population's purchasing power, which brings affordability to the new kind of residential premises too luxurious to dream of before the new force field has come into being. This is one exam-ple of the underlying causalities that a founder entrepreneur would have to watch.

The net result of the new force field is the vertical up-shoot of demand and fixed land supply. While the pocket, pace and purchasing power might not be entirely predictable, the level of certainty this analysis could bring about is such that it could assure an entrepreneur to bet on this future Once the entrepreneur is made assured that these pre-conditions and the reproductive mechanisms are not going away, then this constitute a base on which we could exercise the transactional imagination.

The two sides of the transactional reality could now come together to give a two sided picture. On the one side, the understanding of the demand formation mechanism and reproduction cycles, which is our level five concerns. On the other side, the readiness and ingenuity to construct large scale transactional structures, which is our level four concerns. Inter relating these two give us a more comprehensive picture: mass transaction requires mass demand as pre-condition.

For the specific entrepreneurs in question, the possibilities for servicing the real estate need with critical shortage in sight now call for another level of ingenuity. His effort has been translated into a multiplex of win-win structures in different extended form. He then inter-related these structures into a holistic cluster to be able to serve the flood of demand, leveraging on his insight. Let us see the range of symbiotic structures which he could consider building up:

- *Structure one*: From construction to real estate develop-ment to interior design & decoration to property management

- *Structure two*: The land acquisition to land conversion value chains
- *Structure three*: Land financing, construction financing, mortgage financing, to re-mortgage financ-ing provide a foundation for interlinking banks, real estate developer, users, speculators together
- *Structure four*: Government land sales, tax, stamp duties, land titles administration to be working in harmony with real estate development need.
- *Structure five*: Real estate developer and lawyers on the property right side
- *Structure six*: Real estate developer and the real estate sales agencies, banks and finance company over the creation of the primary and secondary market.

Impact of Transactional Imagination Combining the context restructuring work with the contextual shift leveraging work has lead this entrepreneurs in question into a leading player in Hong Kong. The powerfulness of playing with our imaginative faculty on both sides of the transactional reality could play off handsomely. All of the above requires extensive interpretation of and intervention into the external context. Given the limited space of this chapter, we have only distilled the basic forms without going into a lot of con-tents.

Implications for Theory

The nature of the firm: the dual core metaphor Viewed from the angle of this discovery, our dominant literature in strategy, management, organization and entrepreneurship has missed out on the transactional imperative. The underlying model of the firm would need to be reconceived. Our dominant metaphor, which has informed theoretical formulation through the concept of the firm, has been based on that of a single nucleated image.

There are various expressions of that metaphor: There are different ways of seeing the firms, but most are based on an underlying image of a single nucleus the transformational core:

- An input—transformation core —output model
- A core and peripheral model (core competencies) (Hamel and Prahalad)
- A technical core and the need to protect the stability of the core (Thompson)
- The operating core concept as at the base of all organizational forms, which is a synthesis of most of organization literature up to that time (Mintzberg)

Our finding indicates that our dominant metaphor has better be changed, if we want to make our knowledge relevant and useful to entrepreneurs. There are so many entrepreneurs who started the enterprises with a misconception that only one set of core competencies will make it work. There is a huge area of knowledge, competencies, relationships that need to be in place that are missing entirely from the literature.

The information technology, for example, is full of entrepreneurs passionate about the promise of technological transformation, but has no clues on how to get those wonderful ideas to the market. We are proposing that if we want to see to it that a firm could be alive and kicking, it has to have two cores. One core will remain the same: playing the operational role. The other core will have to play the transactional role. To make a distinction between the two cores, we will consider the first one as being engaged in transformational role.

The core process for the second one is the conversion process. Making the conversion core visible If we take this dual core metaphor, it would means what it takes to make the thing could be conceived as entirely different what it takes to sell the things. It requires two kinds of core competencies.

It is subjected to two sets of logics. Performance breakthroughs, like those in the transformational side, also require paradigm shifts.

So far our knowledge on the second core is still very sketchy. But the transactional horizon is full of amazing creativity and masterly acts, waiting for us to explore. The roles of the founder entrepreneurs: dual task model. If we follow the argument above, we need to think about the roles of the founder entrepreneur in new ways.

There are now at least two core sets of roles:

- To ensure transactional success
- To ensure transformational success.

What we need to think about is whether the two core sets of role might actually demand different sets of knowledge, competencies and network base. That whether asking the core competence to be from the same person would be too much of a stretch.

What we have discovered is the issue of cumulative advantage in the transactional sphere. Our observation of the job of transactional innovator indicates that solution generation resourcefulness is critically dependent on knowledge, competencies and relationships, in particularly those who could produce and reproduce a cumulative and ever-widening network of contacts.

Just having knowledge would not bring in a lot of solution resourcefulness. Because the construction of symbiotic structures requires a lot of mixes and matches, you need to have a lot of relationships, or a large pool to draw on for information, ideas, pattern of evolving trends in order than this could be multiple. Pure theoretical knowledge and rapid learning through books will limit the innovative possibility.

The analogy with Lego is instructive; you need to have pools of concrete building block in order that you could build out the structures. New knowledge building tradition needed: The founder, micro-foundations and macro-structures. The founder entrepreneurs are probably among those who are most critically in need of the kind of knowledge which are conceived and formulated on a philosophical foundation which stresses actor-dependent causalities, on micro-foundations and on macro-structures. This kind of knowledge could turn a situation from death to life, from low to spectacular performance.

Let us reconsider what 25 kind of knowledge challenge is being put before us if we want to help founder entrepreneurs do what they have to do? Perhaps the most critical one is for founders to ensure that the new born could earn its birthright. But unlike biological procreation, which is a result of thousands of years of encoded evolu-tionary knowledge, entrepreneurial creation regularly come into being without all the necessarily in-gredients for survival.

It is a contrived existence, based on limited understanding, and from what we have discovered, a lot of misconceptions. The statistics of venture procreation is littered with high mortality, as much as ninety per cent. In this research, we have identified how actor could play a part in flipping a situation from failure to conclude deals to creating value through contracts, by finding win-win structures.

We have also seen actor could change the transactional reality by re-structuring the contextual elements. And we have seen that spectacular performance could result from interpreting the context in intelligent manner. The theoretical link between actor and macro-structure could be established.

NEW IMMIGRANT ENTREPRENEURS

The legend of the diligent and successful immigrant is repeated in many present-day industry articles written about Silicon Valley entrepreneurs. Indian and Chinese immigrants are an important factor of production in the runaway high-tech US economy of the 1990s.

Immigration and entre-preneurship: is there really some mutually enforcing interdependence between these two proud elements of American heritage and history? Does immigration really inspire entrepreneurship? Does it in some way fuel change and therefore stimulate the "creative destruction" - the foundation of capitalism?

It is widely reported that more than one-third of Silicon Valley engineers are foreign-born, most from India or China. Business Week reported in its December 7, 1998 issue that nearly 40 per cent of the Silicon Valley startups in the 1990s have at least one founder of Indian origin.

Throughout history, waves and waves of immigrants have strengthened the US economy – and there is very little evidence that this will change any time soon. Annalee Saxenian is an associate professor in the Department of City and Regional Planning at the University of California, Berkeley. In the early nineties, she wrote a widely successful book, Regional Advantage: Culture and Competition In Silicon Valley And Route 128. She is widely accepted as the foremost authority on Silicon Valley economics. Over the last two years, in a project sponsored by the Public Policy Institute of California, Saxenian has been researching how Chinese and Indian engineers are creating a new model of immigrant entrepreneurship in Silicon Valley. The following are excerpts from our discussions with her on this theme.

Thomas Kurian: Your recent research has focused on explaining California's new immigrant entrepreneurs, most particularly Indian and Chinese immigrants in Silicon Valley. Could you expand on what the scope and objective of your work is?

Annalee Saxenian: My current research explores why we are seeing increasing numbers of immigrant entrepreneurs in Silicon Valley.

The shift is the result of two convergent factors: First, in contrast to their predecessors, these Chinese and Indian immigrants are highly educated. Many are educated in the elite engineering institutions of their home countries, as well as holding graduate degrees from the US.

Their growing presence reflects changes in US immigration law that, since the mid-1960s, encouraged privileged skilled immigrants.

Second, these immigrants have found their way to Silicon Valley, which has perhaps the most open and meritocratic labour markets and work culture in the world. This has made it possible for recent immigrants to quickly gain business experience and contacts in the technology world.

The most distinctive characteristic of the "new" immigrant entrepreneurs is their continued reliance on traditional ethnic networks within the region (in the form of professional groups like The Indus Entrepreneur that provide sources of capital, information, skill, and role models) alongside a comparable reliance on technologies that allow them to be connected to individuals, businesses, and regions anywhere in the world.

While immigrants often stayed in touch with family and friends in their countries of origin, these new immigrants are building close business ties to formerly poor regions of the world and in the process, are transforming the economic opportunities in those regions as well.

In previous generations, immigrants like Andrew Carnegie have been instrumental in creating wealth and economic progress through entrepreneurship. Is this trend in Silicon Valley different to previous ones? How? Silicon Valley's immigrants are certainly creating wealth and economic progress through entrepreneurship, just as previous waves of immigrants did.

The primary difference is that the scale of entrepreneur--ship and wealth creation is far greater than in the past because of the tremendous dynamism of Silicon Valley and its greater openness to immigrant contributions.

There is a knowledge gap from being a student or engineer in India to becoming an entrepreneur in Silicon Valley. How do immigrants develop these skill sets once they are in Silicon Valley? Most immigrant engineers in Silicon Valley work for at least 5 to 10 years in established technology companies before attempting to start their own firms. In the process, they learn about how business is done in Silicon Valley and about market opportunities.

They also develop their own networks of contacts who they then rely on once they start a company. In addition, the professional associations that I mentioned above, such as TiE, consciously seek to provide the skills, mentorship, role models and even capital needed for Indian immigrants to become entrepreneurs. The venture capital community probably plays a significant role. What is their role in the development of immigrant entrepreneurs?

The mainstream venture capital community in Silicon Valley was historically not a significant source of funding for immigrant entrepreneurs, largely because immigrants lacked contacts or confidence to approach them. So the early immigrant entrepreneurs tended to bootstrap businesses with their own funds and contributions from friends and family members.

As a result, a small number of venture capital funds such as Walden International Investment Group, Draper International and Alpine Technology Ventures emerged in the 1980s and early 1990s to support Chinese and Indian entrepreneurs in particular. Groups like TiE have also played an active role in funding Indian entrepreneurs.

Finally, with growing recognition of the entrepreneurial contributions of immigrants, the mainstream venture capital community has increasingly targeted the Chinese and Indian immigrant populations.

Is the entrepreneurial role of immigrants more prono-unced in Silicon Valley when compared to other high tech regions like Route 128, North Carolina or Austin? I don't have data on this, but I would be surprised if it were not the case. To begin with, there is more immigrant engineers in Silicon Valley than in the other technology regions of the US. Moreover, my sense is that the networks in Silicon Valley remain more open than elsewhere.

Obviously, immigrants in Silicon Valley have contributed to the US economic progress. What are the lessons learned? What changes in public policy, if any, could accelerate this economic dynamism? This economic success suggests that there is a need to recognize the mutually beneficial connections between immigration policy, trade policy and economic development. I believe that the US should continue to encourage skilled immigration because it contributes to wealth and job creation as well as to trade and economic development.

METHODS OF FINANCIAL MANAGEMENT

In the field of financing there are various methods to procure funds. Funds may be obtained from long-term sources as well as from short-term sources. Long-term funds may be availed by owners that are shareholders, lenders by issuing debentures, from financial institutions, banks and public at large. Short-term funds may be availed from commercial banks, public deposits, etc. Financial leverage or trading on equity is an important method by which a finance manager may increase the return to common shareholders.

At the time of evaluating capital expenditure projects methods like average rate of return, pay back, internal rate of returns, net present value and profitability index are used. A firm can increase its profitability without affecting its liquidity by an efficient utilization of the current resources at the disposal of the firm.

A firm can increase its profitability without affecting its liquidity by an efficient management of working capital. Similarly for the evaluation of a firm's performance there are different methods. Ratio analysis is a popular technique to evaluate different aspects of a firm. An investor takes in to account various ratios to know wheather investment in a particular company will be profitable or not. These ratios enable him to judge the profitability, solvency, liquidity and growth aspect of the firm.

FINANCIAL MANAGEMENT IN INDIA

In the country like India there is a changing scenario of financial management. As the economy is opening up and global participation is increasing very fast, the opportunities have no limits. Presently financial management passes through an era of experimentation as a larger part of finance activities are carried out.

A few highlights in this context:

- Interest rates are free from regulations.
- Rupee is fully convertible in current account.
- Optimum debt equity mix is possible.
- Maintaining share prices are also crucial. In liberalized scenario the capital market is an important avenue of funds for business.
- Ensuring management control is vital especially in the light of foreign participation.

CORPORATE VALUATION

Use Equity Multiples (as opposed to Enterprise Multiples). In order to consider how valuing a Financial Institution's balance sheet is different from a non-Financial firm. Consider how an industrials firm wields capital machinery (asset) and the loans it used to finance that asset (liabilities). The line is blurred in Financial Institutions, which must hold deposit accounts (assets) to fuel the issuance of loans. The same accounts are considered loans as they are held in ownership not of the bank, but of the individual client.

Discounted Cash Flow (DCF) Model

You'll need the FCFE (Free Cash Flow for Equity), which is the amount of money that is returned to shareholders. Calculate a FCFF (Free Cash Flow to the Firm): EBIT(1-tax rate)-Capital Expenditures+(Depreciation & Amortization) - (Net increase in working capital)= FCFF

FCFF-Debt+Cash=FCFE

Use the Capital Asset Pricing Model, not the Weighted Average Cost of Capital (for the same reasons one uses Equity Multiples in relative valuation) to determine the cost of equity (the return required by shareholders in order to make the decision to invest in a financial institutions)

Bank

The First Provincial Bank of Taiwan in Taipei, Republic of China was formerly the central bank of the Republic of China and issued the New Taiwan dollar. A bank is a business that provides banking services for profit. Traditional banking services include receiving deposits of money, lending money and processing transactions. Some banks (called Banks of Issue) issue banknotes as legal tender. Many banks offer ancillary financial services to make additional profit; for example: selling insurance products, investment products or stock broking.

Currently in most jurisdictions the business of banking is regulated and banks require permission to trade. Authorisation to trade is granted by bank regulatory authorities and provide rights to conduct the most fundamental banking services such as accepting deposits and making loans. There are also financial institutions that provide banking services without meeting the legal definition of a bank. Banks have a long history, and have influenced economies and politics for centuries.

The word bank comes from the early modern English banke, from French banque, an adaptation of Italian banca feminine, "used side by side," and in same sense, with banco masculine; adaptation of Teutonic bank, banc, "bench." The double form and gender in Romanic, cf. Italian, Spanish, Portuguese banco, banca, Provençal banc, banca, French banc, banche, are apparently original (cf. medieval Latin bancus, banca), and due to the double gender of the German: Old High German der, diu banch, Middle High German der, die banc, early modern and dialect German der, die bank.

The original meaning "shelf, bench" was extended in Italian to that of "tradesman's stall, counter, money-changer's table, mensa argentaria, whence "money-shop, bank," a use of the word which passed, with the trade of banking, from Italy into other countries. In this sense, Italian uses both banco and banca, Spanish and Portuguese the masculine banco; but in French the Italian feminine banca was adapted as banque, whence English banke, bank. The word is thus ultimately identical with Bench and Bank.

Italian, monte "mount, heap, amount, stock," was used in some of the senses of "bank," the notion that the name banco, banca, originated in a German rendering of monte is erroneous: German bank had no such sense as "mount, heap," only that of "bench, shelf." Rather is it the fact, that in the development of banking, the banco of the money-changer, and the monte or "joint-stock capital" were at length combined, and bank applied in English to both. The terms bankrupt and "broke" are similarly derived from banca rotta, which refers to an out-of-business bank, having its bench physically broken. Money lenders in Northern Italy originally did business in open areas, or big open rooms, with each lender working from his own bench or table.

Traditionally, a bank generates profits from transaction fees on financial services and from the interest it charges for lending. In recent history, with historically low interest rates limiting banks' ability to earn money by lending deposited funds, much of a bank's income is provided by overdraft fees and riskier investments.

BOARD COMPOSITION

Some researchers have found support for the relationship between frequency of meetings and profitability. Others have found a negative relationship between the proportion of external directors and firm performance, while others found no relationship between external board membership and performance. In a recent paper Bagahat and Black found that companies with more independent boards do not perform better than other companies. It is unlikely that board composition has a direct impact on firm performance.

Remuneration/Compensation

The results of previous research on the relationship between firm performance and executive compensation have failed to find consistent and significant relationships between executives' remuneration and firm performance. Low average levels of pay-performance alignment do not necessarily imply that this form of governance control is inefficient. Not all firms experience the same levels of agency conflict, and external and internal monitoring devices may be more effective for some than for others.

Some researchers have found that the largest CEO performance incentives came from ownership of the firm's shares, while other researchers found that the relationship between share ownership and firm performance was dependent on the level of ownership. The results suggest that increases in ownership above 20% cause management to become more entrenched, and less interested in the welfare of their shareholders.

Firm performance has been found to be positively associated with share option plans. These plans direct managers' energies and extend their decision horizons toward the long-term, rather than the short-term, performance of the company.

Attention to Corporate Governance

Corporate governance issues are receiving greater attention in both developed and developing countries as a result of the increasing recognition that a firm's corporate governance affects both its economic performance and its ability to access long-term, low-cost investment capital. In response to calls by OECD ministers, a revised version of its "Principles of Corporate Governance" was produced in 2004.

Numerous high-profile cases of corporate governance failure have focused the minds of governments, companies and the general public on the threat posed to the integrity of financial markets, although it is not clear that any system will or should prevent business failures, or that it is possible to provide a guarantee against fraud.

Corporate Governance concerns have been widely studied. For the United States, an analysis of these concerns has been published by the New York Society of Securities Analysts in their 2003 Corporate Governance Handbook. What constitutes good and bad corporate governance is an on-going debate in politics, civil society, and academia. For an international survey of the scientific literature see Becht, Bolton and Roell 2002.

The OECD publishes an annual paper on corporate governance. First issued in 1999, this chapter has provided the framework for regional corporate governance roundtables in cooperation with the World Bank around the world. It has been endorsed as one of the Financial Stability Forum's 12 key standards, and form the basis for the World Bank's Review of Observance of Standards and Codes.

Principal-agent Problem

In economics, the principal-agent problem treats the difficulties that arise under conditions of incomplete and asymmetric information when a principal hires an agent. Various mechanisms may be used to try to align the interests of the agent with those of the principal, such as piece rates/commissions, profit sharing, efficiency wages, the agent posting a bond, or fear of firing. The principal-agent problem is found in most employer/employee relationships, for example, when stockholders hire top executives of corporations.

Overview

In economics, the problem of motivating one party to act on behalf of another is known as 'the principal-agent problem'. The principal-agent problem arises when a principal compensates an agency for performing certain acts that are useful to the principal and costly to the agent, and where there are elements of the performance that are costly to observe.

This is the case to some extent for all contracts that are written in a world of information asymmetry, uncertainty and risk. Here, principals do not know enough about whether (or to what extent) a contract is or has been satisfied. The solution to this information problem – closely related to the moral hazard problem – is to ensure (as far as possible) the provision of appropriate incentives so that agents act in the way principals wish. In terms of game theory, it involves changing the rules of the game so that the self-interested rational choices that the principal predicts the agent will make coincide with the choices the principal desires. Even in the limited arena of employment contracts, the difficulty of doing this in practice is reflected in a multitude of compensation mechanisms ('the carrot') and supervisory schemes ('the stick'), as well as in critique of such mechanisms as e.g. Deming expresses in his Seven Deadly Diseases of management.

Employment Contract

In the context of the employment contract, individual contracts form a major method of restructuring incentives, by connecting as closely as is optimal the information available about employee performance, and the compensation for that performance. Because of differences in the quantity and quality of information available about the performance of individual employees, the ability of employees to bear risk, and the ability of employees to manipulate evaluation methods, the structural details of individual contracts vary widely, including such mechanisms as "piece rates, options, discretionary bonuses, promotions, profit sharing, efficiency wages, deferred compensation, and so on."

Typically, these mechanisms are used in the context of different types of employment: salespeople often receive some or all of their remuneration as commission, production workers are usually paid an hourly wage, while office workers are typically paid monthly or semimonthly (and if paid overtime, typically at a higher rate than the hourly rate implied by the salary). The way in which these mechanisms are used is different in the two parts of the economy which Doeringer and Piore called the "primary" and "secondary" sectors.

The secondary sector is characterised by short-term employment relationships, little or no prospect of internal promotion, and the determination of wages primarily by market forces. In terms of occupations, it consists primarily of low or unskilled jobs, whether they are blue-collar (manual-labour), white-collar (e.g. filing clerks), or service jobs (e.g. waiters). These jobs are linked by the fact that they are characterized by "low skill levels, low earnings, easy entry, job impermanence, and low returns to education or experience."

Non-financial Compensation

Part of this variation in incentive structures and supervisory mechanisms may be attributable to variation in the level of intrinsic psychological satisfaction to be had from different types of work. Sociologists and psychologists frequently argue that individuals take a certain degree of pride in their work, and that introducing performance-related pay can destroy this "psycho-social compensation", because the exchange relation between employer and employee becomes much more narrowly economic, destroying most or all of the potential for social exchange. Evidence for this is inconclusive – Deci, and Lepper, Greene and Nisbett find support for this argument; Staw suggests other interpretations of the findings.

Team Production

On a related note, Drago and Garvey use Australian survey data to show that when agents are placed on individual pay-for-performance schemes, they are less likely to help their coworkers. This negative effect is particularly important in those jobs that involve strong elements of 'team production', where output reflects the contribution of many individuals, and individual contributions cannot be easily identified, and compensation is therefore based largely on the output of the team.

In other words, pay-for-performance increases the incentives to free-ride, as there are large positive externalities to the efforts of an individual team member, and low returns to the individual. The negative incentive effects implied are confirmed by some empirical studies, eg Newhouse for shared medical practices (costs rise and doctors work fewer hours as more revenue is shared), and Leibowitz and Tollison find that larger law partnerships typically result in worse cost containment.

As a counter, peer pressure can potentially solve the problem, but this depends on peer monitoring being relatively costless to the individuals doing the monitoring/censuring in any particular instance (unless one brings in social considerations of norms and group identity and so on). Studies suggest that profit-sharing, for example, typically raises productivity by 3-5%, although there are some selection issues (Prendergast).

Empirical Evidence

There is however considerable empirical evidence of a positive effect of compensation on performance (although the studies usually involve "simple" jobs where aggregate measures of performance are available, which is where piece rates should be most effective).

In one study, Lazear saw productivity rising by 35% (and wages by 12%) in a change from salary to piece rates, with a third of the productivity gain due to worker selection effects.

Paarsch and Shearer also find evidence supportive of incentive and productivity effects from piece rates, as do Banker, Lee, and Potter, although the latter do not distinguish between incentive and worker selection effects. Fernie and Metcalf find that British jockeys perform significantly better when offered prizes for winning races compared to being on fixed retainers. McMillan, Whalley and Zhu and Groves et al look at Chinese agricultural and industrial data respectively and find significant incentive effects. Kahn and Sherer find that better evaluations of white-collar office workers were achieved by those employees who had a steeper relation between evaluations and pay. Nikkinen and Sahlstrom find empirical evidence that agency theory can be used, at least to some extent, to explain financial audit fees internationally.

Four principles of Contract Design

Milgrom and Roberts identify four basic principles of contract design:

- The Informativeness Principle,
- The Incentive-Intensity Principle,
- The Monitoring Intensity Principle, and
- The Equal Compensation Principle.

Informativeness Principle

In the absence of a world of perfect information, Holmstrom developed what became known as the Informativeness Principle. This essentially states that any measure of performance that (on the margin) reveals information about the effort level chosen by the agent should be included in the compensation contract.

This includes, for example, Relative Performance Evaluation – measurement relative to other, similar agents, so as to filter out some common background noise factors, such as fluctuations in demand.

By removing some exogenous sources of randomness in the agent's income, a greater proportion of the fluctuation in the agent's income falls under his control, increasing his ability to bear risk. If taken advantage of, by greater use of piece rates, this should improve incentives.

Incentive-Intensity Principle

However, setting incentives as intense as possible is not necessarily optimal from the point of view of the employer. The Incentive-Intensity Principle states that the optimal intensity of incentives depends on four factors: the incremental profits created by additional effort, the precision with which the desired activities are assessed, the agent's risk tolerance, and the agent's responsiveness to incentives. According to Prendergast, "the primary constraint on performance-related pay is that provision imposes additional risk on workers."

A typical result of the early principal-agent literature was that piece rates tend to 100% (of the compensation package) as the worker becomes more able to handle risk, as this ensures that workers fully internalize the consequences of their costly actions.

In incentive terms, where we conceive of workers as self-interested rational individuals who provide costly effort (in the most general sense of the worker's input to the firm's production function), the more compensation varies with effort, the better the incentives for the worker to produce.

Monitoring Intensity Principle

The third principle – the Monitoring Intensity Principle – is complementary to the second, in that situations in which the optimal intensity of incentives is high correspond to situations in which the optimal level of monitoring is also high. Thus employers effectively choose from a "menu" of monitoring/incentive intensities. This is because monitoring is a costly means of reducing the variance of employee performance, which makes more difference to profits in the kinds of situations where it is also optimal to make incentives intense.

Equal Compensation Principle

The final principle is the Equal Compensation Principle, which essentially states that activities equally valued by the employer should be equally valuable (in terms of compensation, including non-financial things such as pleasantness) to the employee. This relates to the problem that employees may be engaged in several activities, and if some of these are not monitored or are monitored less heavily, these will be neglected, as activities with higher marginal returns to the employee are favoured.

This can be thought of as a kind of "disintermediation" – targeting certain measurable variables may cause others to suffer. For example, teachers being rewarded by test scores of their students are likely to tend more towards teaching 'for the test', and de-emphasise less relevant but perhaps equally or more important aspects of education; while AT&T's practice at one time of rewarding programmers by the number of lines of code written resulted in programs that were longer than necessary – i.e. Programme efficiency suffering.

Following Holmstom and Milgrom (1990) and Baker (1992), this has become known as "multi-tasking" (where a subset of relevant tasks is rewarded, non-rewarded tasks suffer relative neglect). Because of this, the more difficult it is to completely specify and measure the variables on which reward is to be conditioned, the less likely that performance-related pay will be used: "in essence, complex jobs will typically not be evaluated through explicit contracts." Where explicit measures are used, they are more likely to be some kind of aggregate measure, for example, baseball and American Football players are rarely rewarded on the many specific measures available, but frequently receive bonuses for aggregate performance measures such as Most Valuable Player.

The alternative to objective measures is subjective performance evaluation, typically by supervisors. However, there is here a similar effect to "multi-tasking", as workers shift effort from that subset of tasks which they consider useful and constructive, to that subset which they think gives the greatest appearance of being useful and constructive, and more generally to try to curry personal favour with supervisors. (One can interpret this as a destruction of organizational social capital – workers identifying with, and actively working for the benefit of, the firm – in favour of the creation of personal social capital – the individual-level social relations which enable workers to get ahead.

A linear model

The four principles can be summarised in terms of the simplest (linear) model of incentive compensation:

$$w = a + b(e + x + g \times y)$$

where w stands for the wage, e for (unobserved) effort, x for unobserved exogenous effects on outcomes, and y for observed exogenous effects; while g and a represent the weight given to y, and the base salary, respectively. The interpretation of b is as the intensity of incentives provided to the employee.

Nonlinearities

The above discussion on explicit measures assumed that contracts would create the linear incentive structures summarised in the model above. But while the combination of normal errors and the absence of income effects yields linear contracts, many observed contracts are nonlinear. To some extent this is due to income effects as workers rise up a tournament/hierarchy: "Quite simply, it may take more money to induce effort from the rich than from the less well off." In addition, the marginal return to effort may increase: it is more important for a CEO to work hard than for a shop floor worker (eg Murphy 1998 highlights the importance of bonuses for executives). Similarly, the threat of being fired creates a nonlinearity in wages earned versus performance.

Moreover, many empirical studies illustrate inefficient behaviour arising from nonlinear objective performance measures, or measures over the course of a long period (eg a year), which create nonlinearities in time due to discounting behaviour. This inefficient behaviour arises because incentive structures are varying: for example, when a worker has already exceeded a quota or has no hope of reaching it, versus being close to reaching it – eg Healy (1985), Oyer (1997), Leventis (1997). Leventis shows that New York surgeons, penalised for exceeding a certain mortality rate, take less risky cases as they approach the threshold. Courty and Marshke (1997) provide evidence on incentive contracts offered to agencies, which receive bonuses on reaching a quota of graduated trainees within a year. This causes them to 'rush-graduate' trainees in order to make the quota.

OBJECTIVE AND SUBJECTIVE PERFORMANCE EVALUATION

The major problem in measuring employee performance in cases where it is difficult to draw a straightforward connection between performance and profitability is the setting of a standard by which to judge the performance.

One method of setting an absolute objective performance standard - rarely used because it is costly and only appropriate for simple repetitive tasks - is time-and-motion studies, which study in detail how fast it is possible to do a certain task. These have been used constructively in the past, particularly in manufacturing. More generally, however, even within the field of objective performance evaluation, some form of relative performance evaluation must be used. Typically this takes the form of comparing the performance of a worker to that of his peers in the firm or industry, perhaps taking account of different exogenous circumstances affecting that

Subjective Performance Evaluation

Subjective performance evaluation allows the use of a subtler, more balanced assessment of employee performance, and is typically used for more complex jobs where comprehensive objective measures are difficult to specify and/or measure. Whilst often the only feasible method, the attendant problems with subjective performance evaluation have resulted in a variety of incentive structures and supervisory schemes.

One problem, for example, is that supervisors may under-report performance in order to save on wages, if they are in some way residual claimants, or perhaps rewarded on the basis of cost savings. This tendency is of course to some extent offset by the danger of retaliation and/or demotivation of the employee, if the supervisor is responsible for that employee's output. As an example, there have been numerous cases where net profits were apparently underreported on successful Hollywood films, where actors or writers had been promised a percentage of net profits – Cheatham, David, and Cheatham.

Another problem relates to what is known as the "compression of ratings". Two related influences – centrality bias, and leniency bias - have been documented (Landy and Farr 1980, Murphy and Cleveland 1991). The former results from supervisors being reluctant to distinguish critically between workers (perhaps for fear of destroying team spirit), while the latter derives from supervisors being averse to offering poor ratings to subordinates, especially where these ratings are used to determine pay, not least because bad evaluations may be demotivating rather than motivating.

However, these biases introduce noise into the relationship between pay and effort, reducing the incentive effect of performance-related pay. Milkovich and Wigdor (1991) suggest that this is the reason for the common separation of evaluations and pay, with evaluations primarily used to allocate training.

BANKS IN THE ECONOMY

ROLE IN THE MONEY SUPPLY

A bank raises funds by attracting deposits, borrowing money in the interbank market, or issuing financial instruments in the money market or a capital market. The bank then lends out most of these funds to borrowers. However, it would not be prudent for a bank to lend out all of its balance sheet. It must keep a certain proportion of its funds in reserve so that it can repay depositors who withdraw their deposits.

Bank reserves are typically kept in the form of a deposit with a central bank. This behaviour is called fractional-reserve banking and it is a central issue of monetary policy. Some governments (or their central banks) restrict the proportion of a bank's balance sheet that can be lent out, and use this as a tool for controlling the money supply. Even where the reserve ratio is not controlled by the government, a minimum figure will still be set by regulatory authorities as part of bank regulation.

Size of Global Banking Industry

Worldwide assets of the largest 1,000 banks grew 15.5% in 2005 to reach a record $60.5 trillion. This follows a 19.3% increase in the previous year. EU banks held the largest share, 50% at the end of 2005, up from 38% a decade earlier. The growth in Europe's share was mostly at the expense of Japanese banks whose share more than halved during this period from 33% to 13%. The share of US banks also rose, from 10% to 14%. Most of the remainder was from other Asian and European countries.

The US had by far the most banks (7,540 at end-2005) and branches (75,000) in the world. The large number of banks in the US is an indicator of its geographical dispersity and regulatory structure resulting in a large number of small to medium sized institutions in its banking system. Japan had 129 banks and 12,000 branches. In 2004, Germany, France, and Italy had more than 30,000 branches each—more than double the 15,000 branches in the UK.

Bank Crises

Banks are susceptible to many forms of risk which have triggered occasional systemic crises. Risks include liquidity risk (the risk that many depositors will request withdrawals beyond available funds), credit risk (the risk that those that owe money to the bank will not repay), and interest rate risk (the risk that the bank will become unprofitable if rising interest rates force it to pay relatively more on its deposits than it receives on its loans), among others.

Banking crises have developed many times throughout history when one or more risks materialize for a banking sector as a whole. Prominent examples include the U.S. Savings and Loan crisis in 1980s and early 1990s, the Japanese banking crisis during the 1990s, the bank run that occurred during the Great Depression, and the recent liquidation by the central Bank of Nigeria, where about 25 banks were liquidated.

Regulation

The combination of the instability of banks as well as their important facilitating role in the economy led to banking being thoroughly regulated. The amount of capital a bank is required to hold is a function of the amount and quality of its assets. Major banks are subject to the Basel Capital Accord promulgated by the Bank for International Settlements. In addition, banks are usually required to purchase deposit insurance to make sure smaller investors are not wiped out in the event of a bank failure.

Another reason banks are thoroughly regulated is that ultimately, no government can allow the banking system to fail. There is almost always a lender of last resort—in the event of a liquidity crisis (where short term obligations exceed short term assets) some element of government will step in to lend banks enough money to avoid bankruptcy.

Public Perceptions of Banks

In United States history, the National Bank was a major political issue during the presidency of Andrew Jackson. Jackson fought against the bank as a symbol of greed and profit-mongering, antithetical to the democratic ideals of the United States.

Currently, many people consider that various banking policies take advantage of customers. Specific concerns are policies that permit banks to hold deposited funds for several days, to apply withdrawals before deposits or from greatest to least, which is most likely to cause the greatest overdraft, that allow backdating funds transfers and fee assessments, and that authorize electronic funds transfers despite an overdraft.

In response to the perceived greed and socially-irresponsible all-for-the-profit attitude of banks, in the last few decades a new type of banks called ethical banks have emerged, which only make social-responsible investments (for instance, no investment in the arms industry) and are transparent in all its operations. In the US, Credit unions have also gained popularity as an alternative financial resource for many consumers. Also, in various European countries, cooperative banks are regularly gaining market share in retail banking.

Profitability

Large banks in the United States are some of the most profitable corporations, especially relative to the small market shares they have. This amount is even higher if one counts the credit divisions of companies like Ford, which are responsible for a large proportion of those companies' profits.

For example, the largest bank, Citigroup, which for the past 3 years has made more profit than any other company in the world, has only a 5% market share. If Citigroup were to be as dominant in its industry as a Home Depot, Starbucks, or Wal Mart in their respective industries, with a 30% market share — and if its profit margins scaled up proportionally — it would make more money than the top ten non-banking U.S. industries combined.

In the past 10 years in the United States, banks have taken many measures to ensure that they remain profitable while responding to ever-changing market conditions. First, this includes the Gramm-Leach-Bliley Act, which allows banks again to merge with investment and insurance houses. Merging banking, investment, and insurance functions allows traditional banks to respond to increasing consumer demands for "one stop shopping" by enabling cross-selling of products (which, the banks hope, will also increase profitability). Second, they have moved toward risk-based pricing on loans, which means charging higher interest rates for those people who they deem more risky to default on loans.

This dramatically helps to offset the losses from bad loans, lowers the price of loans to those who have better credit histories, and extends credit products to high risk customers who would have been denied credit under the previous system. Third, they have sought to increase the methods of payment processing available to the general public and business clients.

These products include debit cards, pre-paid cards, smart-cards, and credit cards. These products make it easier for consumers to conveniently make transactions and smooth their consumption over time (in some countries with under-developed financial systems, it is still common to deal strictly in cash, including carrying suitcases filled with cash to purchase a home).

However, with convenience there is also increased risk that consumers will mismanage their financial resources and accumulate excessive debt. Banks make money from card products through interest payments and fees charged to consumers and companies that accept the cards. The banks' main obstacles to increasing profits are existing regulatory burdens, new government regulation, and increasing competition from non-traditional financial institutions.

ROLE OF THE ACCOUNTANT

Financial reporting is a crucial element necessary for the corporate governance system to function effectively. Accountants and auditors are the primary providers of information to capital market participants. The directors of the company should be entitled to expect that management prepare the financial information in compliance with statutory and ethical obligations, and rely on auditors' competence.

Current accounting practice allows a degree of choice of method in determining the method of measurement, criteria for recognition, and even the definition of the accounting entity. The exercise of this choice to improve apparent performance (popularly known as creative accounting) imposes extra information costs on users. In the extreme, it can involve non-disclosure of information.

One area of concern is whether the accounting firm acts as both independent auditor and management consultant to the firm they are auditing. This may result in a conflict of interest which places the integrity of financial reports in doubt due to client pressure to appease management. The power of the corporate client to initiate and terminate management consulting services and, more fundamentally, to select and dismiss accounting firms contradicts the concept of an independent auditor.

The Enron collapse is an example of misleading financial reporting. Enron concealed huge losses by creating illusions that a third party was contractually obliged to pay the amount of any losses. However, the third party was an entity in which Enron had a substantial economic stake. In discussions of accounting practices with Arthur Andersen, the partner in charge of auditing, views inevitably led to the client prevailing.

However, good financial reporting is not a sufficient condition for the effectiveness of corporate governance if users don't process it, or if the informed user is unable to exercise a monitoring role due to high costs.

Regulation

Rules Versus Principles

Rules are typically thought to be simpler to follow than principles, demarcating a clear line between acceptable and unacceptable behaviour. Rules also reduce discretion on the part of individual managers or auditors.

In practice rules can be more complex than principles. They may be ill-equipped to deal with new types of transactions not covered by the code. Moreover, even if clear rules are followed, one can still find a way to circumvent their underlying purpose - this is harder to achieve if one is bound by a broader principle.

Enforcement

Enforcement can affect the overall credibility of a regulatory system. They both deter bad actors and level the competitive playing field. Nevertheless, greater enforcement is not always better, for taken too far it can dampen valuable risk-taking. In practice, however, this is largely a theoretical, as opposed to a real, risk.

5

Entrepreneurial Development Project Identification and Selection

MEANING OF PROJECT

A project in business and science is a collaborative enterprise, frequently involving research or design, that is carefully planned to achieve a particular aim. The word project comes from the Latin word projectum from the Latin verb proicere, "to throw something forwards" which in turn comes from pro-, which denotes something that precedes the action of the next part of the word in time and iacere, "to throw".

The word "project" thus actually originally meant "something that comes before anything else happens".When the English language initially adopted the word, it referred to a plan of something, not to the act of actually carrying this plan out. Something performed in accordance with a project became known as an "object".

SPECIFIC USES

School and University

At school, educational institute and university, a project is a research assignment given to a student which generally requires a larger amount of effort and more independent work than is involved in a normal essay assignment. It requires students to undertake their own fact-finding and analysis, either from library/internet research or from gathering data empirically. The written report that comes from the project is usually in the form of a dissertation, which will contain parts on the project's inception, methods of inquiry, analysis.

Engineering Project

The engineering project is a particular type of technological system, embedded in the context of technological systems in general. Engineering projects are, in many countries, specifically defined by legislation, which requires that such projects should be carried out by registered engineers and/ or registered engineering companies. That is, companies with license to carry out such works as design and construction of buildings, power plants, industrial facilities, installation and erection of electrical grid networks, transportation infrastructure and the like.

The scope of the project is specified in a contract between the owner and the engineering and construction parties. As a rule, an engineering project is broken down into design and construction phases. The outputs of the design process are drawings, calculations, and all other design documentation necessary to carry out the next phase.

Project Management

In project management a project consists of a temporary endeavor undertaken to create a unique product, service or result. Another definition is a management environment that is created for the purpose of delivering one or more business products just as to a specified business case. Project objectives define target status at the end of the project, reaching of which is considered necessary for the achievement of planned benefits.

They can be formulated as SMART criteria: Specific, Measurable (or at least evaluable) achievement, Achievable (recently Agreed-to or Acceptable are used regularly as well), realistic (given the current state of organizational resources) and Time terminated (bounded). The evaluation (measurement) occurs at the project closure.

However a continuous guard on the project progress should be kept by monitoring and evaluating. It is also worth noting that SMART is best applied for incremental type innovation projects. For radical type projects it does not apply as well. Goals for such projects tend to be broad, qualitative, stretch/ unrealistic and success driven.

PROJECT IDENTIFICATION

The first step in the project cycle is to identify an issue that a project could address. This usually involves a 'needs assessment' which finds out what community needs are and whom they affect. Only when we know what people really want can we develop an effective project. The needs assessment is followed by a 'capacity assessment' to see what strengths the community has which it can use to address its problems.

The project should seek to strengthen any weaknesses. Some people prefer to use 'appreciative enquiry' instead of needs assessment and capacity assessment. This, in effect, starts with a capacity assessment by asking community members to identify the resources they have and then asks them how they want to use them in the future.

The project can then aim to help the community achieve part of its vision. We might already have a good idea of local needs. They might be quite obvious, or we might have become aware of them during a past project. On the other hand, we might have no idea what a community's needs are. It is important to carry out a needs assessment before planning development work, whether we think we know what the needs are or not.

- The project should come out of what people say they want and not from assumptions that we make.
- Sometimes the needs are not immediately clear or cannot be easily understood.
- By talking to different people, as suggested, be able to understand how problems affect people differently. For example, poor access to clean water may affect women more than men because women have to walk a long way to fetch water.
- *Circumstances change*:
  - There may be new people in the community.
  - There may be new needs.
  - Old needs might have been addressed.
  - Problems might be affecting people differently.
- Needs assessment gives people an opportunity to prioritise their needs, which leads to a more sustainable development project.

The time spent carrying out a needs assessment may vary just as to the contact we have had with a community in the past. In general, needs assessment is done fairly quickly. At this stage, we are trying to gain an impression of needs and who the project beneficiaries might be. We are not looking for too much detail. Further research into stakeholders and causes and effects of the problem is carried out during the design phase of the project cycle.

Try to talk to a variety of people, such as key community members or representatives of community groups. Or use methods that can draw out the views of many people in a short space of time, such as community mapping. We do not want to be raising expectations or wasting people's time. Make sure that the people we talk to include women, men, girls, boys, the elderly, people with disabilities etc. There are many tools that enable communities to identify their needs.

TOOLS

LISTENING

By listening for the issues about which people have the strongest feelings, it is possible to identify the issues that they most want addressed and projects which they are most likely to participate in. A team of people (development workers or village members) ask a community or group questions to find out what people are worried, sad, happy, fearful, hopeful or angry about. The questions should be open-ended. It is important to have a clear idea about what we are looking for so we can make sense of the answers.

INTERVIEWING

This tool helps us to gain greater understanding of the issues. It involves talking to key people in the community in order to discuss their knowledge, experience and understanding of the issues.

These people might already be involved in community development activities, they might be people that the community turn to in times of crisis or those who are seen as the heart of the community. Key people include health workers, traders, religious leaders, village chiefs, pastors and teachers.

When choosing people to interview, make sure their views and opinions are likely to represent those of others in the community. Take care not only to interview the powerful, but also to interview those whose views are not usually heard.

Use open-ended questions such as:

- What are the main problems you face in your area of work?
- What are the main pressures that people in the community face?
- What simple things could be done to improve the situation?

FOCUS GROUPS

This tool is used with a group of 10 –20 people. It helps them to understand and voice some of the problems they face and the needs they have. A focus group enables people with different views to discuss their differences, challenge assumptions and come to a collective understanding of the needs of the community.

By exploring issues together from the start, communities start to own the development intervention.

Questions to stimulate discussion could include the following:

- What are the main pressures that people in the community are facing?
- What simple things could be done to improve the situation?
- If you could change one thing in this community, what would it be? Why?

COMMUNITY MAPPING

This tool involves community members drawing a map of their community to tell their story together. They draw either on the ground, using whatever resources are available. They are given little guidance of what to include.

The important point of the exercise is to discuss what people have drawn. The map might show the natural and physical resources in the area – forests, rivers, roads, houses, wells. It might show important people and organisations.

Once the map has been drawn, encourage discussion by asking questions such as:

- How did you decide what to include? What was excluded?
- What was emphasised? Which are the most important parts?
- What was difficult to represent?
- What were the areas of disagreement?
- What can we learn from the map about the needs of the community?

To gain greater understanding of the issues facing different groups within the community, the groups should work separately. A map by young people may show very different information from that of older women.

Questions for discussion could include:

- What differences are there between the maps?
- Why are there differences?
- How does the information from each map help to make a more complete picture of the community?

Once the needs have been identified, community members should be given the opportunity to say which needs they feel are a priority. Ask them to group their needs into general issues such as water, health, land and food. It does not necessarily matter how they are grouped, but it is important that people can see how their concerns have been included.

Once the needs have been grouped, community members can decide which of the issues should be given priority. Write all of the issues onto separate pieces of paper. Community members then place them in order in a line from the most important to the least important.

Encourage them to discuss and negotiate with each other and to move the pieces of paper around until they all agree. Alternatively, write or draw the needs on separate paper bags. Give each person six seeds, stones or beads to use as counters. Each person in turn is invited to put their counters in the relevant bags, just as to their priorities.

They should put three counters for their first priority, two for their second and one for their third priority. The counters in each bag are then counted and the results announced. The needs are ranked just as to the results. tata hara kiji lila This tool should help to identify the main issue to address. There may be more than one priority issue to start with and the group will have to choose whether to take all priority issues at once or focus on one at a time.

CAPACITY ASSESSMENT

Communities should be encouraged to use their own capacities and resources to address the problems they face. It is therefore important to carry out a capacity assessment after needs assessment to identify strengths that the community could use to address the problems they identified earlier. The project, if needed, should focus on strengthening the community's capacities to address their problems. By doing this, we are facilitating the community to address their problems rather than addressing their problems for them.

Capacity assessment involves six types of assets:

- *Human*: These enable people to make use of their other resources. They include skills, knowledge, ability to work and good health.
- *Social*: These are based on relationships and include organisations and groups within the community, political structures and informal networks.
- *Natural*: These form the local environment and include land, trees, water, air, climate and minerals.
- *Physical*: These are man-made, such as building, transport, water supply and sanitation services, energy sources and telecommunications.
- *Economic*: These are things that people can use to sustain their livelihoods, such as money and savings, grain stores, livestock, tools and equipment.
- *Spiritual*: These include faith, scripture, guidance and prayer.

Using participatory techniques, such as those used for the needs assessment, ask community members to identify their capacities. Remember to ask a range of community members, as different people have different perspectives. Write the capacities onto a large piece of paper and ask community members to identify how they could be used to address the problems identified during the needs assessment. Then ask community members to think about which capacities should be strengthened so that they can start to address their priority problems themselves. This is what the project should focus on.

PROJECT SELECTION

Project selection is the process of evaluating individual projects or groups of projects, and then choosing to implement some set of them so that the objectives of the parent organization will be achieved. This same systematic process can be applied to any area of the organization's business in which choices must be made between competing alternatives.

For example, a manufacturing firm can use evaluation/selection techniques to choose which machine to adopt in a part-fabrication process; a TV station can select which of several syndicated comedy shows to rerun in its 7:30 P.M. weekday time-slot; a construction firm can select the best subset of a large group of potential projects on which to bid; or a hospital can find the best mix of psychiatric, orthopedic, obstetric, and other beds for a new wing. Each project will have different costs, benefits, and risks. Rarely are these known with certainty. In the face of such differences, the selection of one project out of a set is a difficult task. Choosing a number of different projects, a portfolio, is even more complex.

We discuss several techniques that can be used to help senior managers select projects. Project selection is only one of many decisions associated with project management.

To deal with all of these problems, we use decisionaiding models.We need such models because they abstract the relevant issues about a problem from the plethora of detail in which the problem is embedded. Reality is far too complex to deal with in its entirety. An"idealist" is needed to strip away almost all the reality from a problem, leaving only the aspects of the"real" situation with which he or she wishes to deal. This process of carving away the unwanted reality from the bones of a problem is called modeling the problem. The idealized version of the problem that results is called a model. The model represents the problem's structure, its form. Every problem has a form, though often we may not understand a problem well enough to describe its structure.

Models may be quite simple to understand, or they may be extremely complex. In general, introducing more reality into a model tends to make the model more difficult to manipulate. If the input data for a model are not known precisely, we often use probabilistic information; that is, the model is said to be stochastic rather than deterministic.

Again, in general, stochastic models are more difficult to manipulate. [Readers who are not familiar with the fundamentals of decision making might find a book such as The New Science of Management Decisions (Simon, 1977) or Quantitative Business Modeling (Meredith, Shafer, and Turban, 2002) useful.] We live in the midst of what has been called the"knowledge explosion." We frequently hear comments such as"90 per cent of all we know about physics has been discovered since Albert Einstein published his original work on special relativity"; and"80 per cent of what we know about the human body has been discovered in the past 50 years."

In addition, evidence is cited to show that knowledge is growing exponentially. Such statements emphasize the importance of the management of change. To survive, firms should develop strategies for assessing and reassessing the use of their resources. Every allocation of resources is an investment in the future. Because of the complex nature of most strategies, many of these investments are in projects. To cite one of many possible examples, special visual effects accomplished through computer animation are common in the movies and television shows we watch daily. A few years ago they were unknown. When the capability was in its idea stage, computer companies as well as the firms producing movies and TV shows faced the decision whether or not to invest in the development of these techniques. Obviously valuable as the idea seems today, the choice was not quite so clear a decade ago when an entertainment company compared investment in computer animation to alternative investments in a new star, a new rock group, or a new theme park. The proper choice of investment projects is crucial to the long-run survival of every firm.

Daily we witness the results of both good and bad investment choices. In our daily newspapers we read of Cisco System's decision to purchase firms that have developed valuable communication network software rather than to develop its own software.

We read of Procter and Gamble's decision to invest heavily in marketing its products on the Internet; British Airways' decision to purchase passenger planes from Airbus instead of from its traditional supplier, Boeing; or problems faced by school systems when they update student computer labs-should they invest in Windows®- based systems or stick with their traditional choice, Apple®.

But can such important choices be made rationally? Once made, do they ever change, and if so, how? These questions reflect the need for effective selection models. Within the limits of their capabilities, such models can be used to increase profits, select investments for limited capital resources, or improve the competitive position of the organization.

They can be used for ongoing evaluation as well as initial selection, and thus are a key to the allocation and reallocation of the organization's scarce resources.

When a firm chooses a project selection model, the following criteria, based on Souder (1973), are most important:

- Realism The model should reflect the reality of the manager's decision situation, including the multiple objectives of both the firm and its managers. Without a common measurement system, direct comparison of different projects is impossible. For example, Project A may strengthen a firm's market share by extending its facilities, and Project B might improve its competitive position by strengthening its technical staff. Other things being equal, which is better? The model should take into account the realities of the firm's limitations on facilities, capital, personnel, and so forth. The model should also include factors that reflect project risks, including the technical risks of performance, cost, and time as well as the market risks of customer rejection and other implementation risks.
- Capability The model should be sophisticated enough to deal with multiple time periods, simulate various situations both internal and external to the project (*e.g.*, strikes, interest rate changes), and optimize the decision. An optimizing model will make the comparisons that management deems important, consider major

risks and constraints on the projects, and then select the best overall project or set of projects.

- Flexibility The model should give valid results within the range of conditions that the firm might experience. It should have the ability to be easily modified, or to be self-adjusting in response to changes in the firm's environment; for example, tax laws change, new technological advancements alter risk levels, and the organization's goals change.
- Ease of use The model should be reasonably convenient, not take a long time to execute, and be easy to use and understand. It should not require special interpretation, data that are difficult to acquire, excessive personnel, or unavailable equipment. The model's variables should also relate one-to-one with those real-world parameters the managers believe significant to the project. Finally, it should be easy to simulate the expected outcomes associated with investments in different project portfolios.
- Cost Data-gathering and modeling costs should be low relative to the cost of the project and must surely be less than the potential benefits of the project. All costs should be considered, including the costs of data management and of running the model.
- Easy computerization It should be easy and convenient to gather and store the information in a computer database, and to manipulate data in the model through use of a widely available, standard computer package such as Excel®, Lotus 1-2-3®, Quattro Pro®, and like programmes. The same ease and convenience should apply to transferring the information to any standard decision support system.

In what follows, we first examine fundamental types of project selection models and the characteristics that make any model more or less acceptable. Next we consider the limitations, strengths, and weaknesses of project selection models, including some suggestions of factors to consider when making a decision about which, if any, of the project selection models to use.

We then discuss the problem of selecting projects when high levels of uncertainty about outcomes, costs, schedules, or technology are present, as well as some ways of managing the risks associated with the uncertainties. Finally, we comment on some special aspects of the information base required for project selection. Then we turn our attention to the selection of a set of projects to help the organization achieve its goals and show this with a technique called the Project Portfolio Process.

PROJECT SELECTION MODEL

Projects are undertaken for various reasons. Each project should have clear justification and methods defined to show its'worth' taking it. Strategic goals of organization, Market Need, Technological Advancement, Competitive Advantage, Profitability, Project/Portfolio Management Office (PMO), Sponsors are key in project selection.

We presented the gist of few widely-used project selection methods. Decisions are made based on the best information in hand about a particular project at a given point of time.

One can use either Benefit Measurement Methods (Comparative approach) or Constrained Optimization Methods (Mathematical approach) or both to arrive conclusion on project selection. Out of these two benefit measurement method is most commonly used. Benefit measurement methods are based on measuring the benefits in taking up the project and comparing the results against other projects or a strategy benchmark.

Cost-Benefit Analysis, Scoring Models, Economic Models, Discounted Cash Flow(DCF), Net Present Value (NPV), Internal Rate of Return are different types under Benefit measurement methods. Constrained optimization methods uses complex mathematical calculation based on different worst/best case scenarios and probability of outcome and then selecting project on best results.

Generally known methods are Linear programming, nonlinear programming, multi objective programming.

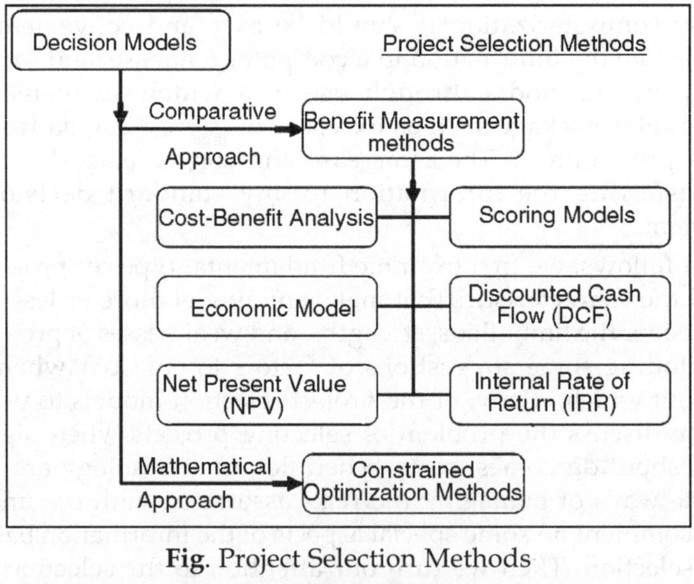

Fig. Project Selection Methods

TYPES OF PROJECT SELECTION MODELS

Of the two basic types of selection models (numeric and nonnumeric), nonnumeric models are older and simpler and have only a few subtypes to consider. We examine them first.

Nonnumeric Models

The Sacred Cow

In this case the project is suggested by a senior and powerful official in the organization. Often the project is initiated with a simple comment such as,"If you have a chance, why don't you look into...," and there follows an undeveloped idea for a new product, for the development of a new market, for the design and adoption of a global data base and information system, or for some other project requiring an investment of the firm's resources.

The immediate result of this bland statement is the creation of a"project" to investigate whatever the boss has suggested. The project is"sacred" in the sense that it will be maintained until successfully concluded, or until the boss, personally, recognizes the idea as a failure and terminates it.

The Operating Necessity

If a flood is threatening the plant, a project to build a protective dike does not require much formal evaluation, which is an example of this scenario. XYZ Steel Corporation has used this criterion (and the following criterion also) in evaluating potential projects. If the project is required in order to keep the system operating, the primary question becomes: Is the system worth saving at the estimated cost of the project? If the answer is yes, project costs will be examined to make sure they are kept as low as is consistent with project success, but the project will be funded.

The Competitive Necessity

Using this criterion, XYZ Steel undertook a major plant rebuilding project in the late 1960s in its steel-bar-manufacturing facilities near Chicago. It had become apparent to XYZ's management that the company's bar mill needed modernization if the firm was to maintain its competitive position in the Chicago market area. Although the planning process for the project was quite sophisticated, the decision to undertake the project was based on a desire to maintain the company's competitive position in that market.

In a similar manner, many business schools are restructuring their undergraduate and MBA programmes to stay competitive with the more forward-looking schools. In large part, this action is driven by declining numbers of tuition-paying students and the need to develop stronger programmes to attract them. Investment in an operating necessity project takes precedence over a competitive necessity project, but both types of projects may bypass the more careful numeric analysis used for projects deemed to be less urgent or less important to the survival of the firm.

The Product Line Extension

In this case, a project to develop and distribute new products would be judged on the degree to which it fits the firm's existing product line, fills a gap, strengthens a weak link, or extends the line in a new, desirable direction. Sometimes careful calculations of profitability are not required. Decision makers can act on their beliefs about what will be the likely impact on the total system performance if the new product is added to the line.

Comparative Benefit Model

For this situation, assume that an organization has many projects to consider, perhaps several dozen. Senior management would like to select a subset of the projects that would most benefit the firm, but the projects do not seem to be easily comparable. For example, some projects concern potential new products, some concern changes in production methods, others concern computerization of certain records, and still others cover a variety of subjects not easily categorized (*e.g.*, a proposal to create a daycare centre for employees with small children). The organization has no formal method of selecting projects, but members of the Selection Committee think that some projects will benefit the firm more than others, even if they have no precise way to define or measure "benefit."

The concept of comparative benefits, if not a formal model, is widely adopted for selection decisions on all sorts of projects. Most United Way organizations use the concept to make decisions about which of several social programmes to fund.

Senior management of the funding organization then examines all projects with positive recommendations and attempts to construct a portfolio that best fits the organization's aims and its budget. Of the several techniques for ordering projects, the Q-Sort (Helin and Souder, 1974) is one of the most straightforward. First, the projects are divided into three groups—*good, fair,* and *poor*—just as to their relative merits. If any group has more than eight members, it is subdivided into two categories, such as *fair-plus* and *fair-minus*. When all categories have eight or fewer members, the projects within each category are ordered from best to worst. Again, the order is determined on the basis of relative merit.

The rater may use specific criteria to rank each project, or may simply use general overall judgment. The process described may be carried out by one person who is responsible for evaluation and selection, or it may be performed by a committee charged with the responsibility. If a committee handles the task, the individual rankings can be developed anonymously, and the set of anonymous rankings can be examined by the committee itself for consensus.

It is common for such rankings to differ somewhat from rater to rater, but they do not often vary strikingly because the individuals chosen for such committees rarely differ widely on what they feel to be appropriate for the parent organization. Projects can then be selected in the order of preference, though they are usually evaluated financially before final selection. There are other, similar nonnumeric models for accepting or rejecting projects. Although it is easy to dismiss such models as unscientific, they should not be discounted casually.

These models are clearly goal-oriented and directly reflect the primary concerns of the organization. The sacred cow model, in particular, has an added feature; sacred cow projects are visibly supported by "the powers that be." Full support by top management is certainly an important contributor to project success (Meredith, 1981). Without such support, the probability of project success is sharply lowered.

Numeric Models: Profit/Profitability

As noted earlier, a large majority of all firms using project evaluation and selection models use profitability as the sole measure of acceptability. As suggested, consider these models first, and then discuss models that surpass the profit test for acceptance.

Payback Period

The payback period for a project is the initial fixed investment in the project divided by the estimated annual net cash inflows from the project. The ratio of these quantities is the number of years required for the project to repay its initial fixed investment. For example, assume a project costs $100,000 to implement and has annual net cash inflows of $25,000. Then Payback period =$100,000/$25,000 = 4 years

This method assumes that the cash inflows will persist at least long enough to pay back the investment, and it ignores any cash inflows beyond the payback period. The method also serves as an (inadequate) proxy for risk. The faster the investment is recovered, the less the risk to which the firm is exposed.

Average Rate of Return

Often mistaken as the reciprocal of the payback period, the average rate of return is the ratio of the average annual profit (either before or after taxes) to the initial or average investment in the project. Because average annual profits are usually not equivalent to net cash inflows, the average rate of return does not usually equal the reciprocal of the payback period. Assume, in the example just given, that the average annual profits are $15,000:

Average rate of return = $15,000/$100,000 = 0.15

Neither of these evaluation methods is recommended for project selection, though payback period is widely used and does have a legitimate value for cash budgeting decisions.

The major advantage of these models is their simplicity, but neither takes into account the time-value of money. Unless interest rates are extremely low and the rate of inflation is nil, the failure to reduce future cash flows or profits to their present value will result in serious evaluation errors.

Other Profitability Models

There are a great many variations of the models just described. These variations fall into three general categories:

1. Those that subdivide net cash flow into the elements that comprise the net flow;
2. Those that include specific terms to introduce risk (or uncertainty, which is treated as risk) into the evaluation;
3. Those that extend the analysis to consider effects that the project might have on other projects or activities in the organization.

Several comments are in order about all the profit-profitability numeric models.

First, let us consider their advantages:

- The undiscounted models are simple to use and understand.
- All use readily available accounting data to determine the cash flows.
- Model output is in terms familiar to business decision makers.
- With a few exceptions, model output is on an "absolute" profit/ profitability scale and allows "absolute" go/no-go decisions.
- Some profit models account for project risk.

The disadvantages of these models are the following:

- These models ignore all nonmonetary factors except risk.
- Models that do not include discounting ignore the timing of the cash flows and the time–value of money.
- Models that reduce cash flows to their present value are strongly biased towards the short run.
- Payback-type models ignore cash flows beyond the payback period.
- The internal rate of return model can result in multiple solutions.
- All are sensitive to errors in the input data for the early years of the project.
- All discounting models are nonlinear, and the effects of changes (or errors) in the variables or parameters are generally not obvious to most decision makers.
- All these models depend for input on a determination of cash flows, but it is not clear exactly how the concept of cash flow is properly defined for the purpose of evaluating projects.

A complete discussion of profit/profitability models can be found in any standard work on financial management. In general, the net present value models are preferred to the internal rate of return models. Despite wide use, financial models rarely include non-financial outcomes in their benefits and costs.

In a discussion of the financial value of adopting project management (that is, selecting as a project the use of project management) in a firm, Githens (1998) notes that traditional financial models "simply cannot capture the complexity and value-added of today's process-oriented firm." The commonly seen phrase "return on investment," or ROI, does not denote any *specific* method of calculation. It usually involves NPV or internal rate of return (IRR) calculations, but we have seen it used in reference to undiscounted average rate of return models and (incorrectly) payback period models.

In our experience, the payback period model, occasionally using discounted cash flows, is one of the most commonly used models for evaluating projects and other investment opportunities. Managers generally feel that insistence on short payout periods tends to minimize the *risks* associated with outstanding monies over the passage of time.

While this is certainly logical, we prefer evaluation methods that discount cash flows and deal with uncertainty more directly by considering specific risks. Using the payout period as a cash-budgeting tool aside, *its primary virtue is its simplicity.*

Real Options

Recently, a project selection model was developed based on a notion well known in financial markets. When one invests, one foregoes the value of alternative future investments. Economists refer to the value of an opportunity foregone as the "opportunity cost" of the investment made.

Numeric Models: Scoring

In an attempt to overcome some of the disadvantages of profitability models, particularly their focus on a single decision criterion, a number of evaluation/selection models that use multiple criteria to evaluate a project have been developed. Such models vary widely in their complexity and information requirements. The examples discussed show some of the different types of numeric scoring models.

Choosing a Project Selection Model

Selecting the type of model to aid the evaluation/selection process depends on the philosophy and wishes of management. Liberatore and Titus (1983) conducted a survey of 40 high-level staff persons from 29 *Fortune 500* firms. Eighty per cent of their respondents report the use of one or more financial models for R & D project decision making. Although their sample is small and nonrandom, their findings are quite consistent with the present authors' experience. None of the respondent firms used mathematical programming techniques for project selection or resource allocation. We strongly favour weighted scoring models for three fundamental reasons. First, they allow the multiple objectives of all organizations to be reflected in the important decision about which projects will be supported and which will be rejected. Second, scoring models are easily adapted to changes in managerial philosophy or changes in the environment.

Third, they do not suffer from the bias towards the short run that is inherent in profitability models that discount future cash flows. This is not a prejudice against discounting and most certainly does not argue against the inclusion of profits/ profitability as an important factor in selection, but rather *it is an argument against the exclusion of nonfinancial factors* that may require a longer-run view of the costs and benefits of a project.

For a powerful statement of this point. It is also interesting to note that Liberatore and Titus found that firms with a significant amount of contract research funded from outside the organization used scoring models for project screening much more frequently than firms with negligible levels of outside funding.

It was also found that firms with significant levels of outside funding were much less likely to use a payback period. The structure of a weighted scoring model is quite straightforward. Its virtues are many. Nonetheless, the actual use of scoring models is not as easy as it might seem. Decision makers are forced to make difficult choices and they are not always comfort able doing so. They are forced to reduce often vague feelings to quite specific words or numbers. Multiattribute, multiperson decision making is not simple. Finally, a multiattribute, multiperson decision model could be constructed from Åstebro's study of key characteristics of technological R & D projects

PROJECT FORMULATION

Project reporting is an essential task for any project and the most frequent report is project status. The project manager will normally write the report and deliver it as a written e-mail update or presentation or perhaps a combination of both. The information will be from the project team and must be current and accurate. Consequently a project manager must ensure that they are fully in touch with project status.

The project report format needs to address the key goals for project reporting:

- Current, accurate and complete information on project progress and the project's RAG [Red, Amber, Green] Status
- Barriers to successful project delivery and what the project team is doing to remove those barriers or prevent them from having an impact
- Understanding of business impact and change
- What actions stakeholders need to take, if any

RAG Status is a simple way to indicate the project status using a traffic light metaphor:

- Red = project is either very delayed or significantly over budget or both
- Amber = project is delayed or over budget or both
- Green = project is on track to deliver as scheduled and within budget tolerances [*i.e.* +/- 10%]

[The actual definitions should be agreed or well-defined beforehand and this RAG status is useful for dashboard style reporting of multiple projects, especially for senior management.]

PROJECT REPORT FORMAT EXAMPLE FOR PROJECT STATUS

The project status report should include current project status, key risks, project metrics and work done, work in progress and work to be started. It should be targeted at the intended audience and contain the level of detail appropriate for that audience.

The frequency, method of update [written, verbal or both] and who gives the project report should be defined beforehand. The following is an example the project report format being used.

PROJECT STATUS

Project is on track to successfully deliver as planned. Slight delay to sign-off of test report but this will not impact final delivery. The project will now move to the deployment phase and the relevant experts have already started these tasks. Current risks are being managed and no final risks have emerged to delay the Go Live date.

KEY RISKS

- Training schedule being delayed by the list of department users not being scheduled. Mitigation is to divert a project team member to accelerate tasks to define list of users to be trained
- Deployment of system to multiple countries is delayed by expert resources not being available as scheduled. Mitigation is to arrange backup people with vendor who will be on call in the event of a resource problem

PROJECT METRICS

- Project schedule is on target with 0 days time delay. 80% of project schedule is now complete
- Project cost is on target. Total project cost variance is -5% and 90% of the budget has been spent

WORK COMPLETED

- Acceptance test phases one and two were completed as scheduled
- Test Report has been produced and is in final approval
- Test environment has now been taken down and will be prepared to support the production use of the new system

WORK IN PROGRESS

- Deployment has started with the installation and configuration of the production environment
- Training material has been finished and is available for online and classroom training.
- Identification of training needs and scheduling of training has just started

WORK TO BE STARTED

- Technical installation report for the production environment will start next week as scheduled
- Preparation of the production training environment will begin following completion of the production environment
- Project closure report and release of resources will start next week

PROJECT REPORT FORMAT EXAMPLE FOR PROJECT STATUS

This audience requires the right level information, which needs to be succinct and focus on the few things that matter rather than everything that can be reported. In particular, the audience will want to know if the project is on track and whether it needs any help with any risks or issues.

In the final analysis the presentation, content and level of detail needs to be determined for the audiences. However, a project will want to "standardise" on a report format to simplify the production and delivery of project information and in particular to not have multiple reports, report formats and potentially giving different or confusing information dependent on which report is read. Following a single report format and adjusting the level of detail for the audience will help to achieve consistency and clarity for all concerned.

IMPORTANCE OF PROJECT REPORT

- It act like a reference guide.
- It is a basis for obtaining loans.
- The government sanction license or certificate of registration.
- It is like a controlling device.

- It supplies information.
- It is used as a basis by promoter to take investment decisions.
- It enables to evaluate the soundness of the project.

SIGNIFICANCE OF PROJECT REPORT

Importance of projects can be highlighted with the following main points:

- Projects serve as catalytic agent of economic development and growth.
- Projects initiative the process of development.
- Projects provide framework for future activities of enterprise.
- Projects also determine the nature of future pattern of services.
- Projects facilitate development of basic infrastructure and environment.
- Projects identification bring about necessary changes in society over period of time.
- Projects help in accelerating the pace of socio cultural development.

After gaining knowledge about the business environment and the role of small scale sector an enterprising individual can think in terms of taking certain concrete steps for taking up his own enterprise.

FORMULATION OF PROJECT

- Taking a first look carefully and critically at the project idea
- Carefully weighing its various components
- Analysing with the assistance of specialists or consultants
- Assessment of the various aspects of an investment proposition
- It is an important stage in the pre-investment phase

STAGES OF PROJECT FORMULATION

- Feasibility Analysis
- Techno-Economic Analysis
- Project Design and Network Analysis
- Input Analysis
- Financial Analysis
- Cost-Benefit Analysis
- Pre-Investment Analysis

Feasibility Analysis:

- First stage in project formulation

- Examination to see whether to go in for a detailed investment proposal or not
- Screening for internal and external constraints

Conclusion could be:

- The project idea seems to be feasible
- The project idea is not a feasible one
- Unable to arrive at a conclusion for want of adequate data

Techno-Economic Analysis:

- *Screens the idea to*:
  - Estimate of potential of the demand for goods/services
  - Choice of optimal technology
  - This analysis gives the project a platform for preparation of
  - Detailed project design

Project Design and Network Analysis:

- It is the heart of the project entity
- It defines the sequence of events of the project
- Time is allocated for each activity
- It is presented in a form of a network drawing
- It helps to identify project inputs, finance needed and cost-benefit profile of the project

Input Analysis:

- Its assesses the input requirements during the construction and operation of the project
- It defines the inputs required for each activity
- Inputs include materials, human resources
- It evaluates the feasibility of the project from the point of view of the availability of necessary resources
- This aids in assessing the project cost

Financial Analysis:

- It involves estimating the project costs, operating cost and fund requirements
- It helps in comparing various project proposals on a common scale
- Analytical tools used are discounted cash flow, cost-volume- profit relationship and ratio analysis
- Investment decisions involve commitment of resources in future, with a long time horizon
- It needs caution and foresight in developing financial forecasts

Cost- Benefit Analysis:

- The overall worth of a project is considered
- The project design forms the basis of evaluation
- It considers costs that all entities have to bear and the benefit connected to it

Pre-investment Analysis:

- The results obtained in previous stages are consolidated to arrive at clear conclusions
- Helps the project-sponsoring body, the project- implementing body and the external consulting agencies to accept/reject the proposal

PLANNING COMMISSIONS GUIDELINES FOR FORMULATION A PROJECT REPORT

In arrange to procedure venture proposals and arrive at investment choices, the planning commission of India has also issued a number of guidelines for preparing formulating realistic industrial projects. The projects formulation stage involves the identification of investment options by the enterprise and in consultation with the Administrative Ministry, the planning commission and other concerned authorities.

The following are the guidelines as given by planning commission of Indian for the formulation of a project Report:

- *General Information*: The feasibility report should include an analysis of industry to which the project belongs It should deal with the past performance of the industry, the description of the type of industry, increase production role of the public sector, allocation of funds, choice of technique etc.
- *Preliminary Analysis of Alternatives*: This should contain present data on the gap between demand and supply for the output, which are to be produced, data on the capacity that would be available from the projects that are in production or under implementation at the time. The report is prepared a complete list of existing plants in the industry giving their capacity and level of production actually attended
- *Project Description*: The feasibility report should provide a brief description of the technology process chosen for the project. Information relevant to determining optimality of the location chose should also be included. The report should contain a list of operational requirement of personal organizational structure envisaged transport costs, activity wise phasing of construction and factor affecting it.
- *Marketing plan*: It should contain the following items. Data in

marketing plan. Demand and prospective plan in each of the areas to be served. The method and data used for making estimates of domestic supply and selection of market areas should be presented estimates of the degree of price sensitively should be presented.

- *Capital Requirements and Costs*: The estimates should be reasonability compete and properly classified. Information on all items of costs should be collected and presented.
- *Operating Requirements and costs*: Operating costs, are essentially those which are incurred after the commencement of commercial production. Information about all items of operating costs should be collected. Operating costs relate to the costs of raw-materials and intermediates, fuel, utilities, labours, repair and maintenance, setting expanses and other expanses.
- *Financial Analysis*: The purpose of this analysis is to present some measures to assess the financial viability of the project. A Preformed balance sheet should be presented. Depreciation should be allowed on the basis specified by the Bureau of public enterprises.
- *Economic Analysis*: Social profitability analysis needs some adjustment in the data relating to the costs and returns to the enterprise. One significant kind of investment involving a correction in input and costs to reproduce the accurate value of foreign exchange labour and capital.

PROJECT APPRAISAL

Project appraisal is a generic term that refers to the process of assessing, in a structured way, the case for proceeding with a project or proposal. In short, project appraisal is the effort of calculating a project's viability. It often involves comparing various options, using economic appraisal or some other decision analysis technique.

Importance of project appraisal:

- It is a capital investment decision
- It has long term effects
- Decision once taken is irreversible
- Expenditures are high

Difficulties in respect of project appraisal:

- Measurement of costs and potential benefits are difficult
- High degree of uncertainty
- Long term spread – time value of money

Process:

- Initial Assessment

- Define problem and long-list
- Consult and short-list
- Develop options
- Compare and select Project

Types of appraisal:

- Financial
  - Cost-benefit analysis
- Economic appraisal
  - Cost-effectiveness analysis
  - Scoring and weighting

METHODS OF PROJECT APPRAISAL

ECONOMIC ANALYSIS

Economic analysis is a process whereby strengths and weaknesses of an economy are analysed. Economic analysis is important in order to understand exact condition of an economy. It can cover a number of important economic issues that keep cropping up within a particular economy, which is being analysed.

Macroeconomics and Economic Analysis

Macroeconomic issues are important aspects of economic analysis process. However, economic analysis can also be done at a microeconomic level. Macroeconomic analysis helps in understanding fundamentals of an economy. Since such a form of analysis operates on a wide scale, it helps one to analyse strengths and weaknesses of particular economies.

Macroeconomic analysis takes into account growth achieved by a particular economy or rather a particular sector of that economy. It tries to find out reasons behind a particular economic phenomena like growth or reversal of economy.

Inflation and Economic Analysis

Many countries of world are plagued by a rising rate of inflation. Economic analysis helps in providing an explanation of why inflation has taken place.

It also suggests ways in which rate of inflation could be brought down, so that economic development could continue.

Economic Analysis and Governmental Policies

Governmental policies and plans, pertaining to economy, have always been an important part of economic analysis. Since policies and plans adopted by a particular government is responsible for shaping an economy, they are always closely scrutinized by various processes of economic analysis.

Economic Ratings and Economic Analysis

Economic rating is another important part of economic analysis, as it provides an accurate picture of how an economy was faring when those ratings were being calculated .

Economic Analysis and Comparison of Economic Policies

It is a good way to analyse an economy by comparing its policies with those followed by other economies. This is all more applicable in case of economies that are of similar types, for example developing economies.

FINANCIAL ANALYSIS

Financial analysis (also referred to as financial statement analysis or accounting analysis) refers to an assessment of the viability, stability and profitability of a business, sub-business or project.

It is performed by professionals who prepare reports using ratios that make use of information taken from financial statements and other reports.

These reports are usually presented to top management as one of their bases in making business decision:

- Continue or discontinue its main operation or part of its business;
- Make or purchase certain materials in the manufacture of its product;
- Acquire or rent/lease certain machineries and equipment in the production of its goods;
- Issue stocks or negotiate for a bank loan to increase its working capital;
- Make decisions regarding investing or lending capital;
- Other decisions that allow management to make an informed selection on various alternatives in the conduct of its business.

Goals

Financial analysts often assess the firm's:

- Profitability - its ability to earn income and sustain growth in both short-term and long-term. A company's degree of profitability is usually based on the income statement, which reports on the company's results of operations;
- Solvency - its ability to pay its obligation to creditors and other third parties in the long-term;
- Liquidity - its ability to maintain positive cash flow, while satisfying immediate obligations;

- Stability- the firm's ability to remain in business in the long run, without having to sustain significant losses in the conduct of its business. Assessing a company's stability requires the use of both the income statement and the balance sheet, as well as other financial and non-financial indicators.

Methods

Financial analysts often compare financial ratios (of solvency, profitability, growth, etc.):

- *Past Performance*: Across historical time periods for the same firm (the last 5 years for example),
- *Future Performance*: Using historical figures and certain mathematical and statistical techniques, including present and future values, This extrapolation method is the main source of errors in financial analysis as past statistics can be poor predictors of future prospects.
- *Comparative Performance*: Comparison between similar firms.

These ratios are calculated by dividing a (group of) account balance(s), taken from the balance sheet and/ or the income statement, by another, for example:

- Net income/ equity = return on equity (ROE)
- Net income/ total assets = return on assets (ROA)
- Stock price/ earnings per share = P/E ratio
- Comparing financial ratios is merely one way of conducting financial analysis.

Financial ratios face several theoretical challenges:

- They say little about the firm's prospects in an absolute sense. Their insights about relative performance require a reference point from other time periods or similar firms.
- One ratio holds little meaning. As indicators, ratios can be logically interpreted in at least two ways. One can partially overcome this problem by combining several related ratios to paint a more comprehensive picture of the firm's performance.
- Seasonal factors may prevent year-end values from being representative. A ratio's values may be distorted as account balances change from the beginning to the end of an accounting period. Use average values for such accounts whenever possible.
- Financial ratios are no more objective than the accounting methods employed. Changes in accounting policies or choices can yield drastically different ratio values.
- Fundamental analysis.

Financial analysts can also use percentage analysis which involves reducing a series of figures as a percentage of some base amount. For example, a group of items can be expressed as a percentage of net income. When proportionate changes in the same figure over a given time period expressed as a percentage is known as horizontal analysis.

Vertical or common-size analysis, reduces all items on a statement to a "common size" as a percentage of some base value which assists in comparability with other companies of different sizes. Another method is comparative analysis. This provides a better way to determine trends. Comparative analysis presents the same information for two or more time periods and is presented side-by-side to allow for easy analysis.

MARKET ANALYSIS

The goal of a market analysis is to determine the attractiveness of a market and to understand its evolving opportunities and threats as they relate to the strengths and weaknesses of the firm.

David A. Aaker outlined the following dimensions of a market analysis:

- Market size (current and future)
- Market growth rate
- Market profitability
- Industry cost structure
- Distribution channels
- Market trends
- Key success factors

Market Size

The size of the market can be evaluated based on present sales and on potential sales if the use of the product were expanded.

The following are some information sources for determining market size:

- Government data
- Trade associations
- Financial data from major players
- Customer surveys

Market Growth Rate

A simple means of forecasting the market growth rate is to extrapolate historical data into the future. While this method may provide a first-order estimate, it does not predict important turning points. A better method is to study growth drivers such as demographic information and sales growth in complementary products. Such drivers serve as leading indicators that are more accurate than simply extrapolating historical data. Important inflection points in the market growth rate sometimes can be predicted by constructing a product diffusion curve.

The shape of the curve can be estimated by studying the characteristics of the adoption rate of a similar product in the past. Ultimately, the maturity and decline stages of the product life cycle will be reached. Some leading indicators of the decline phase include price pressure caused by competition, a decrease in brand loyalty, the emergence of substitute products, market saturation, and the lack of growth drivers.

Market Profitability

While different firms in a market will have different levels of profitability, the average profit potential for a market can be used as a guideline for knowing how difficult it is to make money in the market. Michael Porter devised a useful framework for evaluating the attractiveness of an industry or market.

This framework, known as Porter's five forces, identifies five factors that influence the market profitability:

1. Buyer power
2. Supplier power
3. Barriers to entry
4. Threat of substitute products
5. Rivalry among firms in the industry

Industry Cost Structure

The cost structure is important for identifying key factors for success. To this end, Porter's value chain model is useful for determining where value is added and for isolating the costs.

The cost structure also is helpful for formulating strategies to develop a competitive advantage.

For example, in some environments the experience curve effect can be used to develop a cost advantage over competitors.

Distribution Channels

The following aspects of the distribution system are useful in a market analysis:

- Existing distribution channels - can be described by how direct they are to the customer.
- Trends and emerging channels - new channels can offer the opportunity to develop a competitive advantage.
- Channel power structure - for example, in the case of a product having little brand equity, retailers have negotiating power over manufacturers and can capture more margin.

Market Trends

Changes in the market are important because they often are the source of new opportunities and threats. The relevant trends are industry-dependent, but some examples include changes in price sensitivity, demand for variety, and level of emphasis on service and support. Regional trends also may be relevant.

Key Success Factors

The key success factors are those elements that are necessary in order for the firm to achieve its marketing objectives.

A few examples of such factors include:

- Access to essential unique resources
- Ability to achieve economies of scale
- Access to distribution channels
- Technological progress

It is important to consider that key success factors may change over time, especially as the product progresses through its life cycle.

TECHNICAL FEASIBILITY

Evaluation Goal

Need for Evaluation

A feasibility study is an important phase in the development of business related services. The need for evaluation is great especially in large high-risk information service development projects.

A feasibility study focuses in the study of the challenges, technical problems and solution models of information service realisation, analyses the potential solutions to the problems against the requirements, evaluates their ability to meet the goals and describes and rationalises the recommended solution.

The term "technical feasibility" establishes that the product or service can operate in the desired manner. Technical feasibility means "achievable". This has to be proven without building the system. The proof is defining a comprehensive number of technical options that are feasible within known and demanded resources and requirements. These options should cover all technical sub-areas.

Goal for Evaluation

The goal of a feasibility study is to outline and clarify the things and factors connected to the technical realisation of a information service system. It is good to outline, recognise and possibly solve these things before the actual design and realisation.

Other goals for feasibility studies are:

- Produce sufficient information:
  - Is the development project technically feasible?
  - Produce base data for the requirement definition phase. *E.g.* what technical requirements does the production of the service place on the clients' current technology *i.e.* help direct research and development investments to right things.
  - What are the realisation alternatives?
  - Is there a recommended realisation alternative?

Evaluation Answers

The evaluation of technical feasibility tries to answer whether the desired information service is feasible and what are the technical matters connected to the feasibility:

- Technical feasibility from the organisation viewpoint.
- How practical is the technical solution?
- The availability of technical resources and know-how?

The evaluation backs the selection of the most suitable technical alternative. The feasibility study is a critical document defining the original system concepts, goals, requirements and alternatives. The study also forms the framework for the system development project and creates a baseline for further studies.

Evaluation Process Description, Scope and Viewpoints

The described evaluation process focuses only on the technical viewpoint. Also other evaluations (profitability, reliability etc.) should be carried out on the recommended information service implementation.

The evaluation process can be utilised at different stages of an information service development project:

- At the beginning of an information service development project: evaluation of the technical feasibility of the desired information service and the implementation alternatives based on the available information. Usually a more concise evaluation.
- At the beginning of an information service development project alongside requirement definition (and partly after): Produces data for requirement definition and utilises the data produced by the requirement definition process. A more demanding and in-depth evaluation process.

Evaluation Methods and Instruments

- *Feasibility analysis matrix (pre. feasibility)*:

  - Comparison of different system alternatives. The matrix defines the factors used in the feasibility evaluation and their weight is evaluated for each system. The total weight is calculated at the end defining the order of the evaluated systems.
- Economical feasibility
  - Cost-benefit analysis
  - Return on investments percentage (ROI)

Presentation of Evaluation Results

The evaluation of the technical feasibility of an information system produces information and answers e.g. the following points:

- Definitions of feasible alternatives for information service system design and development.
- Identifies, raises and clarifies issues connected to the technical implementation of an information system.
- Produces data for requirement definition *i.e.* complements and utilises the information service requirement definition.

Conclusions, Recommendations and Reporting

The evaluation results are reported textually. The scope of the report depends on the scope and complexity of the evaluated information system.

Connection to Other Modules

The feasibility evaluation studies the information system from different viewpoints:

- Technical feasibility
- Financial feasibility
- Operational feasibility

The other modules connected to the "Technical feasibility" module are thus:

- Markets and foresight (technology foresight, mega-trends)
- Risk analyses (reliability, technical risks)
- Revenue and finance (economical profitability and project feasibility)

MANAGERIAL COMPETENCE

In recent years managers have become more concerned about personal effectiveness and legitimately so since career progress is rightfully tied to ability. How well managers are able to accomplish the objectives for which they are accountable, the degree to which they do so in a cost-effective manner, how their practices affect the willingness and ability of those they manage to perform productively - all of these are related to effectiveness. In addition, such considerations most often serve as evaluation criteria for managerial performance *per se*. Managers move up or out on the basis of how well they have administered the managerial process. Knowing this, most managers are legitimately preoccupied with finding the best way they can to accomplish work through others.

But most managers are ambivalent, both eager and dubious, in contemplating new managerial technologies: maybe at last they will hit upon the fail-safe solution to their career progress; but what if it does not work? What if a change to some new, less comfortable and familiar approach is not for the better? What if their current style is the best they are capable of, even if it does not always produce the desired effect? The issue of managerial effectiveness is not without some attending trauma.

What Is Effective Management

The whole issue of managerial performance is loaded - emotionally and factually. Managers are expected to be effective, but the guideposts to effectiveness are often inconsistent or lacking altogether. As treated in the literature, managerial effectiveness appears to be one part data, several parts personal bias, and several more parts pure emotion.

In the final analysis, it is impossible to talk about managerial effectiveness unless it is defined. Even so, this does not solve the problem entirely. Pragmatists define effectiveness as whatever approach seems to work in a given situation; humanists define it as any approach that promotes growth, raises consciousness, and gratifies personal impulse; shareholders view it in terms of top dollar earnings per share; and more than a few managers define it in terms of personal power and control. And yet most managers and those they manage agree on one point - they want to be effective. The fundamental consideration in assessing the effectiveness of any approach to management lies in specifying the goal to be served.

If getting a certain amount of work out within a certain period of time is the objective - regardless of quality, cost, morale, absenteeism, or turnover - then any given style of management could be thought of as effective so long as the work arrives before the deadline. By the same token, if effectiveness is fudged only in terms of being liked by subordinates - again regardless of other considerations - some other approach might be deemed effective.

But no one lives in such a simple world. Simplistic definitions of managerial effectiveness yield simplistic results: they are short-lived; they only treat symptoms; they fail to generalize; they ignore the greater proportion of reality. And they are often disastrous because they isolate managers from their true impacts as they become more distant from the real complexities of organizational life.

The Competence Alternative

If an effectiveness criterion leads to simplistic and expedient ideas and practices, perhaps a more encompassing set of criteria based on the idea of competence would be more profitable. Competence implies a modal view, one which takes into account not the extremes of performance and other improbable considerations but, rather, a definition which addresses the broad range of managerial events and personalities which managers are most likely to encounter in their work. Hence, a modal definition of managerial competence, based on those most frequent occurrences and concerns of management, would encompass those practices which work with most of the people most of the time. Such a definition not only generalizes across organizational situations, but lends itself to verification along empirical lines as well.

Competent management is an approach to managing others which seeks to make optimal use of available resources in meeting organizational objectives on a sustained basis. Three key phrases appear in the definition of managerial competence: optimal implies the best of which people are capable; available means those resources typically at the manager's disposal for meeting the organization's goals; and sustained means over the long haul, not just for fleeting moments, as people go about their work.

This assumes a typical management situation where objectives are neither so ill-defined nor exotic as to require extra special considerations and personnel are average, neither extraordinary nor chronically sub-caliber.

Rather the concern is with day-to-day effectiveness on the important but common issues and events where most managers spend 99% of their time. It may be more stimulating to inject a moment of drama into the otherwise mundane world of management by focusing as many writers do on improbable dilemmas and make-or-break decisions, but to do so would simply miss-portray management as most managers know it.

Management is not always exciting. But this does not mean it is easy or unimportant. Competent management is very likely the single most important ingredient contributing to organizational well-being, despite its workaday place in the total scheme of things. If personal competence is achieved at the daily level of performance, more dramatic instances may be handled with even greater aplomb. How can this be done?

If theory and supporting research are correct, the answer begins with the following conditions under which people will optimize - remembering that people are our most varying and costly available resource - and what the manager might do to facilitate the existence of such conditions:

- Most people work at their highest level when they find meaning and challenge in their work; when they are able to derive a sense of personal identity from doing what they do and doing it well; when they enjoy a sense of community, mutual respect and reliance; and are free of the distractions caused by deprivations or undue sensitivity to peripheral considerations surrounding their work.

- Most people put forth their best efforts when they enjoy a sense of dominion over their work, when their ideas and feelings are incorporated into the design and procedures governing their work, and when they have a sense of generative involvement in the accomplishment of objectives.
- Most people, to perform at their best level, require opportunities for interchange and collaborative comparisons with those with whom they work - superior, co-worker, and subordinate - so that understanding of the tasks at hand is enhanced while reservations, anxieties, and related misgivings are worked through as well; the resulting climate enables people to address their work more directly without distracting apprehensions about failure of internal noises stemming from unexpressed feelings or opinions.
- Most people put forth their best efforts when they see themselves as - and indeed are - collaborators in the enterprise before them; when their needs and objectives are met by achieving the goals of their of their organization (or their part of it) and these are attended to via an assurance of a problem-solving posture under which all contribute to and participate in generating solutions.

The effects have been confirmed time and again both in basic research and in ongoing organizations. The intention here is not to prove again the veracity of such statements; the literature is compelling. More important is the fact that for such conditions to exist, as known from data, managers must behave in particular ways.

From research with subordinate personnel, for example, we know that the manager - both in outlook and practices - greatly influences the extent to which such conditions and consequent predilections will characterize the work force.

In fact, simply by reviewing the practice-effect insights gained from this research, specific managerial acts can be identified which are likely to result in those desirable circumstances where most people put forth their best efforts most of the time.

A behavioural equations is: if we have some idea of the effects we wish to obtain and reliable information about the various effects which stem from a number of diverse practices, we can then reduce this information to a statement of which practices evoke which effects.

A review of earlier research on managerial expectations, motivation, gatekeeping, interpersonal competence, management styles, and the synthesis of all these - with the emphasis on data rather than on theory - reveals that the managerial practices with the highest levels are the following:

Positive Prophecies

Management acts which are founded in an unfragmented, internally consistent, Theory Y view of the nature of those people who populate the work place, *i.e.*, practices based on an anticipation that people are both capable and desirous of doing well.

Meaningful Work

Approaches to employee motivation which take into consideration employee self-esteem, potential for growth and capacities for both finding and responding constructively to positive stimulations accruing from the nature of work and the context within which it is imbedded; *i.e.*, major managerial emphasis on the belonging, ego, and actualization needs of people in both design and administration of work processes.

Involvement

Managerial recognition of the power and significance of ego-involvement on the part of employees and its dependence on managerial Gatekeeping for release into the workflow, *i.e.*, management practices which harness the energies, both physical and psychological, which characterize that generative involvement to which most people aspire in the doing of the organization's work.

Interpersonal Competence

Competent management of the face-to-face relationships which characterize any coordinated activity; *i.e.*, practices which promote owning up to personal ideas and feelings, sharing these openly with pertinent parties, being receptive to and encouraging others to do the same so that an interpersonal climate free of power and performance constraints prevails.

When combined, of course, such acts amount to a total social technology of competent management in which motivator-seeking behaviour is supported, participative techniques are used via sustained Gatekeeping practices, and wherein a strong personal reliance on both exposure and feedback-solicitation processes is combined with encouragement for others to do the same.

Such acts constitute a set of criteria for evaluating the various technologies which emerged from the synthesis research project. Those management styles which meet the most criteria may be deemed the most competent...the ones which work best with most of the people most of the time.

PREDICTING COMPETENCE

A check list of critical managerial attributes and practices can be used to evaluate each style of management...both in terms of the degree to which managers themselves profess to employ the various practices and the extent to which their subordinates report the effects as demonstrated by their own practices and attitudes. Information is available from some 2,000 managers and over 3,500 of their subordinates. Rearranging the results from the synthesis research in a more simple format reveals an estimate of the competence of each managerial style described by Blake and Mouton in their Managerial Grid model.

Competence Criteria

Clearly, an estimate of competence should proceed just as to behavioural criteria on one hand and probability theory on the other, noting what managers do and how this impacts on their subordinates. This is consistent with the view that managers' expectations regarding employee potential and performance effect both their own behaviours towards subordinates and subsequent subordinate behaviours in relating to managers and in doing the work of the organization.

Therefore, parameters of competence include:

- Whether or not the manager operates from a set of Theory Y expectations regarding those who populate the workplace;
- The consistency and internal congruity of personal beliefs;
- The degree to which the manager attends to and emphasizes those constructive incentives most characteristic of mature adults, *viz.*, belongingness, ego status, and actualization;
- The extent to which, in turn, subordinates respond inkind by exhibiting responsive potential to those same higher level and most constructive needs;
- The degree to which subordinates report that they enjoy participative opportunities of the type found to be important in the incidence of ego involvement and commitment;
- Managerial estimates of their interpersonal competence as it reflects a reliance on and employment of both exposure and feedback process in relating to others in the workplace; and, finally,
- The level of interpersonal competence which their subordinates report as characterizing their practices in relating to managers.

Decision Rules

Statisticians often use a technique called a"hit" table in making predictive estimates of the type required to assess management competence. The notion is that in predicting an outcome, one is primarily interested in accuracy or the number of"hits" obtained as opposed to the number of misses. By using a very similar procedure, it is possible to estimate the probable competence of the five management styles studied in the synthesis research.

A point system is first established for measuring"hits" on competence criteria. For example, should a manager report a reliance on the well-knit Theory X orientation? He or she should at least receive a one point hit for the authenticity and clarity of beliefs but no points for the Theory X view. No points are given for X-Y confusion. When scoring multifaceted criteria, as in the case of motivational dynamics, weighted points are given for hits on each of three potentially important need systems.

By employing such a system, the proportion of actual hits to possible hits across the seven parameters of competence may be taken as an index of probable managerial competence. When this type of logic is applied to the data from the synthesis research, different estimates of competence result for the five management styles described by Blake and Mouton. The results of the hit analysis indicate that the basic technologies underlying each of the Grid styles differ dramatically in overall managerial competence.

6

Ownership Structures of Entrepreneurial Activity

PROPRIETORSHIP

'Sole' means single and 'proprietorship' means ownership. It means only one person or an individual becomes the owner of the business. Thus, the business organisation in which a single person owns, manages and controls all the activities of the business is known as sole proprietorship form of business organisation. The individual who owns and runs the sole proprietorship business is called a 'sole proprietor' or 'sole trader'.

A sole proprietor pools and organises the resources in a systematic way and controls the activities with the sole objective of earning profit. Is there any such shop near your locality where a single person is the owner? Small shops like vegetable shops, grocery shops, telephone booths, chemist shops, etc. are some of the commonly found sole proprietorship form of business organisation.

Apart from trading business, small manufacturing units, fabrication units, garages, beauty parlors, etc., can also be run by a sole proprietor. This form of business is the oldest and most common form of business organisation.

CHARACTERISTICS OF SOLE PROPRIETORSHIP

Sole proprietorship form of business organisations have the following characteristics:

- Single Ownership
- No sharing of Profit and Loss
- One-man's Capital
- One-man Control
- Unlimited Liability
- Less legal formalities

Now we shall discuss each of the characteristics in details:

- *Single Ownership*: A single individual always owns sole proprietorship form of business organization. That individual owns all assets and properties of the business. Consequently, he alone bears all the risk of the business. Thus, the business of the sole proprietor comes to an end at the will of the owner or upon his death.
- *No sharing of Profit and Loss*: The entire profit arising out of sole proprietor ship business goes to the sole proprietor. If there is any loss it is also to be borne by the sole proprietor alone. Nobody else shares the profit and loss of the business with the sole proprietor.
- *One man's Capital*: The capital required by a sole proprietorship form of business organisation is totally arranged by the sole proprietor. He provides it either from his personal resources or by borrowing from friends, relatives, banks or other financial institutions.
- *One-man Control*: The controlling power in a sole proprietorship business always remains with the owner. The owner or proprietor alone takes all the decisions to run the business. Of course, he is free to consult any body as per his liking.
- *Unlimited Liability*: The liability of the sole proprietor is unlimited. This implies that, in case of loss the business assets along with the personal properties of the proprietor shall be used to pay the business liabilities.
- *Less Legal Formalities*: The formation and operation of a sole proprietorship form of business organisation requires almost no legal formalities. It also does not require to be registered. However, for the purpose of the business and depending on the nature of the business, the sole proprietorship has to have a seal. He may be required to obtain a licence from the local administration or from the health department of the government, whenever necessary.

ADVANTAGES OF SOLE PROPRIETORSHIP

The sole proprietorship form of business is the most simple and common in our country.

It has the following advantages:

- *Easy to Form and Wind up*: A sole proprietorship form of business is very easy to form. With a very small amount of capital you can start the business. There is no need to comply with any legal formalities except for those businesses which required licence from local authorities or health department of government. Just like formation it is also very easy to wind up the business. It is your sole discretion to form or wind up the business at any time.

- *Direct Motivation*: The profits earned belong to the sole proprietor alone and he bears the risk of losses as well. Thus, there is a direct link between effort and reward. If he works hard, then there is a possibility of getting more profit and of course, he will be the sole beneficiary of this profit. Nobody will share this reward with him. This provides strong motivation for the sole proprietor to work hard.
- *Quick Decision and Prompt Action*: In a sole proprietorship business the sole proprietor alone is responsible for all decisions. Of course, he can consult others. But he is free to take any decision on his own. Since no one else is involved in decision making it becomes quick and prompt action can be taken on the basis of this decision.
- *Better Control*: In sole proprietorship business the proprietor has full control over each and every activity of the business. He is the planner as well as the organiser, who co-ordinates every activity in an efficient manner. Since the proprietor has all authority with him, it is possible to exercise better control over business.
- *Maintenance of Business Secrets*: Business secrecy is an important factor for every business. It refers to keeping the future plans, technical competencies, business strategies, etc. secret from outsiders or competitors. In the case of sole proprietorship business, the proprietor is in a very good position to keep his plans to himself since management and control are in his hands. There is no need to disclose any information to others.
- *Close Personal Relation*: The sole proprietor is always in a position to maintain good personal contact with the customers and employees. Direct contact enables the sole proprietor to know the individual likes, dislikes and tastes of the customers. Also, it helps in maintaining close and friendly relations with the employees and thus, business runs smoothly.
- *Flexibility in Operation*: The sole proprietor is free to change the nature and scope of business operations as and when required as per his decision. A sole proprietor can expand or curtail his business just as to the requirement. Suppose, as the owner of a bookshop, you have been selling books for school students. If you want to expand your business you can decide to sell stationery items like pen, pencil, register, etc. If you are running an STD booth, you can expand your business by installing a fax machine in your booth.
- *Encourages Self-employment*: Sole proprietorship form of business organisation leads to creation of employment opportunities for

people. Not only is the owner self-employed, sometimes he also creates job opportunities for others. You must have observed in different shops that there are a number of employees assisting the owner in selling goods to the customers. Thus, it helps in reducing poverty and unemployment in the country.

LIMITATIONS OF SOLE PROPRIETORSHIP

One-man business is the best form of business ogranisation because of the advantages. Still there are certain disadvantages too.

Let us learn those limitations:

- *Limited Capital*: In sole proprietorship business, it is the owner who arranges the required capital of the business. It is often difficult for a single individual to raise a huge amount of capital. The owner's own funds as well as borrowed funds sometimes become insufficient to meet the requirement of the business for its growth and expansion.
- *Unlimited Liability*: In case the sole proprietor fails to pay the business obligations and debts arising out of business activities, his personal properties may have to be used to meet those liabilities. This restricts the sole proprietor from taking risks and he thinks cautiously while deciding to start or expand the business activities.
- *Lack of Continuity*: The existence of sole proprietorship business is linked to the life of the proprietor. Illness, death or insolvency of the owner brings an end to the business. The continuity of business operation is therefore uncertain.
- *Limited Size*: In sole proprietorship form of business organisation there is a limit beyond which it becomes difficult to expand its activities. It is not always possible for a single person to supervise and manage the affairs of the business if it grows beyond a certain limit.
- *Lack of Managerial Expertise*: A sole proprietor may not be an expert in every aspect of management. He/she may be an expert in administration, planning, etc., but may be poor in marketing. Again, because of limited financial resources it is also not possible to employ a professional manager. Thus, the business lacks benefits of professional management.

SUITABILITY OF SOLE PROPRIETORSHIP FORM OF BUSINESS

Let us consider the type of businesses where sole proprietorship form is most suitable.

Sole proprietorship form of business organisation is suitable:

- Where the market for the product is small and local. For example, selling grocery items, books, stationery, vegetables, etc.

- Where customers are given personal attention, just as to their personal tastes and preferences. For example, making special type of furniture, designing garments, etc.
- Where the nature of business is simple. For example, grocery, garments business, telephone booth, etc.
- Where capital requirement is small and risk involvement is not heavy. For example, vegetables and fruits business, tea stall, etc.
- Where manual skill is required. For example, making jewellery, haircutting or tailoring, cycle or motorcycle repair shop, etc.

PARTNERSHIP

A partnership is an arrangement where entities and/or individuals agree to cooperate to advance their interests. In the most frequent instance, a partnership is formed between one or more businesses in which partners (owners) co-labour to achieve and share profits or losses. Partnerships are also frequent regardless of and among sectors.

Non-profit organizations, for example, may partner together to increase the likelihood of each achieving their mission. Governments may partner with other governments to achieve their mutual goals, as may religious and political organizations. In education, accrediting agencies increasingly evaluate schools by the level and quality of their partnerships with other schools and across sectors. Partnerships also occur at personal levels, such as when two or more individuals agree to domicile together. Partnerships between governments, interest-based organizations, schools, businesses, and individuals, or some combination thereof, have always been and remain commonplace. Partnerships have widely varying results and can present partners with special challenges.

Levels of give-and-take, areas of responsibility, lines of authority, and overarching goals of the partnership must all be negotiated. While partnerships stand to amplify mutual interests and success, some are considered ethically problematic, or at least debatable. When a politician, for example, partners with a corporation to advance the corporation's interest in exchange for some benefit, a conflict of interest may make the partnership problematic from the standpoint of the public good.

Developed countries often strongly regulate certain partnerships via anti-trust laws, so as to inhibit monopolistic practices and foster free market competition. Among developed countries, business partnerships are often favoured over corporations in taxation policy, since dividend taxes only occur on profits before they are distributed to the partners.

However, depending on the partnership structure and the jurisdiction in which it operates, owners of a partnership may be exposed to greater personal liability than they would as shareholders of a corporation.

COMMON LAW

Under common law legal systems, the basic form of partnership is a general partnership, in which all partners manage the business and are personally liable for its debts. Two other forms which have developed in most countries are the limited partnership (LP), in which certain limited partners relinquish their ability to manage the business in exchange for limited liability for the partnership's debts, and the limited liability partnership (LLP), in which all partners have some degree of limited liability.

There are two types of partners. General partners have an obligation of strict liability to third parties injured by the Partnership. General partners may have joint liability or joint and several liability depending upon circumstances. The liability of limited partners is limited to their investment in the partnership. A silent partner is one who still shares in the profits and losses of the business, but who is uninvolved in its management, and/or whose association with the business is not publicly known; these partners usually provide capital.

Hong Kong

A partnership in Hong Kong is a business entity formed by the Hong Kong Partnerships Ordinance, which defines a partnership as "the relation between persons carrying on a business in common with a view of profit" and is not a joint stock company or an incorporated company. If the business entity registers with the Registrar of Companies it takes the form of a limited partnership defined in the Limited Partnerships Ordinance. However, if this business entity fails to register with the Registrar of Companies, then it becomes a general partnership as a default.

Australia

Summarising s. 5 of the Partnership Act 1958 (Vic) (hereinafter the "Act"), for a partnership in Australia to exist, four main criteria must be satisfied. *They are*:

- Valid Agreement between the parties;
- To carry on a business – this is defined in s. 3 as "any trade, occupation or profession";
- In Common – meaning there must be some mutuality of rights, interests and obligations;
- View to Profit – thus charitable organizations cannot be partnerships (charities are typically incorporated associations under Associations Incorporations Act 1981 (Vic))

Partners share profits and losses. A partnership is basically a settlement between two or more groups or firms in which profit and loss are equally divided

United Kingdom Limited Partnership

A limited partnership in the United Kingdom consists of:

- One or more people called general partners, who are liable for all debts and obligations of the firm; and
- One or more people called limited partners, who contribute a sum/ sums of money as capital, or property valued at a stated amount. Limited partners are not liable for the debts and obligations of the firm beyond the amount contributed.

Limited partners may not:

- Draw out or receive back any part of their contributions to the partnership during its lifetime; or
- Take part in the management of the business or have power to bind the firm.

If they do, they become liable for all the debts and obligations of the firm up to the amount drawn out or received back or incurred while taking part in the management, as the case may be.

India and Pakistan

The section 4 of the Partnership Act of 1932, which applies in both India and Pakistan, "Partnership is defined as the relation between two or more persons who have agreed to share the profits and losses just as to their ratio of business run by all or any one of them acting for all". This definition superseded the previous definition given in section 239 of Indian Contract Act 1872 as – "Partnership is the relation which subsists between persons who have agreed to combine their property, labour, skill in some business, and to share the profits thereof between them".

The 1932 definition added the concept of mutual agency. A partnership firm is not a legal entity apart from the partners constituting it. It has limited identity for the purpose of tax law as per section 4 of the Partnership Act of 1932.

USA

The federal government of the United States does not have specific statutory law governing the establishment of partnerships. Instead, each of the fifty states as well as the District of Columbia has its own statutes and common law that govern partnerships.

These states largely follow general common law principles of partnerships whether a general partnership, a limited partnership or a limited liability partnership. In the absence of applicable federal law, the National Conference of Commissioners on Uniform State Laws has issued non-binding models laws (called uniform act) in which to encourage the adoption of uniformity of partnership law into the states by their respective legislatures. This includes the Uniform Partnership Act and the Uniform Limited Partnership Act. Although the federal government does not have specific statutory law for establishing partnerships, it has an extensive and hyperdetailed statutory scheme for the taxation of partnerships in the Internal Revenue Code.

COMPANY

A company is a form of business organization. It is a collection of individuals and physical assets with a common focus and an aim of gaining profits. This collection exists in Law and therefore a company is considered a "Legal Person".In the United States, a company is a corporation—or, less commonly, an association, partnership, or union—that carries on an industrial enterprise."

Generally, a company may be a "corporation, partnership, association, joint-stock company, trust, fund, or organized group of persons, whether incorporated or not, and (in an official capacity) any receiver, trustee in bankruptcy, or similar official, or liquidating agent, for any of the foregoing." In English law, and therefore in the Commonwealth realms, a company is a form of body corporate or corporation, generally registered under the Companies Acts or similar legislation.

It does not include a partnership or any other unincorporated group of persons.

MEANING AND ETYMOLOGY

A company can be defined as an "artificial person", invisible, intangible, created by Law, with a discrete legal entity, perpetual succession and a common seal. It is not affected by the death, insanity or insolvency of an individual member.

The English word company has its origins in the Old French military term compaignie (first recorded in 1150), meaning a "body of soldiers", originally taken from the Late Latin word companio "companion, one who eats bread with you", first attested in the Lex Salica as a calque of the Germanic expression *gahlaibo (literally, "with bread"), related to Old High German galeipo "companion" and Gothic gahlaiba "messmate".

By 1303, the word referred to trade guilds. Usage of company to mean "business association" was first recorded in 1553 and the abbreviation "co." dates from 1769.

HISTORY

"It may be formed by Act of Parliament, by Royal Charter, or by registration under company law." In the United Kingdom, the main regulating laws are the Companies Act 1985 and the Companies Act 2006. Reportedly, "a company registered under this Act has limited liability: its owners (the shareholders) have no financial liability in the event of winding up the affairs of the company, but they might lose the money already invested in it". In the

USA, companies are registered in a particular state—Delaware being especially favoured—and become Incorporated (Inc). In North America, two of the earliest companies were The London Company—an English joint stock company established by royal charter by James I of England on April 10, 1606 with the purpose of establishing colonial settlements in North America—and Plymouth Company that was granted an identical charter as part of the Virginia Company.

The London Company was responsible for establishing the Jamestown Settlement, the first permanent English settlement in the present United States in 1607, and in the process of sending additional supplies, inadvertently settled the Somers Isles, alias Bermuda, the oldest-remaining English colony, in 1609.

TYPES

There are various types of company that can be formed in different jurisdictions, but the most common forms of company (generally formed by registration under applicable companies legislation) are:

- A company limited by guarantee. Commonly used where companies are formed for non-commercial purposes, such as clubs or charities. The members guarantee the payment of certain (usually nominal) amounts if the company goes into insolvent liquidation, but otherwise they have no economic rights in relation to the company. This type of company is common in England.
- A company limited by shares. The most common form of company used for business ventures. Specifically, a limited company is a"company in which the liability of each shareholder is limited to the amount individually invested" with corporations being"the most common example of a limited company." This type of company is common in England.
- A company limited by guarantee with a share capital. A hybrid entity, usually used where the company is formed for non-commercial purposes, but the activities of the company are partly funded by investors who expect a return. This type of company may no longer be formed in the UK, although provisions still exist in law for them to exist.
- A limited-liability company."A company-statutorily authorized in certain states-that is characterized by limited liability, management by members or managers, and limitations on ownership transfer", *i.e.,* L.L.C.
- An unlimited company with or without a share capital. A hybrid entity, a company where the liability of members or shareholders for the debts (if any) of the company are not limited.

Less commonly seen types of companies are:

- Companies formed by letters patent. Most corporations by letters patent are corporations sole and not companies as the term is commonly understood today.
- Charter corporations. Before the passing of modern companies legislation, these were the only types of companies. Now they are relatively rare, except for very old companies that still survive (of which there are still many, particularly many British banks), or modern societies that fulfil a quasi regulatory function (for example, the Bank of England is a corporation formed by a modern charter).
- Statutory Companies. Relatively rare today, certain companies have been formed by a private statute passed in the relevant jurisdiction.

Note that"Ltd after the company's name signifies limited company, and PLC (public limited company) indicates that its shares are widely held." In legal parlance, the owners of a company are normally referred to as the"members". In a company limited or unlimited by shares (formed or incorporated with a share capital), this will be the shareholders. In a company limited by guarantee, this will be the guarantors. Some offshore jurisdictions have created special forms of offshore company in a bid to attract business for their jurisdictions. Examples include"segregated portfolio companies" and restricted purpose companies.

There are however, many, many sub-categories of types of company that can be formed in various jurisdictions in the world. Companies are also sometimes distinguished for legal and regulatory purposes between public companies and private companies. Public companies are companies whose shares can be publicly traded, often (although not always) on a regulated stock exchange. Private companies do not have publicly traded shares, and often contain restrictions on transfers of shares. In some jurisdictions, private companies have maximum numbers of shareholders.

COOPERATIVE

A cooperative is a business organization owned and operated by a group of individuals for their mutual benefit. Cooperatives are defined by the International Co-operative Alliance's Statement on the Co-operative Identity as autonomous associations of persons united voluntarily to meet their common economic, social, and cultural needs and aspirations through jointly owned and democratically controlled enterprises. A cooperative may also be defined as a business owned and controlled equally by the people who use its services or by the people who work there. Cooperative enterprises are the focus of study in the field of cooperative economics.

ORIGINS

Cooperation dates back as far as human beings have been organizing for mutual benefit. Tribes were organised as cooperative structures, allocating jobs and resources among each other, only trading with the external communities. Pre-industrial Europe is home to the first co-operatives from an industrial context.

In 1761, the Fenwick Weavers' Society was formed in Fenwick, East Ayrshire, Scotland to sell discounted oatmeal to local workers. Its services expanded to include assistance with savings and loans, emigration and education. In 1810, Welsh social reformer Robert Owen, from Newtown in mid-Wales, and his partners purchased New Lanark mill from Owen's father-in-law David Dale and proceeded to introduce better labour standards including discounted retail shops where profits were passed on to his employees. Owen left New Lanark to pursue other forms of co-operative organization and develop co-op ideas through writing and lecture.

Co-operative communities were set up in Glasgow, Indiana and Hampshire, although ultimately unsuccessful. In 1828, William King set up a newspaper, The Cooperator, yash rathi The Rochdale Society of Equitable Pioneers, founded in 1844, is usually considered the first successful co-operative enterprise, used as a model for modern co-ops, following the'Rochdale Principles'.

A group of 28 weavers and other artisans in Rochdale, England set up the society to open their own store selling food items they could not otherwise afford. Within ten years there were over 1,000 co-operative societies in the United Kingdom. Other events such as the founding of a friendly society by the Tolpuddle Martyrs in 1832 were key occasions in the creation of organized labour and consumer movements.

SOCIAL ECONOMY

In the final year of the 20th century, cooperatives banded together to establish a number of social enterprise agencies which have moved to adopt the multi-stakeholder cooperative model. In the last 15 years (1994-2009) the EU and its member nations, have gradually revised national accounting systems to"make visible" the increasing contribution of social economy organizations.

ORGANIZATIONAL AND IDEOLOGICAL ROOTS

The roots of the cooperative movement can be traced to multiple influences and extend worldwide. In the Anglosphere, post-feudal forms of cooperation between workers and owners, that are expressed today as"profit-sharing" and"surplus sharing" arrangements, existed as far back as 1795. The key ideological influence on the Anglosphere branch of the cooperative movement, however, was a rejection of the charity principles that underpinned welfare reforms when the British government radically revised its Poor Laws in 1834. As both state and church institutions began to routinely distinguish between the'deserving' and'undeserving' poor, a movement of friendly societies grew throughout the British Empire based on the principle of mutuality, committed to self-help in the welfare of working people. Friendly Societies established forums through which one member, one vote was practiced in organisation decision-making.

The principles challenged the idea that a person should be an owner of property before being granted a political voice. Throughout the second half of the nineteenth century (and then repeatedly every 20 years or so) there has been a surge in the number of cooperative organisations, both in commercial practice and civil society, operating to advance democracy and universal suffrage as a political principle. Friendly Societies and consumer cooperatives became the dominant form of organization amongst working people in Anglosphere industrial societies prior to the rise of trade unions and industrial factories.

Weinbren reports that by the end of the 19th century, over 80% of British working age men and 90% of Australian working age men were members of one or more Friendly Society. From the mid-nineteenth century, mutual organisations embraced these ideas in economic enterprises, firstly amongst tradespeople, and later in cooperative stores, educational institutes, financial institutions and industrial enterprises.

The common thread (enacted in different ways, and subject to the constraints of various systems of national law) is the principle that an enterprise or association should be owned and controlled by the people it serves, and share any surpluses on the basis of each members' cooperative contribution (as a producer, labourer or consumer) rather than their capacity to invest financial capital.

The cooperative movement has been fueled globally by ideas of economic democracy. Economic democracy is a socioeconomic philosophy that suggests an expansion of decision-making power from a small minority of corporate shareholders to a larger majority of public stakeholders. There are many different approaches to thinking about and building economic democracy.

Both Marxism and anarchism, for example, have been influenced by utopian socialism, which was based on voluntary cooperation, without recognition of class conflict. Anarchists are committed to libertarian socialism and they have focused on local organization, including locally managed cooperatives, linked through confederations of unions, cooperatives and communities.

Marxists, who as socialists have likewise held and worked for the goal of democratizing productive and reproductive relationships, often placed a greater strategic emphasis on confronting the larger scales of human organization. As they viewed the capitalist class to be prohibitively politically, militarily and culturally mobilized in order to maintain an exploitable working class, they fought in the early 20th century to appropriate from the capitalist class the society's collective political capacity in the form of the state, either through democratic socialism, or through what came to be known as Leninism. Though they regard the state as an unnecessarily oppressive institution, Marxists considered appropriating national and international-scale capitalist institutions and resources (such as the state) to be an important first pillar in creating conditions favourable to solidaristic economies. With the declining influence of the USSR after the 1960s, socialist strategies pluralized, though economic democratizers have not as yet established a fundamental challenge to the hegemony of global neoliberal capitalism.

MEANING

Cooperatives as Legal Entities

A cooperative is a legal entity owned and democratically controlled by its members. Members often have a close association with the enterprise as producers or consumers of its products or services, or as its employees.

In some countries, *e.g.* Finland and Sweden, there are specific forms of incorporation for co-operatives. Cooperatives may take the form of companies limited by shares or by guarantee, partnerships or unincorporated associations. In the USA, cooperatives are often organized as non-capital stock corporations under state-specific cooperative laws.

However, they may also be unincorporated associations or business corporations such as limited liability companies or partnerships; such forms are useful when the members want to allow:

- Some members to have a greater share of the control, or
- Some investors to have a return on their capital that exceeds fixed interest,

Neither of which may be allowed under local laws for cooperatives. Cooperatives often share their earnings with the membership as dividends, which are divided among the members just as to their participation in the enterprise, such as patronage, instead of just as to the value of their capital shareholdings (as is done by a joint stock company).

Aspects of Economic Rationale

If cooperatives/mutuals succeed, that success may reflect not the characteristics of the cooperative/mutual form itself but the existence of a long term regulated competitive environment that created the space and margins which allowed them to adopt welfare objectives different from those of profit maximising competitors.

Llewellyn and Holmes (1991) argue that, in the absence of a clear efficiency advantage, mutual building societies, for example, would need to behave in a manner substantially similar to banks and mutual life insurers similarly to Plc life insurers: "Only if mutuals have a substantial efficiency advantage compared with their Plc competitors are they able to set objectives significantly different from their Plc competitors. In the absence of this, competitive pressures force a convergence of behaviour and remove the major behavioural distinctions between mutuality and Plc's". From this point of view, competition and narrow margins are inimical to the mutual form because they erode behavioural difference.

These issues are complicated in the case of UK building societies and mutual life insurers because they require judgement about whether they really have behaved differently in these two areas. If banks may be different from building societies, that may not be so in the case of, for example, the UK Plc 'Prudential' life insurer and its mutual competitors. But, what is clear is that building societies (like mutual life insurers) have operated in regulated areas where returns on capital are high, so that mutuals can choose different objectives.

This discretion, of course, greatly complicates outcomes because mutuals can set objectives in terms of prices received or paid or in terms of market access to those who would be denied access or disadvantaged by other providers. There is also the complication that if (as in the case of building societies in the late-1980's), mutuals dominate the field, the behaviour of non-mutual competitors has to be conjectured. Consumer attitudes and behaviour are also relevant when competition is weak. Consumers may prefer cooperatives/mutuals like building societies if they fear that surplus distributing banks might try to 'rip them off.'

The point is made in the building society mutual context by Armitage (1991): "In theory, in a free market with well-informed participants, competition ensures competing services are priced just as to their value to the consumer; if not they do not sell. Therefore, consumers are never 'ripped off'.

However to the extent that a market is less than competitive in this sense, sellers have opportunities for exploiting customers., which their duty to shareholders should oblige them to take if they are companies, and their duty to members should oblige them not to take if they are mutuals. The mortgage and deposit markets are competitive, but not perfectly so. In particular, customers have incomplete information and face search costs. So there is scope for institutional policies to make a difference to customers' welfare without always paying or gaining in terms of loss or gain of custom". The fact that most small depositors are ill-informed (as building society depositors certainly were) may also explain the importance of mutuals in the savings markets.

The Uninformed Depositor Model of Rasmusen (1988) does appear to offer explanation for why small savers prefer mutuals. In banking markets, there is usually information asymmetry whereby managers are relatively informed as to risk, such as asset risk and maturity transformation/interest yield mismatch risk, and depositors are left relatively ignorant. In this case, the cost of virtually any monitoring by small savers is practically unsustainable. The 'free rider' effect in building societies is a manifestation of this kind of unsustainable monitoring cost where the cost of meaningful involvement in building society affairs (even attendance at the annual meeting) really quite outweighs benefits to be obtained through involvement, as Ingham and Thompson 4 point out.

In earlier times, some building societies resorted to fining members for not attending annual meetings, in order to get the members to turn out. But once the roll was checked many promptly adjourned to the nearest pub ('bar'). Under these risk-monitoring circumstances, depositors will prefer a mutual where they perceive that what they understand to be moderate or no risk attaches, due to regulation, as compared to more risky less regulated banks.

Also, they may understand that managers in mutuals are less motivated to take risk, as suggested by Rasmusen (1988) below and by Masulis (1987). It could be claimed that part of the success of mutuals is due to simplified agency relationships resulting from the absence of external shareholders or to the ability to distribute surplus through product price (not 'Plc' dividend). These arguments are not conclusive, as the presence of external claimants may result in considerable pressure for cost economies, especially if there is a market for corporate control.

It is doubtful that the operating cost leadership of UK building societies, which is so much a factor in the dominance of the mutual form in the savings banking and home mortgage financing market, has much to do with lower agency costs or efficiency. Before deregulation, the objective was not efficiency but growth through retained earnings which was in the management interest; and the finance directors attributed their funding cost advantage to the accident of mixed funding.

Much of this detail may not matter to an uninformed depositor. As Rasmusen (1988) observes: "In the Uninformed Depositor Model the depositor does not have to distinguish motives: the advantage of the mutual is that the interests of depositors and managers roughly coincide, and whether managers are conservative to protect their perks or their depositors is a minor point".

Masulis (1987) also refers to the motivations of managers in relation to risk in the terms with reference to American style mutual savings and loan banks where his references to 'owners' and boards of directors, in the MS&L [mutual savings and loan] context, are references to management: "Since MS&L owners (boards of directors) are only able to extract a portion of a S&L's current and accumulated earnings [through salary and perks], they have less incentive to take risks than the owners of stock companies [*e.g.* Plc banks] who can capture the entire stream of accumulated and expected future profits by selling their stock.

Identity

Cooperatives are based on the cooperative values of "self-help, self-responsibility, democracy and equality, equity and solidarity" and the seven cooperative principles:

1. Voluntary and Open Membership
2. Democratic Member Control
3. Member Economic Participation
4. Autonomy and Independence
5. Education, Training and Information
6. Cooperation among Cooperatives
7. Concern for Community

In the tradition of their founders, cooperative members believe in the ethical values of honesty, openness, social responsibility and caring for others. Such legal entities have a range of unique social characteristics. Membership is open, meaning that anyone who satisfies certain non-discriminatory conditions may join.

Economic benefits are distributed proportionally just as to each member's level of participation in the cooperative, for instance by a dividend on sales or purchases, rather than divided just as to capital invested. Cooperatives may be generally classified as either consumer cooperatives or producer cooperatives.

Cooperatives are closely related to collectives, which differ only in that profit-making or economic stability is placed secondary to adherence to social-justice principles. Co-ops can sometimes be identified on the Internet through the use of the.coop gTLD. Organizations using.coop domain names must adhere to the basic co-op values.

TYPES OF COOPERATIVE GOVERNANCE

Retailers' Cooperative

A retailers' cooperative (known as a secondary or marketing co-operative in some countries) is an organization which employs economies of scale on behalf of its members to get discounts from manufacturers and to pool marketing. It is common for locally owned grocery stores, hardware stores and pharmacies.

In this case the members of the cooperative are businesses rather than individuals. The Best Western international hotel chain is actually a retailers' cooperative, whose members are hotel operators, although it now prefers to call itself a "nonprofit membership association." It gave up on the "cooperative" label after some courts insisted on enforcing regulatory requirements for franchisors despite its member-controlled status.

Worker Cooperative

A worker cooperative or producer cooperative is a cooperative, that is owned and democratically controlled by its "worker-owners". There are no outside owners in a "pure" workers' cooperative, only the workers own shares of the business, though hybrid forms in which consumers, community members or capitalist investors also own some shares are not uncommon.

In practice, control by worker-owners may be exercised through individual, collective or majority ownership by the workforce, or the retention of individual, collective or majority voting rights (exercised on a one-member one-vote basis). A worker cooperative, therefore, has the characteristic that the majority of its workforce owns shares, and the majority of shares are owned by the workforce. Membership is not always compulsory for employees, but generally only employees can become members either directly (as shareholders) or indirectly through membership of a trust that owns the company.

The impact of political ideology on practice constrains the development of co-operatives in different countries. In India, there is a form of workers' cooperative which insists on compulsory membership for all employees and compulsory employment for all members. That is the form of the Indian Coffee Houses.

This system was advocated by the Indian communist leader A. K. Gopalan. In places like the UK, common ownership (indivisible collective ownership) was popular in the 1970s. Cooperative Societies only became legal in Britain after the passing of Slaney's Act in 1852. In 1865 there were 651 registered societies with a total membership of well over 200,000. There are now more than 400 worker co-operatives in the UK, Suma Wholefoods being the largest example with a turnover of £24 million.

Spanish law permits owner-members to register as self-employed enabling worker-owners to establish regulatory regimes that support co-operative working, but which differs considerably from co-operatives that are subject to Anglo-American systems of law that require the co-operative (employer) to view (and treat) its worker-members as salaried workers (employees). The implications of this are far-reaching, as this requires co-operatives to establish authority driven statutory disciplinary and grievance procedures (rather than democratic mediation schemes), impacting on the ability of leaders to enact democratic forms of management and counter the authority structures embedded in the dominant system of private enterprise centred around the entrepreneur.

Volunteer Cooperative

A volunteer cooperative is a cooperative that is run by and for a network of volunteers, for the benefit of a defined membership or the general public, to achieve some goal. Depending on the structure, it may be a collective or mutual organization, which is operated just as to the principles of cooperative governance. The most basic form of volunteer-run cooperative is a voluntary association. A lodge or social club may be organized on this basis.

A volunteer-run co-op is distinguished from a worker cooperative in that the latter is by definition employee-owned, whereas the volunteer cooperative is typically a non-stock corporation, volunteer-run consumer co-op or service organization, in which workers and beneficiaries jointly participate in management decisions and receive discounts on the basis of sweat equity.

Social Cooperative

A particularly successful form of multi-stakeholder cooperative is the Italian"social cooperative", of which some 7,000 exist."Type A" social cooperatives bring together providers and beneficiaries of a social service as members."Type B" social cooperatives bring together permanent workers and previously unemployed people who wish to integrate into the labour market.

Social cooperatives are legally defined as follows:

- No more than 80% of profits may be distributed, interest is limited to the bond rate and dissolution is altruistic (assets may not be distributed)
- The cooperative has legal personality and limited liability
- The objective is the general benefit of the community and the social integration of citizens
- Those of type B integrate disadvantaged people into the labour market. The categories of disadvantage they target may include physical and mental disability, drug and alcohol addiction, developmental disorders and problems with the law. They do not include other factors of disadvantage such as race, sexual orientation or abuse.
- Type A cooperatives provide health, social or educational services
- Various categories of stakeholder may become members, including paid employees, beneficiaries, volunteers (up to 50% of members), financial investors and public institutions. In type B co-operatives at least 30% of the members must be from the disadvantaged target groups
- Voting is one person one vote

A good estimate of the current size of the social cooperative sector in Italy is given by updating the official Istituto Nazionale di Statistica (Istat) figures from the end of 2001 by an annual growth rate of 10% (assumed by the Direzione Generale per gli Ente Cooperativi). This gives totals of 7,100 social cooperatives, with 267,000 members, 223,000 paid employees, 31,000 volunteers and 24,000 disadvantaged people undergoing integration.

Combined turnover is around 5 billion euro. The cooperatives break into three types: 59% type A (social and health services), 33% type B (work integration) and 8% mixed. The average size is 30 workers.

Consumers' Cooperative

A consumers' cooperative is a business owned by its customers. Employees can also generally become members. Members vote on major decisions, and elect the board of directors from amongst their own number. A well known example in the United States is the REI (Recreational Equipment Incorporated) co-op, and in With its 414,383 employees, 7,736,210 members and a turnover of €50Bn per year growing at a steady rate of 4.41%., Legacoop of Italy is arguably the world's biggest cooperative. The world's largest consumers' cooperative is the Co-operative Group in the United Kingdom, which offers a variety of retail and financial services. The UK also has a number of autonomous consumers' cooperative societies, such as the East of England Co-operative Society and Midcounties Co-operative.

In fact the Co-operative Group is something of a hybrid, having both corporate members (mostly other consumers' cooperatives, as a result of its origins as a wholesale society), and individual retail consumer members. Japan has a very large and well developed consumer cooperative movement with over 14 million members; retail co-ops alone had a combined turnover of 2.519 trillion Yen (21.184 billion US dollars [market exchange rates as of 15 November 2005]) in 2003/4.

(Japanese Consumers' Co-operative Union., 2003). Migros is the largest supermarket chain in Switzerland and keeps the cooperative society as its form of organization. Nowadays, a large part of the Swiss population are members of the Migros cooperative - around 2 million of Switzerland's total population of 7,2 million, thus making Migros a supermarket chain that is owned by its customers.

Coop is another Swiss cooperative which operates the second largest supermarket chain in Switzerland after Migros. In 2001, Coop merged with 11 cooperative federations which had been its main suppliers for over 100 years. As of 2005, Coop operates 1437 shops and employs almost 45,000 people. Bio Suisse, the Swiss organic producers' association, Coop accounts for half of all the organic food sold in Switzerland. EURO COOP is the European Community of Consumer Cooperatives.

Business and Employment Co-operative

Business and employment co-operatives (BECs) are a subset of worker co-operatives that represent a new approach to providing support to the creation of new businesses. Like other business creation support schemes, BECs enable budding entrepreneurs to experiment with their business idea while benefiting from a secure income. The innovation BECs introduce is that once the business is established the entrepreneur is not forced to leave and set up independently, but can stay and become a full member of the co-operative.

The micro-enterprises then combine to form one multi-activity enterprise whose members provide a mutually supportive environment for each other. BECs thus provide budding business people with an easy transition from inactivity to self-employment, but in a collective framework. They open up new horizons for people who have ambition but who lack the skills or confidence needed to set off entirely on their own - or who simply want to carry on an independent economic activity but within a supportive group context.

New Generation Co-operative

New generation co-operatives (NGCs) are an adaptation of traditional co-operative structures to modern, capital intensive industries. They are sometimes described as a hybrid between traditional co-ops and limited liability companies. They were first developed in California and spread and flourished in the US Mid-West in the 1990s. They are now common in Canada where they operate primarily in agriculture and food services, where their primary purpose is to add value to primary products. For example producing ethanol from corn, pasta from durum wheat, or gourmet cheese from goat's milk.

TYPES OF COOPERATIVES

Housing Cooperative

A housing cooperative is a legal mechanism for ownership of housing where residents either own shares (share capital co-op) reflecting their equity in the cooperative's real estate, or have membership and occupancy rights in a not-for-profit cooperative (non-share capital co-op), and they underwrite their housing through paying subscriptions or rent.

Housing cooperatives come in three basic equity structures:

- In Market-rate housing cooperatives, members may sell their shares in the cooperative whenever they like for whatever price the market will bear, much like any other residential property. Market-rate co-ops are very common in New York City.
- Limited equity housing cooperatives, which are often used by affordable housing developers, allow members to own some equity in their home, but limit the sale price of their membership share to that which they paid.
- Group equity or Zero equity housing cooperatives do not allow members to own equity in their residences and often have rental agreements well below market rates.

Building Cooperative

Members of a building cooperative (in Britain known as a self-build housing co-operative) pool resources to build housing, normally using a high proportion of their own labour. When the building is finished, each member is the sole owner of a homestead, and the cooperative may be dissolved. This collective effort was at the origin of many of Britain's building societies, which however developed into "permanent" mutual savings and loan organisations, a term which persisted in some of their names (such as the former Leeds Permanent).

Nowadays such self-building may be financed using a step-by-step mortgage which is released in stages as the building is completed. The term may also refer to worker co-operatives in the building trade.

Utility Cooperative

A utility cooperative is a type of consumers' cooperative that is tasked with the delivery of a public utility such as electricity, water or telecommunications services to its members. Profits are either reinvested into infrastructure or distributed to members in the form of "patronage" or "capital credits", which are essentially dividends paid on a member's investment into the cooperative. In the United States, many cooperatives were formed to provide rural electrical and telephone service as part of the New Deal.

In the case of electricity, cooperatives are generally either generation and transmission (G&T) co-ops that create and send power via the transmission grid or local distribution co-ops that gather electricity from a variety of sources and send it along to homes and businesses.

Agricultural Cooperative

Agricultural cooperatives or farmers' cooperatives are cooperatives where farmers pool their resources for mutual economic benefit. Agricultural cooperatives are broadly divided into agricultural service cooperatives, which provide various services to their individual farming members, and agricultural production cooperatives, where production resources such as land or machinery are pooled and members farm jointly.

Agricultural production cooperatives are relatively rare in the world, and known examples are limited to collective farms in former socialist countries and the kibbutzim in Israel. Agricultural supply cooperatives aggregate purchases, storage, and distribution of farm inputs for their members. By taking advantage of volume discounts and utilizing other economies of scale, supply cooperatives bring down members' costs.

Supply cooperatives may provide seeds, fertilizers, chemicals, fuel, and farm machinery. Some supply cooperatives also operate machinery pools that provide mechanical field services (*e.g.*, plowing, harvesting) to their members. Agricultural marketing cooperatives provide the services involved in moving a product from the point of production to the point of consumption. Agricultural marketing includes a series of inter-connected activities involving planning production, growing and harvesting, grading, packing, transport, storage, food processing, distribution and sale. Agricultural marketing cooperatives are often formed to promote specific commodities.

Credit Unions and Cooperative Banking

Credit unions are cooperative financial institutions that are owned and controlled by their members. Credit unions provide the same financial services as banks but are considered not-for-profit organizations and adhere to cooperative principles. Credit unions originated in mid-19th century Germany through the efforts of pioneers Franz Hermann Schulze-Delitzsch and Friedrich Wilhelm Raiffeisen.

The concept of financial cooperatives crossed the Atlantic at the turn of the 20th century, when the caisse populaire movement was started by Alphonse Desjardins in Quebec, Canada. In 1900, from his home in Lévis, he opened North America's first credit union, marking the beginning of the Mouvement Desjardins. Eight years later, Desjardins provided guidance for the first credit union in the United States, where there are now about 7,950 active status federally insured credit unions, with almost 90 million members and more that $679 billion on deposit.

While they have not taken root so deeply as in Ireland, credit unions are also established in the UK. The largest are work-based, but many are now offering services in the wider community.

The Association of British Credit Unions Ltd (ABCUL) represents the majority of British Credit Unions. British Building Societies developed into general-purpose savings and banking institutions with "one member, one vote" ownership and can be seen as a form of financial cooperative (although nine 'de-mutualised' into conventionally owned banks in the 1980s & 1990s). The UK Co-operative Group includes both an insurance provider CIS and the Co-operative Bank, both noted for promoting ethical investment.

Other important European banking cooperatives include the Crédit Agricole in France, Migros and Coop Bank in Switzerland and the Raiffeisen system in many Central and Eastern European countries. The Netherlands, Spain, Italy and various European countries also have strong cooperative banks.

They play an important part in mortgage credit and professional (*i.e.* farming) credit.

Cooperative banking networks, which were nationalized in Eastern Europe, work now as real cooperative institutions. A remarkable development has taken place in Poland, where the SKOK network has grown to serve over 1 million members via 13,000 branches, and is larger than the country's largest conventional bank. In Scandinavia, there is a clear distinction between mutual savings banks (Sparbank) and true credit unions.

Federal or Secondary Cooperatives

In some cases, cooperative societies find it advantageous to form co-operative federations in which all of the members are themselves cooperatives. Historically, these have predominantly come in the form of cooperative wholesale societies, and cooperative unions. Cooperative federations are a means through which cooperative societies can fulfill the sixth Rochdale Principle, cooperation among cooperatives, with the ICA noting that "Co-operatives serve their members most effectively and strengthen the co-operative movement by working together through local, national, regional and international structures."

Cooperative Wholesale Society

The cooperative economist Charles Gide, the aim of a cooperative wholesale society is to arrange "bulk purchases, and, if possible, organise production." The best historical example of this were the English CWS and the Scottish CWS, which were the forerunners to the modern Co-operative Group.

Cooperative Union

A second common form of co-operative federation is a co-operative union, whose objective is"to develop the spirit of solidarity among societies and... in a word, to exercise the functions of a government whose authority, it is needless to say, is purely moral." Co-operatives UK and the International Co-operative Alliance are examples of such arrangements.

Co-operative Party

In some countries with a strong cooperative sector, such as the UK, cooperatives may find it advantageous to form a parliamentary political party to represent their interests. The British Co-operative Party and the Canadian Co-operative Commonwealth Federation are prime examples of such arrangements.

The British cooperative movement formed the Co-operative Party in the early 20th century to represent members of consumers' cooperatives in Parliament. The Co-operative Party now has a permanent electoral pact with the Labour Party, and has 29 members of parliament who were elected at the 2005 general election as Labour Co-operative MPs. UK cooperatives retain a significant market share in food retail, insurance, banking, funeral services, and the travel industry in many parts of the country.

SELECTION OF AN APPROPRIATE FORM OF OWNERSHIP STRUCTURE

Before setting up any business the entrepreneur required to take an important decision regarding the form of ownership. The decision has got bearing on the availability of resources rights duties and ownership of the stakeholders. There are various options open to the entrepreneur as he has to take decision in the light of the business requirement, size, nature and business. Ownership can be public or private or joint. Factor affecting selection of ownership form: Selection of ownership form depends mainly upon many factors. Right choice of ownership will determine the success or failure of the business.

Various factor affecting choice of ownership form areas under:

- *Nature or type of business*: Sale proprietorship business is best suited for a business requiring personal skill or attention. Large scale business requiring huge funds and professional management can be run effectively and efficiently by under companies form of organization partnership is best suited for medium scale business.
- *Financial Requirement*: Financial requirements at the starting and future expansion or diversification of business will be the deciding factors regarding the choice of form of business small funds are required for sole proprietorship, medium fund for partnership and huge funds for company form of business.
- *Liability*: The entrepreneur before starting the enterprises should anticipate his risk bearing capacity and liability. Sole-traders or partnership firms even sell their personal properties for clearing business liabilities. The liability is unlimited in case of joint stock companies.
- *Flexibility*: While taking decision about form of ownership an entrepreneur must consider the flexibility of operations Maximum flexibility is enjoyed sole proprietor and approval of partner is needed in case of partnership business and various legal formi litias are needed for any change in case of companies.
- *Taxation*: No entrepreneur can afford to ignore taxation aspect while deciding about the form of ownership. Progressive tax system is followed in case of sole proprietor, flat tax rates is followed by partnership firms and companies.
- *Survival or continuity*: An entrepreneur must be concerned with the future or continuity of enterprise. If objective of business is permanent survival company form of business is suitable in case of other forms of business survival depends on the life span of sole proprietors partners.
- *Cnotrol*: An entrepreneur should decided in advance regarding extent of control he is willing to sacrifice in return for resources from others in building up a successful enterprise for full control over business sole propreitor is suitable partnership is suitable if control is to be

shared with other partners/ owners while in case of company the control is in the hands of Board of Directors.

- *Govt. rules and regulations*: Compliance with Govt. Rules and regulations is needed for survival of the enterprise. Sole trader is free from rules and regulations and partnership is also free from rules and regulations and to some extent. A joint stock company is on the other hand is governed by government rules and regulations from its incorporation to its winding up.

OWNERSHIP PATTERN IN THE MICRO SCALE ENTERPRISES IN INDIA

Despite of the growth of large scale industry small or micro scale enterprises has survived and progressed because it has its own specialized areas of operating micro scale enterprises have captured a major part of Indian economy.

So far as the ownership pattern of micro enterprises is concerned it can be classified as under:

- Private enterprise: An enterprise is said to be a private enterprise where it is owned managed and controlled by persons other then Government.
- Public enterprises: An enterprise is said to be public enterprise where it is owned managed and controlled by Government agencies. Examples of public enterprises are as under:
  - Industrial Finance Corporation of India
  - Food corporation of India.
  - State trading corporation.
  - Hindustan Machinery Tools.
- Joint enterprises: An enterprise is said to be joint enterprise, where it is owned, managed and controlled by Government and private enterprises jointly.

Usually small scale or micro industries have private ownership in India because of the following reasons:

- *Profit Motive*: As the profit is the main motive behind any business and small business requires less capital and less risk and hence private entrepreneurs come forward.
- *No state participation*: While establishing a small scale unit there is no need of state participation in the management except the legal formalities. Hence the owners of these units prefer privatization.
- *Private ownership*: Because of private ownership in small scale or micro scale sector all the important decisions are taken at once; There

is no need of getting and guideline or approval from the governments.

- *Independent Management*: The management of private sector is totally in the hands of the owners. There is no outside interference 'regarding any matter relating to the enterprise.
- *Availability of raw material at cheaper rates*: In private sector the purchasing power is in the hands of the owner of the business. Raw -materials are purchased from the market directly keeping in view their prices, quality and quantity. To conclude the ownership pattern of micro scale enterprises is mostly in the hands of private sector.

7

Legal and Tax Issues for the Entrepreneur

LEGAL AND TAX CONSIDERATIONS

Over the last few years, India has emerged as a leading destination for companies wishing to outsource their software development, and business process requirements. International companies have either entered into contracts with Indian service companies or set up their own facilities through Joint Ventures and Indian subsidiaries.

Indian Government has been a catalyst in the growth of the Indian software and BPO industry through the tax incentives provided to exporters. These incentives are aimed largely at maximizing exports, thereby resulting in an inflow of foreign exchange into India. Industrial policy reforms have eliminated the licensing requirements except for certain select sectors, removed restrictions on investment and expansion and facilitated easy access to foreign technology and direct investment. This has contributed to increased inflow of foreign exchange into India.

FOREIGN INVESTMENT POLICY

Foreign investment is permitted in virtually every sector, except those of strategic concern such as defence (opened up recently to a limited extent) and rail transport. Foreign companies are permitted to set up Wholly Owned Subsidiaries in India.

No prior approval from the exchange control authorities (RBI) is required, except for certain specified activities. The investment should be in accordance with the prescribed guidelines and the details of the investment should be filed with the authorities within the prescribed time limit. This investment procedure is commonly known as the "automatic approval route".

Foreign Investment Promotion Board (FIPB) of the Government of India is constituted mainly to promote inflow of FDI into the country, as also to provide appropriate institutional arrangements, transparent procedures and guidelines for investment promotion and to consider and approve proposals for foreign investment.

AUTOMATIC APPROVAL ROUTE AND FIPB ROUTE

Foreign investment into India is governed by the Foreign Direct Investment (FDI) policy of the Government and the Foreign Exchange Management Act, 1999 (FEMA). With increasing liberalisation of the Indian economy, generally, there is no need to obtain prior approval of the Government of India for a fresh investment to be made into an Indian company (only procedural filings have to be made with the Reserve Bank of India (RBI), the Indian central bank).

In certain cases, however, and also for investment in certain specified sectors, prior approval is required. Further, investment in certain specified sectors is subject to foreign equity caps.

Outsourcing vs. Software Development Centre

The determination of whether to outsource to an Indian software services company or set up one's own facility is largely a business decision. A long term requirement could make investment in a subsidiary worthwhile. Recent transfer pricing regulations may however have an impact on the pricing of the services provided by the subsidiary.

A requirement for highly specialized work may also point to setting up one's own facility. The need to exercise control over valuable intellectual property and maintenance of confidentiality is also a key factor. The slowdown since 2001 has also seen some hybrid structures, for e.g. where the Indian company sets up a separate entity, is assured a steady stream of business and grants the customer an option to purchase the business later. This would have the effect of leveraging on the benefits of outsourcing while sheltering the associated risks.

SOFTWARE OUTSOURCING ARRANGEMENTS

Contractual Protection

Where at least one party is a foreign entity, the parties can choose the law governing the contract. The negotiating power of international customers would typically weigh in favour of choosing a governing law of the customer. The parties may also choose a foreign venue for arbitration. A Foreign arbitral award would be recognized in India if the country of venue has signed either the New York or Geneva conventions and has been notified as having reciprocal relations with India in the matter of enforcement of foreign awards. A foreign arbitral award would generally be more easily enforced in India than a foreign court judgment.

If dispute resolution is to be held in India, it is generally recommended that the parties opt for arbitration because litigation in India can be long drawn and subject to delays. However, it is possible to obtain quick injunctive relief in case of intellectual property violations.

Contract Liability Concerns

Indian law does not contain statutory provisions or case law dealing specifically with liability issues arising from development of software. However, customers should keep in mind that under Indian law, compensation can be awarded for breach of contract only in relation to damages that naturally arise in the usual course of things and which the parties knew would result from such breach.

It cannot extend to any remote or indirect losses. Further, Indian courts rarely award large damages for breach of contract. Delays in the justice system also make speedy recovery of money difficult. This may impact the ability of customers to recover fees paid or obtain damages in Indian courts.

Copyright and Protection of Intellectual Property

It is generally difficult to patent software programmes in India. Under copyright law, the software developer, being an independent contractor, would be the author of the works and therefore, the owner. However, Indian law permits the parties to agree that the customer would be the owner of the copyright.

Under Indian law, in the absence of anything to the contrary, it is presumed that an assignment or license of a copyright work would be limited to 5 years and to the territory of India.

Further, the assignment may lapse if the work product is not made use of within one year. Accordingly, the contract would need to mention specific language to overcome these presumptions.

An assignment agreement must also specifically describe the work to be assigned. It is important to note that the knowing violation of copyright in India is a criminal offence. It is possible to obtain reasonably quick injunctive relief from Indian courts for intellectual property violation. However, it is important that the customer chooses an IP friendly jurisdiction.

The Business Software Alliance has had some success in obtaining Anton Pillar orders from Indian courts and conducting raids on distributors of pirated software. Another remedy that could be used is criminal breach of trust, if the developer has misused proprietary software or know-how provided by the customer.

India does not have a statute governing the protection of confidential information and trade secrets. Further, there is no statute dealing with data protection or privacy matters. One would typically obtain protection through a civil action under common law.

Recently, the central government and some state governments have expressed an interest in bringing forth a separate legislation for data protection in an effort to attract more investment in BPO activities. Another option would be to file an action for criminal breach of trust. This is based on the principle that confidential information is provided "in trust" and any misuse would amount to a breach of trust. Criminal action has its advantages in that the individuals involved will be put to inconvenience in terms of personal appearance before the court, the perceived stigma and the restrictions on traveling out of India.

TAX ISSUES

Under Indian law, software and BPO companies would typically be exempt from tax in relation to income earned from export of software out of India if the fees are received in convertible foreign currency.

This may affect certain types of outsourcing arrangements, for example, where the customer wishes to outsource the work from its existing Indian subsidiary. Payment of fees in Indian Rupees could significantly increase the cost, because the developer would seek to recover the tax payable on its margins.

Another important issue is the possibility that the customer may be held to have a permanent establishment in India if it transfers testing equipment to the developer for use while developing the software.

Another relevant issue is the taxation on Information Technology related services. In an attempt to boost the growth of software exporting, Government of India has exempted export of services and also secondary services consumed in exported services from service tax.

As mentioned earlier, India's software companies are largely exempt from tax. However, it is possible that the exemption may be removed or substantially reduced in the future. In such event, the Vendor would seek to increase its fees. The customer must recognize this as a reasonable possibility and perhaps, obtain fixed, tax inclusive costs, at least in the short term.

OUTSOURCING THROUGH OWNERSHIP MODEL

Foreign Investment Regulations

Software development and BPO services is now under the automatic route and no foreign investment approvals are required to set up a wholly owned subsidiary; only certain filings need to be made after receipt and issue of share capital. However, acquisition of shares in an existing Indian company may still require a prior foreign investment approval.

Choice of Vehicle - Private Company

Most foreign corporations set up their subsidiaries as private limited companies with liability limited by share capital. This entity is similar but not identical to an unlisted C Corporation in the USA and has no flow-through taxation. A private company can have a maximum of 50 shareholders (excluding employees), must restrict the transferability of its shares and is prohibited from making invitations to the public for subscription to shares, debentures or deposits. A private company is generally less regulated than a public company. It must have at least 2 shareholders. Regulations relating to personal presence of shareholders at shareholder meetings, and limitations on transfer of shares under exchange control laws would require a careful structuring of share capital investment into the subsidiary.

Funding the Venture

Restrictions imposed by Indian exchange control laws on the ability of an Indian company to obtain short term debt from abroad make it difficult to fund the subsidiary through loan funds.

Inflexible buy back regulations make a buyback of share capital difficult. Hence, the parent would typically seek to fund only the capital costs through share capital. One could possibly consider funding the operating expenses by the holding company making trade advances to the subsidiary for services to be performed.

Software Technology Park Units

Most foreign corporations interested in engaging in development of software and BPO services in India set up their Indian subsidiaries as Software Technology Park Units. This is not a separate legal entity but merely a status obtained from the government.

The STP status entitles the company to substantial tax benefits, subject to it meeting certain export commitments. An STP unit would need to be a customs bonded area.

This means that it can be at a location of the Company's choosing but must be in an area demarcated specifically for STP operations. Some formalities on entry and removal of goods would apply. In practice, most companies handle these requirements with ease.

Activities of an STP

The permitted activities of an STP do not cover just software development activities. An STP's activities could include:

- Software development
- Hardware design, digital signal processing;
- Business process outsourcing, including medical transcription services, customer relations, document processing and call centres.

On site services through deputed personnel would also be covered. Because an STP is supposed to be engaged primarily in export activities, its ability to make sales within the Indian market is limited to the equivalent of 50% of its total exports. Further, restrictions under both STP regulations and tax laws would limit the ability of the Indian subsidiary to outsource work to another Indian STP.

Export Requirements for STP Units

The export related commitments that need to be satisfied by an STP Unit are driven largely by the Government's objective of maximizing the country's foreign exchange reserves.

These commitments are as follows:

- Exports of US$ 0.25 million or 5 times the CIF value of imported capital goods, whichever is higher (if no capital goods are imported, the US$ 0.25 million requirement would apply).
- An annual Net Foreign Exchange Earnings as a Percentage of Exports (NFEP) of 10%. This means that the inflow of foreign exchange earned by the company should be at least 10% more than the outflow of foreign exchange out of India.
- Both the requirements need to be satisfied over a period of 5 years. The value of capital goods would cover the entire CIF value - cost, insurance and freight. However, the value of exports would cover only the landed cost. Further, it may be noted that in considering the outflow of foreign exchange, the dividend distributed to the holding company would also need to be considered.

INCOME TAX BENEFITS

An STP Unit in India would be entitled to enjoy the remainder of a 10 year tax holiday commencing from April 1, 2000 to March 31, 2009. (The Indian tax year runs from April 1 to March 31).

The tax benefit would apply only if the software/service is exported out of India and payment is received in convertible foreign exchange. It would also not cover profits earned from domestic business or income other than from STPI services. The tax holiday will not cover dividend distribution.

The STP Unit cannot be set up as a result of the re-organization or break up of an existing business and not more than 20% of its hardware should constitute hardware previously used by another business. Hence, in an acquisition, a careful structuring may be required in order to preserve the tax holiday.

Transfer Pricing Regulations

Indian tax laws have recently included provisions relating to transfer pricing, requiring pricing of transactions between associated enterprises to be at arms length. Even in the case of a tax exempt software company, this assumes significance because if the tax authorities conclude that the consideration payable to the Indian subsidiary is not at arms length, the enhanced income determined by the authorities would be subject to tax and would be the basis of possible penalties. Typically, companies opt for a cost plus method (between 7-15%) or standard per diem rates. Since these developments are relatively recent, there is no consensus yet on what would be an acceptable pricing formula.

Indirect Tax

An STP company can import capital goods and consumables without payment of any customs duty. However, the higher the value of imported goods, the higher will be the export commitment, as above.

The company would also be exempt from payment of excise duty on manufacture of goods, when purchased from the manufacturer and can claim a refund on sales tax paid by the supplier on sale of the product to the STP.

Tax Benefits for Non-STP Companies

Even if a software exporting company does not have an STP unit, it can avail of the general exemption for profits derived from export of computer software under Indian tax laws. At present, 30% of such export income is tax exempt.

Procedure for Setting up the STP

Setting up the STP Unit involves compliance with numerous regulatory procedures that would typically take about 3 months. After company incorporation, a detailed STP application has to be prepared, that would include the prescribed application form, a project report, projected 5 year accounts and details of expenses and foreign exchange remittances.

This would involve substantial work from the company officials. After obtaining the STP registration, certain other formalities need to be completed relating to customs bonding and obtaining tax registrations.

OPERATING A BUSINESS IN INDIA

Company Law - Indian company law is based on the English Companies Act of 1948. Key requirements include mandatory board and shareholder meetings, shareholder approval in respect of certain matters, appointment of officers, restrictions on loans and investments, etc.

Exchange Control

The Indian Rupee is fully convertible on the current account though control remains on the capital account. Doing business in India involves wading through India's complex exchange control regulations that restrict the remittance of foreign exchange out of India.

Employment Laws

Indian employee laws are considered to be somewhat restrictive in terms of requirements relating to lay offs, closure of business, etc. BPO companies need to be particularly concerned about rules relating to flexible working hours, holidays and employment of women at night as well as regulation of leave policies *Stock Options*: Exchange control restrictions that limited the amount that an employee could remit out of India for purchase of foreign stock have been lifted in the case of listed stock of holding companies. Subject to the employer fulfilling certain requirements, employees receiving foreign stock can also claim a tax status similar to the ISO status in the USA.

India many believe has just the right "climate" for entrepreneurial development and in 2007 India is the place to be in. It provides a great combination of skill and competency. Combine that with the right investment climate and the ever improving technological efficiency, you find that the great Indian time has arrived. The India boom is here to stay. The heat is on and it's only getting hotter.

BUSINESS OPPORTUNITIES IN INDIA

While looking at the prospect of doing business in India it would be prudent to see what options are available to a Non Indian company to invest in India. Since 1991 India has undergone a sea of change in its outlook toward foreign investment and global collaboration.

Add to that the phenomenon called Internet and you really have an explosive combination. It's no wonder that software and Internet services have really led India's outward push. Outsource2india has been providing high-quality and technology-driven services to a wide range of global customers since the year 1999.

Outsource to O2I and get access to proficient, professional and cost-effective services. Outsource 2india provides a range of competent services which include call centre services, data entry services, engineering services, financial services, creative services, web analytics services, healthcare services, digital image editing services, software services, Research and Analysis services and a host of other additional services.

While most of the policies are not specific to any industry, there are special provisions that relate only to the IT industry. Once you have decided to invest in India, the next question is naturally, how do I set up operations? There are primarily 2 ways to get your work done.

- Having your own setup
- Outsource the work to a local company

HAVING YOUR OWN SETUP

Many foreign investors prefer to have their own setup in India. This gives them better control over management of the organization.

It is also the best guarantee that the company's processes are being followed. Furthermore this may in some cases tend to be preferable, especially if the volume of work is large or the work is sensitive in nature.

However there are also disadvantages in this approach. One is regarding flexibility. Often these branches or subsidiaries are bound by the policies of the parent company and this may make it unwieldy when it comes to Indian legal and cultural framework.

Secondly, management of a remote setup is always more difficult, especially if the work involved is intermittent and small in volume.

Basically there are four types of direct foreign investment businesses in India:

- Branch Office
- 100% Subsidiary
- Joint Venture Companies
- Acquiring Existing Indian companies

Branch office:

It's really simple to set up a branch office in India. You are allowed to open a branch office if you are engaged in manufacturing or trading for the following activities:

- To represent your company in various matters in India e.g. acting as buying/selling agents in India, etc.
- To conduct research work in which the parent company is engaged provided the results of the research work are made available to the Indian companies
- To undertake export and import trading activities
- To promote the possible technical and financial collaborations between the Indian companies and overseas companies

Under this setup, you will not be allowed to do any sales in India for any of your products or services. However if you are only looking at doing your software development or IT enabled services, then this is the easiest option.

Wholly Owned Companies (100% Subsidiary):

If you would like to hand over control to the local management or would like to sell your products in India then look at this option. For the software industry, the Government of India allows up to 100% ownership by the Foreign Investor. Also, if you were to set up your office in an Export Processing Zone (EPZ), Software Technology Park (STP) or Electronic Hardware Technology Park (EHTP), then you will automatically be given permission for 100% ownership. The catch though is that you will have to export at least 75% of the final output out of India.

Many of India's States have at least one of these Parks. Automatic approvals are given by the Secretariat for Industrial Approval for setting up 100% Export Oriented Units ("EOU"). These zones are designed to provide internationally competitive infrastructure facilities and duty-free and low cost environment. Various monetary and non-monetary incentives are granted which include import duty exemption, complete tax holiday, decentralized "single window clearance," etc.

Establishing units in EPZ or STPs have the following advantages:

- Duty Free imports
- Tax free income
- Readymade infrastructure
- Housing and living facilities (in some cases)

Joint Venture Companies:

This is a common form of investment, because it allows the Foreign Investor and the Indian partner to do what each does best - the foreign partner brings in technology, systems and products and the Indian partner takes care of Human resources, marketing and legal and tax issues.

This is a special favourite for foreign companies just moving into India, since it gives you the distribution channel to get sales moving quickly. However over the long term you may prefer to move to a 100% subsidiary, to establish greater control. This is commonly done by means of stock buyouts or fresh investments. Both Wholly owned Companies and Joint ventures may be registered as Private Limited Liability (Pvt. Ltd.) or Public Limited Liability (Public Ltd.). Currently the government allows 51% shareholding by foreign companies in all but a small list of companies (these companies are essential to India's national security).

Acquisition of existing Indian Companies:

You have also the option of acquiring a company already existing in India. Such acquisition could take place through the issue of fresh capital and/or transfer of shares of an existing Indian company to the foreign investor with the effect of transferring control. Shares of an Indian company could be acquired from another foreign investor, subject to RBI approval. This will give you the advantage of a readymade setup. The Foreign Exchange Regulations Act (FERA) makes it necessary that Reserve Bank of India (India's Federal Reserve Bank) permission be taken prior to acquisition of shares in an Indian company by a foreign investor.

Similar permission is required in case of transfer of shares from you to a person resident in India. Either the transferor or the transferee can apply for permission. However be careful with this one. If the company is listed on the stock exchange, then you cannot hold more that 5% of the total paid up capital and all Foreign investors and Non Resident Indians (in case there's more than one) cannot own in total more than 24% of the capital.

CORPORATE TAX AND OTHER INCENTIVES

The corporate income tax effective rate for domestic companies is 35% while the profits of branches in India of foreign companies are taxed at 45%. Companies incorporated in India (any setup other than a branch) even with 100% foreign ownership, are considered domestic companies under the Indian laws. However, the New Export-Import Policy of 1992 provides substantial tax incentives for investments in Export. Major exporters are allowed to operate bank accounts abroad to facilitate trade.

Companies that sell in the Indian market as well as international markets may deduct export earnings from their tax liabilities. Exporters and other foreign exchange earners have been permitted to retain 25% of their foreign exchange earnings in foreign currency. For 100% Export Oriented Units and units in Export Processing Zones, Electronic Hardware Technology Parks, retention up to 50% is allowed.

Other incentives include:

- Tax holiday for a period of 5 continuous years in the first 8 years from the year of commencement of production
- Exemption from taxes on exports earnings even after the period of tax holiday
- Exemption from central and state taxes on production and sale
- Permission to install machinery on lease
- Freedom to borrow self-liquidating foreign currency loans at the prime rate of interest
- Inter-unit transfers of finished goods among exporting units

OUTSOURCING YOUR WORK TO INDIA

The other option is to completely outsource your work to Indian companies. This has it's own advantages. For example

- For intermittent jobs, it may make better sense to pay only when you have work
- Also if the volume of work were small, it would always be difficult to achieve economy of scale
- Outsourcing ensures that while you may not be the best in a certain area, you are giving the work to someone who's really good at it. That leaves you to focus on what you do best
- Many Indian companies do a lot of business with International customers, so they would often be able to bring in expertise and advice from their earlier work
- Lastly but definitely not least, you have no legal hurdles to overcome when you outsource

When companies go through M&A (merger and acquisition) deals what are the key tax issues that arise? How far do tax laws and other laws encourage or constrict M&A, inbound and outbound? For starters, inbound deals have a foreign buyer and an Indian target, while outbound deals are the opposite.

"Inbound acquisitions have recently become the flavour of the season with a good number of deals ringing the bells of some of the finest Indian fast-growing corporates," says Mr Girish Vanvari, Executive Director - M&A Tax, KPMG, India.

He cites as examples: Heidelberg's purchase of 51 per cent stake in Mysore Cements, EDS Corp's acquisition of 52 per cent stake of MphasiS BFL, Kohlberg Kravis Roberts (KKR) buying up Indian software unit Flextronics, and Holcim taking up stake in Gujarat Ambuja Cement.

"These transactions require a lot of structuring such that they are tax-efficient, compliant with SEBI (Securities and Exchange Board of India), FDI (Foreign Direct Investment) regulations and so forth," points out Mr Vanvari. "The Heidelberg's acquisition in the BIFR-reported (Board of Industrial and Financial Reconstruction) Mysore Cements triggered off the SEBI takeover code.

Heidelberg compulsorily made an open offer for 22.15 per cent stake at a price higher than their acquisition price," he recounts.

"The acquisition of 51 per cent stake was made on a preferential basis subject to the approval of the shareholders in their extraordinary general meeting." Thus, corporate law provisions come in to full play in deals involving companies. What about the EDS Corp deal? "This merger is subject to the approval of the Bombay and Karnataka High Courts. Also required are sanctions of the stock exchanges, shareholders, creditors, and regulatory authorities," explains Mr Vanvari.

"Tax neutrality of this merger will be on the compliance with the `amalgamation' conditions laid down under Section 2(1B) of the Income-Tax Act, 1961." In contrast, KKR's acquisition of 85 per cent of Flextronics did not trigger the takeover code, distinguishes Mr Vanvari. Because "the Indian entity had applied for voluntary delisting and been delisted from BSE and NSE in 2005."

Not all proposals sail through, as for example the US glassmaker Guardian Industries' idea to set up a separate wholly owned glass venture in the country. "It ran into rough weather with the FIPB (Foreign Investment Promotion Board) since the company already had a joint venture partner in India, and its partner would not grant a no-objection certificate to Guardian," narrates Mr Vanvari. "Any M&A in India has to be carefully planned and executed, cutting through a wide spectrum of tax and regulatory issues such as exchange control, income-tax, capital market regulations and so forth," he opines. "From tax perspective it would be important to structure these transactions into the country in a tax efficient manner, taking into account manner of funding, and choice of the holding company jurisdiction."

OUTBOUND ACQUISITIONS

Recently we have had many outbound acquisitions. Such as: Patni's acquisition of the US-based Cymbal Corporation for about $68 million; Dr Reddy's acquisition of Betapharm in Germany for $570 million, and Terapia in Romania for $324 million; Suzlon's acquisition of Eve Holding in Belgium for $526 million; Aban Loyd's acquisition of Sinvest ASA in Norway for $445 million; and Matrix Labs acquiring Docpharma in Belgium for $320 million. And the deal meter keeps ticking! "Outbound acquisitions are guided not only by the tax laws of the foreign companies but also the political relationships, free trade agreements (FTAs) and double taxation avoidance agreements (DTAAs or tax treaties) between these countries," says Mr Vanvari. "Deal structuring from tax perspective has become one of the most important factors for structuring transactions in the recent times such that the transaction is tax neutral or has minimum tax outflow."

It should enthuse professionals that a lot of tax planning is possible because good tax treaties are in place with many countries. Yet, areas that need appropriate attention, according to Mr Vanvari, are: 'substance' test, tax outflow, capital gains, dividend, interest and royalty, withholding taxes and elimination of double taxation.

"Tax, legal and financial due diligence of the target company is of utmost importance," he alerts. For, such an exercise can result in `a good understanding of the laws governing the target company,' so that you can structure the transactions appropriately.

EVALUATING YOUR BUSINESS'S LEGAL STRUCTURE

One of the many roles you will have to play in your business is that of security guard. You have to make sure that the company remains safe—nothing enters that could harm your business and nothing leaves that could reduce its value. The more you can use legal protections to safeguard your business, the easier this task becomes.

There are many ways to protect the business, its assets, and employees—one critical way is to conduct business within the most appropriate legal framework. The legal framework you use to support your business can affect your tax payments, legal liability, and potential for future investment.

As an entrepreneur, you must make decisions and take legal actions to structure your business. Otherwise, the law will make those decisions for you, and that can be detrimental.

Even if you've never officially selected a legal form for your business, you are operating within the parameters of a legal form. States typically hold undeclared businesses to be sole proprietorships or partnerships, leaving you personally responsible for debts and injuries.

Instead of ignoring this issue, take the time to select an appropriate legal structure after consulting an attorney and accountant. If you are in business, you're currently operating under one of the following legal structures:

- Sole proprietorship
- Partnership
- Corporation
- S corporation

- Limited liability company (LLC)
- Nonprofit corporation

The important question now is whether your legal form is appropriate for your business and its plan for growth. The factors that affect this important decision are listed below. Read these carefully and then complete My Business's Legal Form to see if you should talk with a lawyer and accountant about changing your current legal structure.

FACTORS AFFECTING THE CHOICE OF LEGAL STRUCTURE

While you should consider many factors in choosing the legal structure of your business, not all factors will apply to every business. Several key issues, however, will apply to most:

Control

Who is the decision maker? The decision maker will control management, determine who receives profits, decide whether to get loans or solicit investors, and be solely responsible for the company's financial losses.

Taxes

Tax liability is a major concern for business owners. The amount of taxes paid yearly can make or break a business.

Liability

Some legal structures do not protect personal assets from business debts. If you do not want to personally pay the debts of your business, consider a legal structure that will protect your personal assets.

Transferability of Ownership

Depending upon the legal structure, one person's ownership in a business may be transferred to another owner in whole or in part simply by the exchange of a piece of paper.

Longevity of the Business

Not all business forms are perpetual. Some forms of business cease when the entrepreneur exits the business.

Raising Capital

Simple entities such as sole proprietorships and general partnerships are restricted in their ability to raise capital.

Most often, entrepreneurs are concerned with all of these important issues. The key is to identify the legal structure that best meets your needs and the needs of your business as it grows. This tough decision should not be made without adequate counsel from an attorney, an accountant, and other advisers.

In an ideal world, you would select a legal form of business understanding every legal and tax implication.

The reality is that you must rely on the advice of your attorneys and accountants to make this decision. Attorneys and accountants can anticipate many situations based on their experience and on the information you provide. Still, the legal structure of the business is your decision to make and live with. Use My Business's Legal Form to check that the structure you operate under best covers the factors you are concerned about from the list above and best align with your business's strategy and goals. The legal form of your business can't be an afterthought. Your profits, your peace of mind, and even your business may depend upon using the right structure. Schedule appointments with your lawyer and accountant now to review your company's legal form.

Index